The Logic of Democracy

MICHIGAN STUDIES IN POLITICAL ANALYSIS

Michigan Studies in Political Analysis promotes the development and dissemination of innovative scholarship in the field of methodology in political science and the social sciences in general. Methodology is defined to include statistical methods, mathematical modeling, measurement, research design, and other topics related to the conduct and development of analytical work. The series includes works that develop a new model or method applicable to social sciences, as well as those that, through innovative combination and presentation of current analytical tools, substantially extend the use of these tools by other researchers.

General Editors: John E. Jackson (University of Michigan) and Christopher H. Achen (Princeton University)

The Logic of Democracy

Reconciling Equality, Deliberation, and Minority Protection

Anthony McGann

The University of Michigan Press
Ann Arbor

Published in the United States of America by
The University of Michigan Press
Manufactured in the United States of America
∞ Printed on acid-free paper

2009   2008   2007   2006   4   3   2   1

A CIP catalog record for this book is available from the British Library.

Library of Congress Cataloging-in-Publication Data

McGann, Anthony J.
    The logic of democracy : reconciling equality, deliberation, and
minority protection / Anthony McGann.
        p.   cm. — (Michigan studies in political analysis)
    Includes bibliographical references and index.
    ISBN-13: 978-0-472-09949-8 (cloth : alk. paper)
    ISBN-10: 0-472-09949-3 (cloth : alk. paper)
    ISBN-13: 978-0-472-06949-1 (pbk. : alk. paper)
    ISBN-10: 0-472-06949-7 (pbk. : alk. paper)
    1. Democracy.   2. Representative government and representation.
3. Minorities—Civil rights.   I. Title.   II. Series.

JC423.M384   2006
321.8—dc22   2006001568

For Karen, as promised

Contents

Figures

Tables

Acknowledgments

This book began as a spirited email exchange with Mike Munger and Mike Ensley at Duke University concerning the 2000 presidential election. I would like to thank Bernard Grofman, Donald Saari, Russell Dalton, Duncan Luce, and William Batchelder at the University of California, Irvine for their support and encouragement, and also the Institute for Mathematical Behavioral Science and the Center for the Study of Democracy. I would also particularly like to thank Nicholas Miller for his support and advice over the years. I am grateful to my co-author, Eliora van der Hout, whose work on electoral systems was vital to the conclusions of chapter 3. Chapter 5 draws heavily on my article "The Tyranny of the Supermajority," *Journal of Theoretical Politics* 16, no. 1: 53–77, © Sage Publications, Ltd., London, Thousand Oaks, and New Delhi, 2004, and is used here by permission.

I would like to thank my teachers, particularly Herbert Kitschelt, Hervé Moulin, John Brehm, Emerson Niou, John Aldrich, Romand Coles, Michael Gillespie, David Soskice, and Iain McLean. I would like to thank various colleagues at UCI and elsewhere for their helpful suggestions and conversations, and others for providing encouragement to finish this book. The list includes but is not limited to James Adams, Shaun Bowler, Carter Butts, Linda Cohen, Amihai Glazer, Marek Kaminski, Kamal Sadiq, Wayne Sandholtz, Brian Skyrms, and Rein Taagepera. I would also like to thank various graduate students who participated in the classes and seminars in which some of this material was developed, notably Michael Latner, Bruce Hemmer, Michael Jensen, John Ensch, and Steven Weldon. Finally I would like to thank Karen, Margaret, and Madeleine for being there or not being there, as appropriate.

CHAPTER 1

Introduction

This book provides a unified theory of democracy, bringing together the literatures on normative political philosophy, social choice, and the empirical study of political institutions. It should be possible to take the values that are addressed by normative political philosophy, proceed axiomatically by means of social choice theory to the procedures these values imply, and then consider how practical institutions implement these values and procedures empirically. Unfortunately the relationship between the three literatures has frequently been one of ignorance or indifference, if not outright hostility. However, by bringing the three literatures together it is possible to provide answers for many outstanding problems in all three.

The starting point is Dahl's definition of democracy in *A Preface to Democratic Theory* (1956) as a system of government that satisfies the values of popular sovereignty and political equality. This book works out the logical consequences of this definition. Although the definition seems innocuous, it leads to results that force us to revise the way we think about democracy. This is especially true when it is combined with the social choice results concerning majority-rule cycling (the fact that under majority rule, there is no alternative that cannot be majority-rule defeated by at least one other alternative). Several initially counterintuitive conclusions follow.

- Political equality logically implies a very precise institutional prescription: proportional representation at the electoral stage, and simple majority rule without checks and balances at the decision-making (parliamentary) stage.
- Majority rule is the decision rule that best protects the weakest minority and gives most incentive for reasonable deliberation. Adapting the arguments of Buchanan and Tullock (1962) and N. Miller (1983), it can be shown that majority-rule cycling allows us to escape the problem of majority tyranny. Contra Riker (1982), cycling does not make democracy meaningless but rather allows us to reconcile majority rule and minority protection.

- The deliberative democracy literature has been based on the ideal of consensual decision making. However, Rae (1975) shows that unforced consensus is logically impossible. As a result the logical basis of much of this literature is flawed (in particular Habermas's [1984] "ideal speech situation" is a logical impossibility). It is, however, possible to ground a theory of deliberative democracy on majority rule and get normatively similar results.
- We find the institutional forms required for political equality in the so-called consensual democracies of Western Europe. Whereas Lijphart (1977, 1999) and many others have argued that these systems are based on mutual vetoes, there are actually very few checks and balances that restrain majority rule. Minority protection and a consensual style of politics occur because of majority rule, not in spite of it.

Some of these conclusions are likely to be controversial. If the value of political equality logically implies proportional representation, then first-past-the-post and other electoral systems violate political equality and are, in this sense at least, less democratic. The same applies to constitutional systems that are supermajoritarian, either explicitly or implicitly through the existence of checks and balances or division of powers. Indeed, the conclusion that majority rule provides the most protection for minorities contradicts the usual justification of liberal constitutionalism (that special protections are necessary to protect minorities from majority tyranny). It will be shown that this justification is logically untenable— it is certainly possible for such institutions to protect some minorities at the expense of others, but it is impossible to protect every minority more than every other minority. Empirical political scientists and political philosophers are often studiously agnostic about drawing normative conclusions about political institutions. However, once we accept values such as political equality, such results are logically inescapable.

This book is sympathetic to the idea of deliberative democracy. Indeed, it is argued that democratic procedures have to be understood as rules that structure deliberation, rather than as social choice functions that directly translate preferences into outcomes. However, a great deal of the literature on deliberative democracy (including the work of Rawls and Habermas) rests on a basis that is logically problematic. Following social contract theory it relies on the concept of unforced consensus, something that cannot exist in a political context even as a logical possibility. It is also necessary to critically examine the claims made for the effects of deliberation. While deliberation is an inescapable part of democracy, some of the claims that have been made for the beneficial effects of deliberation have been utopian or even impossible. Fortunately, there is a considerable literature that takes majority rule within real political institutions as the basis of deliberative democracy.

The intent of this book is not utopian. Institutions very similar to those deduced from the requirement of political equality are found in a considerable number of countries—notably the so-called consensual democracies of Western Europe. Furthermore, many questions we are interested in can only be answered if we consider empirical evidence. For example, if we wish to argue that the value of political equality has to be balanced against the value of stability, we need to know whether there is indeed any trade-off between the two values. This means studying the literature on the mechanics of political institutions (the social choice literature) and particularly the literature on the effects of political institutions (the comparative politics literature). If we want to theorize about democracy in an informed manner, we need to learn about *democracies.*

The key to bringing the three literatures together is a correct understanding of the concept of majority-rule cycling. Cycling has typically been portrayed as either a mathematical curiosity or as something intrinsically corrosive to meaningful democratic choice, as in Riker's (1982) *Liberalism Against Populism.* However, it is neither. As Nicholas Miller's (1983) article "Social Choice and Pluralism" argues, cycling is a normal, indeed beneficial, part of democracy as we know it. Cycling is simply the situation where parties or legislators can combine in a variety of different ways to form a majority coalition. As a result, negotiation is necessary to reach an outcome. It is true that this does not give us a single best outcome that we can describe as the "General Will" or as the outcome of a transitive social choice function (the two concepts are logically related), but neither is the result arbitrary or lacking moral force. If we understand cycling as the presence of alternative, overlapping winning coalitions, then we can find solutions to many outstanding problems in democratic theory: We can provide a meaningful justification of democracy without denying the results of social choice; we can reconcile majority rule with minority protection; and we can provide a concept of social reason appropriate for a plural society.

Plan of Book

Chapter 2 justifies defining democracy in terms of procedural political equality, and it compares this to other conceptions of equality and democracy. It shows how the requirement of political equality can be axiomatized in political procedures, both social decision rules (rules for making decisions, such as parliamentary procedures) and seat allocation rules (rules for distributing seats in a legislature). Finally it considers other requirements that political procedures must meet to yield reasonable results.

In part 1, chapters 3 and 4 consider what procedures are required to meet the axioms of political equality laid out in chapter 2. Chapter 3 shows that political equality in seat allocation rules implies proportional representation, drawing on proofs from Hout and McGann (2004). However, it finds that there are many ways of implementing this in practice. Chapter 4 shows that political equality in social decision rules implies majority rule. It also considers in depth the phenomenon of majority-rule cycling. Contra Riker (1982) it argues that cycling does not undermine the case for majority rule and a nonminimal conception of democracy; rather, cycling is essential to the working of democratic decision making.

Parts 2 and 3 (chapters 5, 6, and 7) consider whether there is a trade-off between political equality and other values that we may find important. Chapter 5 considers minority protection, drawing heavily on my 2004 article "The Tyranny of the Supermajority" in the *Journal of Theoretical Politics*. However, far from there being a trade-off between majority rule and minority protection, I argue that majority rule is actually the decision rule that gives most protection to minorities. The chapter also considers supermajoritarian rule, checks and balances, and rights protection. Chapter 6 considers democratic deliberation. Again, I argue that the institutions that satisfy political equality are precisely those most likely to foster reasonable deliberative decision making. Chapter 7 critiques the consensual basis of much of the deliberative democracy literature (particularly the work of Rawls and Habermas) and shows (following Rae 1975) that unforced consensus is logically impossible in a political context. I argue, however, that it is possible to reach similar conclusions using majority rule instead of consensus.

Chapter 8 considers those countries whose political institutions are most similar to those implied by political equality, the so-called consensual democracies of northern Europe. These countries typically have majority-rule parliamentary systems with proportional representation elections. This chapter also considers empirical evidence as to whether there is a trade-off between political equality and qualities such as stability, economic performance, and rights protection.

CHAPTER 2

Groundwork: Political Equality and Political Institutions

This chapter lays out the basic qualities we require for procedures to be called democratic. These qualities are then developed in the next two chapters into a theory of democratic institutions. The remaining chapters consider how institutions can balance the value of democracy so defined with other things we consider valuable, such as rights protection, deliberation, and stability.

We begin with the definition of democracy given by Dahl in *A Preface to Democratic Theory* (1956). A procedure is democratic if it satisfies the properties of popular sovereignty and political equality. Popular sovereignty is satisfied if the people are the final arbiter over every matter, should they choose to be. Thus the people may delegate control over many (indeed most) matters but are always the ultimate authority. Political equality is satisfied when all citizens have equal say on such binding decisions. This is operationalized as everyone's vote being equal, a condition that is harder to meet than it might at first appear. It is not sufficient that everyone have a vote and these votes be equally weighted ("one person, one vote"). It is also necessary that the institutions be so constructed so as not to be biased in favor of any voter (or group of voters) or in favor of any alternative. We will find that this situation is the exception rather than the rule among the countries that are commonly referred to as democracies.

Of course these formal, procedural qualities are not the only criteria we may use to judge how democratic a government is. We may expect a democratic polity to have many other qualities. For example, we may expect it to have high levels of popular participation, a culture favorable to democracy and tolerance, a highly informed populace, a tendency to foster rational social inquiry, a discourse oriented toward impartial rule making rather than special interest pleading, or any number of other qualities. However, formal political equality is more essential, in the sense that it forms a minimal core of what we mean by democracy.

First, it is possible to conceive a government being democratic and lacking the various other qualities listed. For example, it is possible for a government to be democratic even though it has low participation. We may argue that it is a low-quality democracy, but it is a democracy nevertheless. However, if the institutions are systematically rigged in someone's favor, then the system is no longer democratic. For example, if some people have two votes, and others only one, we would not typically refer to this system of government as democratic. If we have a complicated institutional setup that has the same effect as giving some people two votes, we may refer to it as democratic out of ignorance or hypocrisy. But when it is pointed out that the system effectively gives some people a double vote, we can no longer defend it as democratic, although we may be able to defend it on other grounds, such as the superior competence of some people.

Another way of stating the same point is that a minimal requirement for democracy is that elections be free and fair, and that the decision-making process by elected officials (such as parliamentary rules) also be procedurally fair. This requirement is harder to meet than it may at first appear. When we talk about elections being "free and fair," we often demand a very low standard of fairness. Essentially we simply demand that the election be competitive, and that victory by the government is not preordained (for example, by government monopoly control over the media or outright electoral fraud). As a result, all the countries we refer to as "advanced industrial democracies" easily pass the test, as do many others. This rightly leads to the criticism of the concept of "electoral democracy." However, the response to this criticism should be to define electoral fairness more rigorously, before we search for other requirements. If we take the requirement of electoral fairness seriously (in the manner described later), we will see that this is actually a very demanding requirement that very few of the countries we conventionally describe as democracies come close to meeting. Dismissing the requirement that elections be free and fair as trivial may lead us to ignore the fact that many elections are actually not that fair.

A second reason for concentrating on democratic procedures is that procedures can be legislated, whereas other qualities we view as desirable in a democracy cannot be. Procedures are essentially the rules of the democratic game. Qualities such as the level of participation and the quality of deliberation are outcomes of the democratic process; that is, they are products of the way that people choose to play the democratic game. Whereas we can set up the rules of the game, in general we cannot force people to play the game in a specific way. Indeed, to do so would be self-defeating in a democratic setting. The most we can do is to try to influence people to behave in certain ways, either by moral suasion or by the provisions of incentives (which may include the rules and procedures themselves). We can design democratic institutions, but we cannot design the demos to order.

A third and final justification for adopting a procedural approach to democracy is that democratic procedure may be complementary to the other qualities we value in democracy. That is to say, adopting democratic procedures may be the most effective way to promote those other values. This, of course, is a strong assumption and will be dealt with in subsequent chapters. For example, chapter 5 will argue that proportional representation elections to a majority-rule parliament is the institutional configuration most likely to protect minority rights, while chapter 6 will make the case that this configuration provides the greatest incentive for democratic deliberation and the rational social inquiry favored by pragmatists in the tradition of Dewey (1946).

However, there is one set of outcomes that is essential to a process being even minimally democratic: the provision of basic rights. As Dahl (1988) argues, certain rights are implicit to the notion of democracy. It makes no sense to talk about democratic procedures if people are unable to make democratic choices, say because of the threat of physical coercion or the inability to speak freely. Furthermore, some other rights that are not implicit in the notion of democracy may in practice be essential to it. Dahl suggests that a degree of economic independence is such a requirement—if one voter was economically dependent on another in a feudal manner, that voter might be unable to choose freely. As Nino (1996, 138) argues, such rights are outcomes of the democratic process, not "things" that exist before it. Constitutions cannot give people rights in a substantive sense. Indeed many authoritarian regimes have had impressive collections of paper rights guaranteed by a constitution that was never enforced.

Thus we are forced to think about rights in a dynamic perspective. The political process in period t protects basic rights that allow democratic choice in period $t + 1$. For a system to remain minimally democratic therefore requires that it be procedurally democratic and that the practice of democracy does not lead to the violation of basic rights that are a condition of future democratic choice. There are different mechanisms by which basic rights can be protected. It can be argued, in the manner of Mill, Dahl, and Rousseau, that the people are the best protectors of their own liberty and thus that democratic procedures are the least likely to infringe on democratic rights. However, there is another tradition that argues that basic rights require protection from the democratic process. As Dahl (1988) points out, this logically requires some degree of guardianship—a nondemocratic body such as a constitutional court has to decide when basic rights have been infringed. This violates the principle of popular sovereignty but can be defended from a democratic perspective on the grounds that restricting democracy in a few spheres (basic rights) is essential for the maintenance of democracy in all other matters. Alternatively, judicial guardianship can be defended by arguing that the good of defending rights trumps the good of democratic procedure. Chapter 5 considers rights protection in more depth and broadly argues for the democratic view that democratic procedure provides the best defense for democratic rights. However, for current purposes, it is enough to recognize that democratic procedure is a necessary, but not sufficient, condition for democratic government.

Dahl (1956) refers to the theory of democracy based on the axioms of popular sovereignty and political equality as the "populist theory of democracy." After outlining this in chapter 2 of *A Preface to Democratic Theory,* he dismisses it as being of little practical relevance because it is purely axiomatic. In particular the populist theory mandates majority rule, but actual democracies are not direct but representative and so cannot simply use majority rule to make decisions. In place of the populist theory, he outlines a behavioral theory of democracy, which he refers to as polyarchy. This is not, as is sometimes supposed, essentially a description of the American system of government. The "American Hybrid" is dealt with separately in Dahl's chapter 5, and he is explicit that the American system does not meet all of the requirements of polyarchy. Instead polyarchy is an operationalization of the populist theory of democracy laid out in chapter 2.

This chapter and the next two will argue that the axioms of popular sovereignty and political equality can be applied far more directly to political institutions. Furthermore, they can give us very specific prescriptions as to what democratic institutions should look like, as well as specific criteria to judge how democratic the existing institutions are. Contrary to Dahl's assertion, the fact that all modern democracies are representative is not a stumbling block to an axiomatic theory. However, it does force us to separate the democratic process into two sets of procedures. First there are seat allocation rules, whereby the votes of the population are translated into seats in decision-making bodies, such as legislatures or executives. Second, there are social decision rules, by which these bodies make binding decisions. The next section considers this distinction.

Seat Allocation Rules and Social Decision Rules

This book treats seat allocation rules and social decision rules as separate species, to which it is appropriate to apply different standards. This is in contrast with the direction typically taken by social choice theory. (Austen-Smith and Banks 2005 is a notable exception.) Typically, social choice theory looks for a procedure that takes people's preference orderings as an input and produces as an output an ordering of either social states or candidates for office. This approach is usually justified in either epistemic or constitutive terms. That is, the outcome is taken to be the "will of the people" or the correct decision by definition (constitutive) or to be an indicator of it (epistemic). In either case, the procedure takes voters' orderings of alternatives or candidates and is supposed to produce a social ordering that corresponds to the collective will of the voters or the correct ordering of the alternatives based on the voters' assessment of their merits.

For example, Arrow's (1951/1963) work is built around the concept of a social welfare function, which is defined as a procedure that translates voters' preference orderings into a social ordering. Black (1958/1971) uses a statistical analogy, looking for a procedure that produces a suitable "average" based on voters' ranking of the candidates. However, the justification of this is still to produce an ordering of the candidates based on their merits. Going further back, Borda (1770/1995) justifies his proposed procedure in terms of correctly reflecting the will of the people and in terms of ranking the candidates correctly in terms of their merits. Furthermore he explicitly argues that the same procedure should be applied to the selection of candidates as to the choice of alternatives by a committee. Condorcet (1785/1995) argues that an appropriate voting system is one that maximizes the probability of choosing the worthier competitor or correct alternative based on the pairwise rankings of the candidates or alternatives by the voters.

This approach runs into problems for two reasons. First, as Black (1948, 1958/1971) and Arrow (1951/1963) discovered, it is not possible to find a single function that translates individual orderings into social orderings in a satisfactory way. This has led to the conclusion that democracy is meaningless or at least that it can only be defended in the most minimalist terms, in that it merely ensures that governments can sometimes be removed (as argued most notably in Riker 1982). However, this conclusion depends on the epistemic demand that democratic procedures must reveal the true "will of the people" (that is, a single ordering of social preferences). If instead we simply require that procedures satisfy some requirements of fairness, the skeptical conclusion that democracy is empty proves to be unwarranted. Chapter 4 presents an argument for this view.

Second, actual democratic institutions are not social welfare functions, nor should they be. The underlying normative justifications of actual political institutions and theoretical social welfare functions are quite different. Seat allocation rules are not justified because they pick the best 150 or 435 or however many candidates. Instead they are justified in terms of producing an assembly that is representative (in some way) of the voters. Social decision rules in practice are not used to determine outcomes from the raw data of legislators' preferences. They are used to structure a deliberative process in which legislators debate and negotiate outcomes. If we are to talk about what institutions can satisfy the procedural demands of democracy (most notably, political equality) we have to start from the classes of procedure we actually use in representative democracy.

Seat allocation rules are used to choose representatives, who subsequently make social decisions. Given that choice of the representatives is not the final outcome, it makes little sense to talk about the procedure choosing the 150 or however many "best" candidates in any kind of ultimate sense. Rather the goal is to produce an assembly that is representative of the voters. Given that it is impractical for all voters to take part in the final deliberative process, it is necessary for someone to be present for (re-present) them. Of course, there is a tremendous amount of ambiguity in terms of what is meant by *representation*. It could be meant in terms of shades of opinion, or demographic characteristics, or geographical residence, or some other criterion. The most frequently cited work on this (Pitkin 1967) gives a rich typology of conceptions of representation but no definitive conclusion. Nevertheless, it is clear that the process of representation is to some degree distributive, that is, about sharing legislative seats among different groups of people, not simply about choosing the best candidates. This is most obvious in a proportional representation system, where the legislative seats are distributed in proportion to vote strength. However, it is also the case in a district-based plurality system. The Westminster system does not choose the 658 best candidates but gives one representative to each geographical district.

Decision rules in legislatures are used to structure a deliberative decision-making process. No legislature proceeds by collecting each legislator's complete preference schedule and then aggregating them into a social ordering. Rather, debates take place, at the end of which votes are taken. In every existing legislature these votes are up-down votes between two alternatives, but it would be theoretically possible to use other procedures. Typically, many of the real decisions are made as a result of negotiation between the various parties or factions. This does not, however, imply that the voting rule is not important. The voting rule determines which coalitions are large enough to carry an outcome. Thus we can think of the voting rule as a rule defining a coalition game between the various parties or factions.[1] Using this framework, it is not necessary to claim that the procedure produces the objectively "correct" outcome or the "will of the people." To justify such a procedure it is enough to show that it is (1) a fair procedure, satisfying political equality, or (2) a procedure that makes "reasonable" decisions in an environment of limited information about potential alternatives. These criteria are pursued further in chapter 4.

From this point of view, even as an abstraction of what decision ought to be made, the social welfare function is of limited use. From an informational point of view, the demand that legislators have preferences over all possible social states is clearly unrealistic. Indeed, it is almost certainly impossible to enumerate all the possible alternatives. Furthermore, even if we had complete information about all the alternatives, actual legislative negotiation reveals valuable information about intensity of preferences that is not included in the ordinal preference schedules (Buchanan and Tullock 1962). Although this clearly does not overcome the social choice problems outlined by Arrow (see Bernholz 1973; N. Miller 1975, 1977a), it does mean that a social welfare function cannot capture all of the information available to make a social decision. Having said this, the social choice theoretic finding that social decision rules do not give a single determinate outcome, but that instead any alternative can be beaten by some other, will be extremely important, especially in chapter 4.

It is important to distinguish the argument made here from that made by various advocates of "deliberative democracy." Some of these writers (Cohen 1998; Dryzek 2000) have argued that it is possible to distinguish "aggregative" democracy (the type studied by social choice, where preferences are aggregated via a social welfare function) from "deliberative" or "discursive" democracy (where people deliberate and their preferences change). It is argued that if democracy is deliberative, social decision rules are less important, as a consensus may be reached. The problem with this argument (as pointed out by too many authors to list) is that if consensus is not reached, some social decision rule has to be used. In politics decisions typically have to be made, as not making a decision is actually a decision to do nothing (which may well be the decision some people want). Furthermore, the ultimate decision rule will structure the preceding deliberation. If there is a unanimity rule, then people who want (or at least can tolerate) the status quo are under no pressure to compromise and can demand large concessions. If there is majority rule, however, everyone has to look for potential allies. Thus, although the argument here draws heavily on deliberation and negotiation, it does not view these as a substitute for the analysis of social decision rules. Rather, the analysis of social decision rules has to be done in the context of the use of these rules to structure deliberative games.

Let us strictly define what is meant by a seat allocation rule and a social decision rule. Formal definitions are given in the appendix of this chapter. Seat allocation rules map the votes of the population onto an allocation of seats to each alternative (generally a candidate, list, or party), while social decision rules map the votes of the participants (usually legislators) onto a social preference between each pair of legislative alternatives. We can apply the axioms of popular sovereignty and political equality to both these procedures. The application of the axioms, as well as the other qualities we demand of these procedures to render them tractable, will vary for the two types of procedure. The rest of the chapter lays out these qualities.

What We Can Demand of a Democratic Procedure 1: Political Equality

The requirements for popular sovereignty are straightforward. The people must have the final say over any matter, should they choose to exercise it. The concept of political equality requires a bit more work. The conception of equality used here is liberal in that it is specified in terms of individuals and applies to formal political procedures. If we consider individual voters, then the concepts of equality (treating all voters alike), fairness (treating all voters appropriately), and impartiality (not discriminating for inappropriate reasons) are equivalent. Thus we are able to proceed negatively, defining procedures as equal, fair, and impartial if they do not take into account factors that should not be considered. This is the same intuition that underlies Williams's (1962/1971) "relevant reasons" approach to equality and Barry's (1989, 1995) "justice as impartiality." We can then operationalize liberal political equality as the axioms of anonymity (the names of the voters make no difference) and neutrality (the electoral system does not discriminate between alternatives on the basis of their names).

Thus by *liberal political equality* we mean the requirement that procedures treat every individual equally. This may seem the most obvious kind of equality to apply to political institutions, especially in countries with a long tradition of liberal democracy. However, a great deal of the literature on political justice (particularly the electoral systems literature, covered in chapter 3) draws on group conceptions of fairness rather than an individualist conception. Furthermore, various political philosophers, most notably Rawls, have argued that the concept of equality should only be applied to arguments about justice, and not directly to institutions. Finally, some have criticized a liberal conception of equality for being exclusively formal and not taking account of substantive (and in particular, economic) inequality. I will deal with these objections in turn, before considering how to axiomatize a liberal conception of political equality.

If we consider only individual voters, as opposed to the groups they make up, then the concepts of equality (the demand that individuals be treated the same), fairness (the demand that every individual be treated as he or she ought to be), and impartiality (the demand that how someone is treated should not depend on inappropriate factors, such as personal friendship, class, race, or gender) become equivalent. When we consider the rights of individual citizens in a liberal democratic state, it is extremely hard to escape the conclusion that fairness implies equality. It is difficult for us to argue that one citizen deserves more political rights or better treatment than others. This follows from the standard liberal assumptions (see, for example, Dahl 1988 following Mill 1861/1993 that every individual's interest is worthy of equal consideration and that every individual is the best judge of his or her own interests). However, even if we accept that some individuals are more worthy or more qualified than others, we would still have to find a mutually acceptable procedure to determine *which* citizens are better qualified or more deserving. Given that this is likely to be impossible, equality is the only remaining option that can be described as fair (see Barry 1979). Similarly, if we treat individual voters in different ways, we can hardly argue that we are acting impartially, unless the different treatment is handed out in a strictly random way. It is hard to see how we can justify such discrimination *in terms of individual voters.* Of course, many reasons have been given as to why different voters should be treated differently. However, all these arguments rely on fairness and impartiality in terms of groups and thus are not framed in terms of *liberal* equality.

This equivalence of equality, fairness, and impartiality disappears if we consider groups instead of individual voters. For a start, groups can be of different size. It is not clear that it is fair to treat differently sized groups equally (this certainly violates equal treatment of the individual members of the groups). Neither is it obvious that impartiality is violated if we treat differently sized groups unequally, as to argue this it would be necessary to show that the size of the group is an unacceptable criterion for discriminating. In addition to size differences, some groups may be politically salient, while others may not. Furthermore it is possible to divide a population into groups in many different ways. These different sets of groups may overlap or have cross-cutting membership. Therefore, to make an argument about fairness based on groups, it is necessary first to justify why fairness should be seen in terms of a particular partition of the voters into groups. This involves both justifying why fairness should be seen in terms of these groups rather than in terms of individuals and justifying why these groups are more appropriate than other possible sets of groups. Having done this, it is necessary to justify a particular conception of fairness between groups.

Two arguments can be made in favor of preferring liberal equality over some form of group-based fairness. First there is the liberal argument that the rights of individuals should enjoy normative priority over the rights of groups that these individuals make up. However, even if we do not accept this doctrinal liberalism, a case can still be made for liberal equality as a fair means to arbitrate between different conceptions of (group-based) fairness. As we have seen there are multiple forms of group-based fairness depending on which set of groups and which principle of allocation we choose. Who has a right to impose their conception of fairness over everyone else? Liberal equality offers a way out, in that it merely demands that all individuals be treated equally. Individual voters can then decide which group identities are salient to them, as opposed to certain forms of group fairness being imposed by the electoral system. We can compare this to the role that political liberalism plays in Rawls (1993/1996). There political liberalism provides a means for arbitrating between competing "comprehensive doctrines" that lay out the values that define the good life. Here liberal equality provides a means of arbitrating between different conceptions of group-based fairness.

So far we have assumed that the concepts of equality, fairness, and impartiality are to be applied directly to political institutions such as electoral systems and legislative rules. However, some theorists deny this and instead take a "constructivist" position, in which equality and fairness are properly applied to a hypothetical decision situation. This hypothetical decision situation then allows the theorist to derive concepts such as fairness to be applied to actual situations. Most famously, Rawls (1971/1999) argues that principles of political justice can be derived by considering what agents would decide in a situation of equality resulting from ignorance of their own circumstances. Institutions are then chosen so as to maximize the probability of legislation that is just in the terms already determined. Beitz (1989) argues even more strongly that concepts such as political equality and fairness should be applied at the level of arguments and not institutions. However, in place of Rawls's original position, Beitz uses the construction from Scanlon (1982) whereby a norm is justified if no person affected by it could reasonably reject it.

However, there are serious problems with arguing that concepts such as equality, fairness, and impartiality should apply to arguments and not institutions. Most significant is the question of who is to determine what people in a hypothetically constructed decision situation would decide. There is, for example, a large literature arguing that the agents in Rawls's original position would reason quite differently from the way that Rawls argues they would (see Hare 1973/1975 and Harsanyi 1975 for arguments that utilitarianism would be chosen from Rawls's premises). Similarly, as Barry (1995) points out, Scanlon's construction depends heavily on what objections can be considered "reasonable." If different people would come to different conclusions about what would be decided in a hypothetically constructed situation, then we need some means to arbitrate between them. Given that this dispute is to be settled reasonably, without resort to force or authority, we need rules for debate and decision making that are fair. This, however, leads us back to applying the concept of fairness to actual institutions. (This is essentially the argument that Habermas [1995] makes against Rawls [1993/1996], an argument that Rawls [1995/1996] largely accepts.)[2]

Thus there is a strong argument for applying liberal equality directly to institutions. We can accept Barry's (1995) argument that in many cases applying impartiality directly to outcomes leads to ridiculous results, such as the argument that one cannot prefer one's friends over strangers in one's allocation of free time. However, the choice of democratic procedures is precisely the kind of situation where first-level impartiality is appropriate, because it is by these procedures that society determines what is fair and impartial in other circumstances. Fairness requires first-level impartiality because there is no higher court of appeal. (Interestingly, Barry accepts the limitations of theorizing based on a hypothetical construction and argues that these conclusions need to be supplemented by what he refers to as "the empirical method." This involves considering the decisions made in countries where the institutions best approximate the conditions of impartiality. The countries that Barry considers to best meet this criterion are the Scandinavian democracies—that is to say, proportional representation parliamentary systems.)

It could be argued that the emphasis on formal political equality is misguided, as it ignores economic inequalities that can allow certain parts of the political community to dominate others (see Roemer 1999a,b for a recent version of this argument). As Gutmann (1980) argues, it is certainly logically possible for formal and substantive equality to conflict. This creates a situation where we would have to consider the trade-off between the intrinsic value of political equality and the value of substantive justice. We would also have to consider the degree to which formal political equality is meaningful in the presence of severe economic inequality.

However, this trade-off between formal and substantive equality is highly unlikely to manifest itself in practice. If political equality is violated, the resulting inequality is highly unlikely to benefit the otherwise underprivileged. Underprivileged groups are (almost by definition) unlikely to be powerful enough to get the constitution biased in their favor. If any bias in the democratic procedure is likely to work in favor of the privileged, the best the underprivileged can hope for is political equality. Chapter 8 will show that empirically this is indeed the case: The countries that best approximate our definition of political equality (the small European consensual democracies) are the countries that are economically most egalitarian and redistributive.

We now turn to how the concept of liberal equality can be operationalized. The most efficient way to operationalize liberal equality is to proceed negatively, excluding those considerations whose inclusion would violate equality. This is what we do when we consider equality or fairness in terms of impartiality. It is also the basis of Williams's (1962/1971) "relevant reasons" approach to equality—discrimination has to be justified by reasons, and some kinds of reasons cannot be used to morally justify such discrimination. Instead of trying to define what equality is in a specific context, we derive axioms by excluding various considerations.

First, and most obviously, if a social decision rule treats all voters equally, then the outcome should not depend on the names of the voters, or their identities. That is to say, if we permute the names of the voters, this should not change the outcome. Thus the social decision rule needs to satisfy the axiom of *anonymity*. Second, to treat all voters equally, the social decision rule cannot discriminate on the basis of the names or identities of the alternatives. If it did, it would give favorable treatment to the supporters of one alternative over another. Furthermore, such a social decision rule would violate the idea of popular sovereignty. If changing the names of the alternatives changes the result, then the result depends on a built-in bias in the social decision rule, and not solely on the preferences of the voters. Thus political equality also requires the condition of *neutrality*.

Similarly, we can also apply anonymity and neutrality to seat allocation rules. A seat allocation rule is anonymous if changing around the names of the voters does not change the number of seats each alternative receives. A seat allocation rule is neutral if changing the names of the alternatives around does not change the number of seats each receives.

When considering seat allocation rules, the axioms of anonymity and neutrality need to be applied not just to the choice between alternatives, but also to the choice between coalitions of alternatives. This is important because political power is not distributed on the basis of the relative seat share of candidates or parties, but on the relative size of coalitions—or more precisely in terms of which coalitions have a majority (or superma-jority, if required) of seats and are thus able to elect a government or pass legislation. Applying anonymity to coalitions is straightforward—if the electoral system is anonymous with regard to alternatives, it is automati-cally anonymous with regard to coalitions of alternatives. However, neu-trality to coalitions does not follow automatically from neutrality to alter-natives, and actually represents a considerably stronger requirement. Coalition neutrality implies that the electoral system cannot discriminate between different kinds of coalition. Of course, a case can be made that the electoral system should reward coalitions made up of a small number of alternatives, because this promotes consolidation and stability; or that coalitions of a large number of alternatives should be encouraged be-cause this allows for the representation of a greater number of points of view. The liberal defense of coalition neutrality is that this question should not be settled by the electoral system but by the voters themselves. The electoral system should be neutral between coalitions, because the seat share allocated to each coalition should depend only on the voters, not on a bias built into the system.

What We Can Demand of a Democratic Procedure 2: Other Axiomatic Qualities

Apart from the normatively appealing qualities resulting from political equality, there are other axiomatic qualities that are required for social decision rules to be practically useful. Two of these axioms (decisiveness and nonnegative responsiveness) should be uncontroversial and intuitive. However, the other two (binary independence and transitivity) are logi-cally incompatible. I will argue that for social decision rules the require-ment of binary independence is reasonable, but that we can dispense with the requirement of transitivity. For seat allocation rules, however, a tran-sitive result must occur by definition. However, the requirement of binary independence is unreasonable—indeed it is a quality that any reasonable seat allocation should violate.

For a social decision rule, decisiveness (May 1952) is simply the re-quirement that the rule produce a definite result. An alternative either wins, loses, or draws. In the case of seat allocation rules, every seat has to be allocated or be declared a draw. Note that in most practical political situations, a draw is not an acceptable outcome. If we have a draw in par-liament or in an election, the result typically has to be decided somehow. One way to decide a drawn outcome is at random. This indeed is fre-quently the method of last resort for legislative elections. It is also the only method that is compatible with political equality. Another means of breaking a draw is to decide the outcome in a nondemocratic manner. For example, a person or committee may be given ex officio power to be the tiebreaker. This, of course, violates anonymity. Alternatively, one alternative may be privileged over the other. This is the case when in the case of a tie the status quo or the incumbent is allowed to remain, violating neutrality.

Nonnegative responsiveness (also known as weak monotonicity) is the requirement that if some voters switch to an alternative and everything else remains equal, it cannot do worse than before. This is a weakening of the quality of positive responsiveness (May 1952). In the case of a social decision rule, positive responsiveness means that if an alternative is winning and some voters switch to it, then it must still win. If it is drawing and some voters switch, then it must win. We can adapt positive responsiveness to seat allocation rules: If two alternatives are receiving the same seat share and some voters switch to an alternative (either at the expense of another alternative or from abstainers), then this alternative must receive a greater seat share than the other alternative.

Positive responsiveness is a strong condition. In terms of social decision rules, it means that draws are knife-edge results: One vote change will turn the draw into a result for one alternative or the other. For seat allocation rules, positive responsiveness implies that if a party wins one extra vote, it acquires a greater seat share, something that is clearly impossible given that seats are not infinitely divisible. Nurmi (1987) suggests nonnegative responsiveness (weak monotonicity) as a more reasonable requirement. In the case of social decision rules, this means that voters' switching to an alternative does not make that alternative do worse (if it was drawing, it must at least still draw). In the case of seat allocation rules, it means that if some voters switch to a party, all other things being equal, then it must at least maintain its seat share. In both cases, extra votes cannot hurt an alternative, but they may sometimes have no effect. Whereas the requirement that even one extra vote must improve the outcome for an alternative is a strong one, the requirement that winning more support does not hurt it is not. We are surely entitled to think of a procedure as perverse if it punishes an alternative for winning more support.

Binary independence and transitivity require more justification, as they are effectively mutually exclusive. Binary independence is essentially the quality that Arrow (1951/1963) referred to as *independence of irrelevant alternatives*. In the context of social decision rules it means that society's choice between alternatives A and B must only depend on the preference of voters between A and B, and not on how voters rate A and

B relative to any third alternative. This can be adapted to seat allocation rules as follows: a seat allocation rule satisfies binary independence if the relative seat share of two alternatives only depends on the preference of voters between these two alternatives. The intuition normally given for binary independence is that if society prefers A to B, it should still prefer A to B if another option becomes available. Furthermore, if this is not so, it is possible to manipulate the outcome by introducing spurious alternatives that do not get chosen but do affect the choice. However, I will justify it on rather different grounds, namely, that it is simply not possible to enumerate what all the alternatives are, so any decision between two alternatives based on a (probably nonrandom) sample of third alternatives will be arbitrary.

Transitivity is the property that if society prefers A over B, and B over C, then it must prefer A over C. (Strictly speaking we can substitute "prefers or is indifferent to" with regard to either A and B or B and C, and still get the result that A is preferred over C.) This allows us to rank all alternatives and have a single alternative (or set of alternatives if they tie) that is preferred to all the others. From the point of view of making a social choice, transitivity clearly makes our life easier. If it was the case that A was preferred to B, B to C, but C was preferred to A, it would not be possible to say which one was preferred by society. Nevertheless, I will argue that this is a property that we must dispense with in social decision rules. In seat allocation rules, however, the property of transitivity is present by definition. Such rules assign a number of seats to each alternative. If A has more seats than B, which in turn has more seats than C, then A must have more seats than C.

Arrow (1951/1963) showed that transitivity and binary independence are logically incompatible unless at least one other quality essential to democratic choice is violated. Specifically, Arrow showed that a social welfare ordering (which is by definition transitive) could not simultaneously satisfy the properties of independence of irrelevant alternatives, universal domain, unanimity (Pareto optimality), and nondictatorship. It is straightforward to show that the latter three qualities are essential to any reasonably democratic decision rule. Universal domain simply means that voters can have any preference ordering. Restricting the preferences that voters are allowed to have clearly violates the most basic democratic principles. Unanimity (Pareto optimality) is the quality that if all voters prefer A over B, then A must be chosen. Violating this principle violates the principle of popular sovereignty. Nondictatorship simply means that a single agent is not always decisive and is obviously necessary for democratic choice.

A common interpretation of Arrow's theorem has been the rather nihilistic conclusion that there is no nonarbitrary democratic decision rule. Notable among these interpretations are Arrow (1951/1963, 59) himself[3] and Riker's *Liberalism Against Populism* (1982). This reading, however, should be resisted. As Saari (2001) argues, what Arrow's theorem shows is that binary independence and transitivity are mutually incompatible. Arrow's theorem can be seen as a generalization of the famous Condorcet (1788/1995) paradox. Suppose we have three voters making a decision by majority rule, a procedure that satisfies binary independence. Their preferences are as in table 2.1, so that voter 1 prefers candidate a to candidate b to candidate c. Then by majority rule, a beats b, b beats c, but c beats a. What Arrow shows is that any procedure that satisfies binary independence is susceptible to this kind of cycling (strictly speaking, may exhibit intransitivities) or violate one of the other three qualities we have listed as essential to democratic choice. Rather than showing that democratic choice is impossible, Arrow's theorem shows us that we have to make a choice between binary independence and transitivity. We will see that Saari argues for abandoning binary independence, whereas I will argue we need to abandon transitivity in some circumstances.

A possible response to Arrow's result without abandoning transitivity altogether is to weaken this requirement (Sen 1970a). For our purposes, however, this does not help much, as the resulting procedures, although nondictatorial, still seriously violate democratic principles. We can weaken transitivity to quasi transitivity (a beats b, b beats c, implies a beats c, but this is not the case if the relationship between a and b or b and c is one of indifference). This, however, only allows us to replace a dictator with an oligarchy, a single group that is decisive over all social choices (the proof comes from an unpublished paper, Gibbard 1969; see Moulin 1988; Mueller 2003). Alternatively, we could weaken the condition even further to acyclicity (there are no cycles, such that a beats b, b beats c, and c beats a). This dispenses with the need for an oligarchy, but we still have an individual voter who is a veto player if the number of alternatives is greater than the number of voters (Brown 1975; Nakamura 1979). The presence of veto players violates the condition of neutrality,

TABLE 2.1.   The Condorcet Paradox

Voter 1	Voter 2	Voter 3
a	b	c
b	c	a
c	a	b

By majority rule, a beats b, b beats c, and c beats a

in that the status quo can be guaranteed by one voter, but a new alternative cannot. Besides, as we will see in chapter 4, the only binary social decision rule that satisfies the requirement of political equality is majority rule (May 1952), and this clearly is susceptible to cycles. Thus if we want a decision rule that respects political equality, we have to face the choice between binary independence and transitivity.

Binary Independence (Independence of Irrelevant Alternatives)

I will argue that it is appropriate to demand that binary independence be satisfied for social decision rules, but for reasons rather different from those normally given. Arrow (1951/1963, 26–28) justified independence of irrelevant alternatives as a quality we ought to demand of decision rules on the grounds that to do otherwise would be to make the outcome contingent on events that are obviously accidental. If candidate A would win using a certain procedure, it should not make any difference to the outcome if one of the other candidates dies. Arrow criticizes the "rank-order methods frequently used in clubs" on these grounds. Arrow's justification of independence of irrelevant alternatives is similar to Condorcet's (1788/1995, 126) criticism of the Borda procedure.[4]

> But how is it that Paul is not the clear winner when the only difference between himself and Peter is that Peter got thirty-one first places and thirty-nine second, while Paul got thirty-nine first and thirty-one second? Well, out of the thirty-nine voters who put Peter second, ten preferred him to Paul, whereas only one of the thirty-one voters who put Paul second preferred him to Peter. The points method confuses votes comparing Peter and Paul with those comparing either Peter or Paul to James and uses them to judge the relative merits of Peter and Paul. As long as it relies on irrelevant factors to form its judgments, it is bound to lead to error, and that is the real reason why this method is defective for a great many voting patterns, regardless of the particular values assigned to each place. The conventional method is flawed because it ignores elements that should be taken into account and the new one because it takes into account elements which should be ignored.

However, Dummett (1984, 54–59) and Saari (2001) criticize this justification of binary independence on the grounds that comparisons with other alternatives do yield relevant information. Both argue that decisions should not only depend on how many people prefer A to B but also on the intensity with which they prefer. Comparisons to third alternatives may be an imperfect measure of intensity, but if they are the only information about intensity we have, we should not throw this information away. In response to the argument that a procedure should not be influenced by one candidate withdrawing or dying, Dummett argues that if this happens, we have lost valuable information, so it should not be surprising that our choice may be different. In addition to the fact that limiting ourselves to binary comparisons deprives us of (imperfect) information about intensities, Saari (2001) also argues that it deprives us of transitivity information present in the rankings of the voters, essentially "emasculating" the transitivity requirement of individual voters' preferences.

There are situations where it appears reasonable to use nonbinary comparisons to rank alternatives. Indeed this is commonly used in sports leagues, as Arrow (1951/1963, 27) notes. When deciding whether Arsenal or Manchester United ought to be English Football Champions, we do not simply compare the results of the two games between two clubs. We also compare how the two clubs have fared against Newcastle, Chelsea, Liverpool, and so on. Indeed, if we consider other soccer results, there are many intransitivities (Manchester United beat Charlton, Charlton beats Wolves, but Wolves beats Manchester United). Nevertheless, we have no qualms about transitively ordering clubs at the end of the season using comparisons with third clubs. Where we have a fixed number of candidates for a job, we may ask why it would be more inappropriate to consider nonbinary comparisons.

While a case can be made for using nonbinary comparisons for ranking soccer teams and job candidates, violating binary independence is far more problematic in a legislative setting. The reason for this is not that irrelevant alternatives should not be considered, but that they cannot be considered—at least not all of them. Choosing a government policy is different from choosing a candidate. In an election or job search there are a finite number of candidates. However, all the different packages of policies a legislature could consider cannot even be enumerated. Faced with an infinite (indeed uncountable) number of potential alternatives, any decision based on nonbinary comparisons will depend on what subset of third alternatives we use. But how do we decide what the reference group of alternatives should be? We cannot even take a random sample of alternatives, as we have no way to decide what the sample frame to select from is.[5] The alternatives we are likely to propose will in all probability be highly nonrandom, close to the current status quo. In these circumstances, nonbinary comparisons are likely to be highly arbitrary and thus should be disregarded.

The problem of even describing the set of all possible alternatives in a legislative setting is made more severe by the fact that government policy is intrinsically multidimensional and the different dimensions of policy affect one another. All government policies that involve spending money affect each other because there is a common budget constraint—if we spend more on health, we must spend less on education or raise taxes. Furthermore, many policy domains affect each other directly—our policy on education affects income distribution, income distribution affects health policy, which in turn affects labor market policies. What an individual or society would choose on each policy dimension depends on what policies are chosen on other dimensions. Deciding policies on different dimensions independently can lead to very poor policies that do not make any sense together, and it may even lead to policy choices that are mutually impossible (for example, deciding to have high public spending, low taxes, and low borrowing). Thus political decisions are more complex than many other kinds of decision. When a group of middle managers decides who to hire, they can take the overall strategic direction of the firm as given, beyond their control. In politics we cannot do this. Popular sovereignty implies that everything is potentially up for grabs.

Using nonbinary comparisons in a situation where alternatives can be made up in an arbitrary manner exposes us to a kind of manipulation different from that we face when choosing a job candidate. We have to worry not only about strategic voting but also about the strategic manipulation of the set of alternatives under consideration. When we consider job candidates, we may vote strategically, misrepresenting our true preferences to try to get a result we prefer, a ploy to which all nondictatorial voting rules are susceptible (Gibbard 1973; Satterthwaite 1975). However, given the costs of applying for the job, we assume that a candidate will not enter the race just to disadvantage another applicant.

Similarly, in a soccer league, the number of teams is fixed. However, in a legislative setting it is always possible to add new alternatives (indeed, to forbid this violates the principle of popular sovereignty). This encourages not just strategic voting but the introduction of spurious alternatives to manipulate the result. If it is advantageous to introduce spurious alternatives, the agenda will soon be overrun by such spurious alternatives proposed by competing factions. The information required to compare all these alternatives becomes immense. Of course, binary decision rules, such as an amendment procedure, can also be manipulated. However, the number of alternatives considered at one time is limited to two. The voters only need the information required to judge between the two alternatives on the table. Furthermore, to have an effect, the new alternative proposed at least has to be relevant in the sense that it can defeat the measure currently under consideration.

Thus our justification of binary independence for social decision rules does not apply to all situations. We are only concerned with social decision rules used for legislation. Some nonbinary rules have attractive axiomatic qualities (see Young 1974, 1975; Saari 2003 for Borda count; Young 1995 for the Kemeny rule) and may be suitable for some purposes, such as selecting job candidates. However, the number of possible alternatives facing a legislature is not enumerable, and new alternatives can be added in an arbitrary way. In these circumstances, nonbinary rules are either intractable or arbitrary. Thus, binary independence is justified for social decision rules because it provides a tractable basis for legislative bargaining in a world with limited information.

Binary independence is not a quality that we should require of seat allocation rules. Indeed, it is a quality that any reasonable seat allocation rule should violate. Imagine that we have two parties in a legislature, Left and Right, each of which has an equal share of the seats after an election. This means that the ratio of the seat share of the two parties is 1:1. Suppose now that a new party (New Left) enters the legislature. By binary independence, the seat share between Left and Right has to remain 1:1. Thus if New Left receives any seats at all, then the two Left parties between them have a majority. This is clearly unreasonable, as the more left parties enter (or the more existing left parties splinter), the greater the total seat allocation for the left parties. If a new party enters an election, we expect it to win support at the expense of at least one of the existing parties. If New Left enters, but the total vote for the left parties remains constant, it seems reasonable the seat allocation that had gone to Left would be divided between Left and New Left. However, this violates binary independence. Furthermore, in a legislative setting, what matters is not the relative size of parties, but what coalitions they are able to form. In this context, a new party entering the legislature is a potential coalition partner, not an "irrelevant alternative." Binary independence implies that a party can increase its bargaining power by spinning off clones of itself. Therefore any reasonable seat allocation rule will violate binary independence.

Transitivity and Freedom from Cycling

In seat allocation rules as I have defined them transitivity is satisfied automatically. In the case of social decision rules the reasonableness of demanding transitivity (or else a slight relaxation of it such as quasi transitivity or acyclicity) is usually taken for granted. However, I will argue that it can be dispensed with, and (following N. Miller 1983) that cycling is actually normatively appealing. The reason why transitivity is intuitively appealing in social decision rules is that it is assumed as a condition of individual choice being rational. The assumption here is that social rationality and individual rationality are similar. One of the starting points of economic theory is that individuals can rank alternatives in order of preference. Furthermore, if an individual has cyclical preferences, preferring good a to b, b to c, and c to a, it is possible for another individual to keep trading him the more preferred good in the cycle over and over again, every time making a profit. Another reason why transitivity is desirable in social decision rules is that in a situation of social choice we have to make a single decision. Transitivity gives us a single best alternative or at least a set of alternatives that are equally good.

However, the degree to which social decisions should be judged by the same criteria as individual decisions is open to question. Nicholas Miller (1983) was the first to suggest that cycling may actually be a desirable quality in a social decision rule. His argument grows out of confrontation between social choice theory and the empirical study of pluralist democracy. Social choice theory suggests that multidimensional political competition, as we observe in countries with multiple cross-cutting social cleavages (class, religion, ethnicity, language, region), leads to cycling and instability. However, the empirical literature shows countries with such cleavages tend to be politically more stable than those that are polarized on one dimension. Miller explains this by distinguishing between policy stability and systemic stability. Cycling may produce instability in terms of who wins office and what the policy is, although this instability is more bounded than some previous social choice results suggest. However, this instability increases systemic stability. Because of the instability associated with cycling, it is always possible for the opposition to win the next election. Therefore it is in the interest of the opposition to contest the next election, as opposed to starting a civil war. In the absence of cycling, there may be permanent winners and permanent losers, and this unequal stability may lead the losers to reject the political system. Therefore in systemic terms, intransitivity is desirable.

Building on this insight, a broader case can be made for the desirability of cycling. Consider a legislative bargaining situation where different parties are negotiating government policy. Cycling implies that any proposal can be beaten by some other proposal. Alternatively it implies that there are multiple, overlapping winning coalitions. Whatever the current winning coalition is, and whatever proposal is currently on the table, it is possible to find an alternative and an alternative coalition to beat it. That is, it is always possible for those players excluded from the winning coalition to find some alternative that they can agree on and that will split the current winning coalition. I will argue that this has some very appealing normative effects. The fact that there are multiple possible winning coalitions means that it is unwise to try to treat those excluded from the winning coalition too harshly by infringing on their most vital interests. If the winners do this, the losers will be willing to sell their support to part of the winning coalition at a very low price in exchange for protection of their vital interest, splitting the winning coalition. In chapter 5 I argue that cycling allows us to combine majority rule with minority protection. In chapter 6 I argue that cycling encourages reasonable deliberation. Rather than cycling being a problem for democratic theory, it may be that cycling is what makes democracy as we know it possible.

Furthermore, some of the arguments made in favor of transitive procedures do not really apply in a legislative context. The arguments for transitive, nonbinary procedures are frequently couched in epistemic terms (see, for example, Young 1995). A procedure is good if it identifies that alternative that is most likely to be the best one, given the information we have available. However, in a legislative bargaining situation it is hard to see what we would mean by the "best" option. Rather, the decision is often a distributive one. A transitive social decision rule means that we are able to rank alternatives on a single dimension from best to worst. It is hard to see how this applies here. Certainly some alternatives are worse, in that they are inefficient. However, among those alternatives that are efficient (in the sense that it is not possible to make anyone better off without taking something away from someone else), the difference is distributional and thus multidimensional. It may be possible to rank the various alternatives in accordance with how egalitarian they are, but in practice even this is impossible to do objectively, as different people have different conceptions of what a fair division is. If it is the case that the problem does not have a one-dimensional structure, there is no reason to insist on a transitive social decision rule that reduces the problem to a single dimension. Rather, an intransitive social decision rule that preserves the dimensionality of the problem—the cycling that is present in the collective preferences of the voters—may be a better basis for facilitating reasonable bargaining.

In particular, we should reject the notion that transitivity is necessary for social reason. The fact that we define individual rationality in terms of transitivity does not imply that this axiom must apply to the collective. We should not assume that the collective is just like an individual writ large. Indeed this equation of individual and collective is a result of the same sort of anthropomorphism that social choice theory has largely discredited (most notably Riker's 1982 assault on populism and the notion of the collective will). Instead of defining social reason in terms of a transitive general will (something that is no longer tenable), much of the political philosophy literature defines it in terms of a communicative process (notably Dewey 1946; Habermas 1984; Rawls 1993/1996). An outcome is reasonable if it is the type of outcome that reasonable people would agree to under reasonable rules. This does not require a transitive decision rule that "discovers" the "correct" solution, but rather a situation in which agents need to persuade one another, producing a reasonable compromise in a situation where there is no right answer.

What We Can Demand of a Democratic Procedure 3: Protection of Rights, Stability, and Other Desirable Outcomes

This book develops a theory of democratic institutions in terms of the basic value of political equality. However, no one would argue that this or other procedural qualities are the only things we should value in political institutions. Clearly we are also interested in the kinds of outcomes institutions produce. We are concerned that institutions lead to basic rights being respected and minorities having some means to safeguard their interests. We want institutions to produce reasonable, informed debate, producing reasonable policy decisions and keeping public officials accountable. We also value at least a modicum of stability and are interested in economic growth and equity.

A number of influential theorists have argued that democracy can be justified only in terms of such outcomes, and not in terms of intrinsic qualities. For example, Riker (1982) argues that the results of social choice theory render the idea of democratic choice empty. Schumpeter (1942) and Weber (1978) argue that the public is insufficiently informed or involved for democracy to represent an idea of the popular will (see Warren 1988 on Weber). In all these cases, the only value of democracy is that it allows the periodic removal of elites, which in turn restrains government. This book, of course, rejects the idea that democracy can only be justified in such minimal, instrumental terms, arguing in chapter 4 that democracy can be justified in terms of the fairness of its procedures, and perhaps the reasonable deliberation that results from this.

Nevertheless, it is necessary to consider the performance of democratic procedures in terms of these other values. In particular we need to ask whether there is a trade-off between the value of political equality, on one hand, and the qualities of minority protection, reasonable deliberation, stability, accountability, and economic performance, on the other. Thus chapter 5 considers the relationship between political equality, rights, and minority protection. Chapter 6 considers reasonable deliberation and accountability. Chapter 8 considers the empirical evidence for the stability and economic performance (both growth and equality) of the countries whose political systems are closest to the ideals of political equality defined here.

Summary

I have outlined the basic concepts and qualities that define democratic choice. Modern democracies involve two sets of procedures. Seat allocation rules translate the electorate's votes into allocations of seats in decision-making bodies. Social decision rules are used by these bodies to compare policy alternatives and prospective governments. It is important that we not consider democracy a single procedure (a social choice function, in the language of social choice theory) that directly maps people's preferences onto outcomes. Rather, political institutions consist of separate sets of procedures that structure games in which people compete to be representatives, on one hand, and they negotiate and deliberate, on the other.

Following Dahl (1956) we start with the basic assumption that democracy can be defined in terms of popular sovereignty and political equality. I have defined political equality in a liberal sense, in that it is based on procedures treating individual voters equally. This individualism can be defended either in terms of doctrinal liberalism (the individual takes normative precedence over groups individuals make up) or on the grounds that it provides the only neutral way to arbitrate between the claims of different groups. The emphasis on procedure was justified on the grounds that politically fair procedures are a sine qua non of democracy, necessary for any of the other attributes we may consider democratically desirable. It is possible to operationalize this liberal conception of political equality as defined in terms of anonymity (all voters are treated alike) and neutrality (all candidates or alternatives are treated alike). These qualities can be defined to apply to both seat allocation rules and social decision rules.

There are other axiomatic qualities that reasonable democratic procedures must have. Decisiveness and nonnegative responsiveness should be uncontroversial. However, binary independence and transitivity are logically incompatible in a democratic procedure, as demonstrated by Arrow (1951/1963). Which axiom we should choose depends on the type of procedure. I have argued that we should demand that a social decision rule satisfy binary independence, but for a reason quite different from that given by Arrow and most of the social choice literature. Binary independence is necessary because the set of possible government policies cannot be enumerated, which makes binary decision rules necessary for the sake of tractability. Furthermore, political decision making involves a bargaining process, to which binary procedures are well suited. However, I have argued that transitivity is not essential in a social decision rule and that cycling may actually be a good thing, protecting minorities from permanent majorities and preserving the possibility that today's losers could be tomorrow's winners. With seat allocation rules, however, this situation is reversed. Binary independence is a positively undesirable quality in a seat allocation rule, while transitivity is satisfied by definition.

In addition to the qualities intrinsic to democratic procedures, such as political equality, we are also interested in the instrumental effects of democratic institutions. That is, we are interested in whether democracy leads to outcomes like the protection of minorities, accountability of governments, rational decision making, and at least a modicum of stability. It has been argued that democracy only has value in terms of such instrumental benefits, with democratic procedures having no intrinsic value (Schumpeter 1942; Riker 1982). While this book rejects this argument in chapter 4, the instrumental effects of democratic institutions are considered in chapters 5, 6, and 8.

APPENDIX: FORMAL DEFINITIONS OF AXIOMS

SEAT ALLOCATION RULES

Let us define the set of eligible voters as N, with voters numbered $1 \ldots n$, and the set of alternatives A, numbered $1 \ldots a$. The voting correspondence V is defined over the Cartesian product $N \times A$, with $_{i \in N} V_{j \in A}$ reading "i votes for alternative j." Assigning the value 1 for true and 0 for false, $\forall\, i \in N \sum_{j \in A} {}_i V_j \leq 1$. (Each individual either votes for one alternative or does not vote.) The function T maps the voting correspondence into the total vote for each alternative: $T : V \to [0,n]^A$. The function E maps the voting correspondence into the seat share for each alternative: $E : V \to [0,1]^A$. We will assume that seats are infinitely divisible, to abstract from rounding problems.

We can define the following properties of the seat share function E.

Anonymity: Let σ be a function that permutes N. Then E is anonymous if $E(V) = E(\sigma V)$.

Neutrality: Let π be a function that permutes A. Then E is neutral if $\pi E(V) = E(\pi V)$.

Decisiveness: E is decisive iff $\forall\, V, \forall\, i \in A : E_i(V) \in [0,1]$. This is automatically satisfied by the definition of E.

Nonnegative (positive) responsiveness: Let V' be a vote pattern over $N \times A$. Let $V'' = V'$, except that some voters or abstainers have switched to alternative j:

$$(_iV_j' \Rightarrow {}_iV_j''; \exists\, i \in N : {}_iV_j'' \wedge \sim_iV_j'; \forall\, i \in N : \sim_iV_j'', \forall\, k \in A, {}_iV_k' \Leftrightarrow {}_iV_k'').$$

Function E is nonnegatively responsive iff

$$\forall\, (j, k \in A : k \neq j)\ E_j(V') = E_i(V') \Rightarrow E_j(V'') \geq E_i(V'').$$

Function E is positively responsive iff $\forall\, (j, k \in A : k \neq j)\ E_j(V') = E_i(V') \Rightarrow E_j(V'') > E_i(V'')$.

Transitivity: E is transitive iff

$$((E_{i\in A} \geq E_{j\in A}) \wedge (E_{j\in A} \geq E_{k\in A}) \Rightarrow E_{i\in A} \geq E_{k\in A})$$
$$\wedge ((E_{i\in A} \geq E_{j\in A}) \wedge (E_{j\in A} \geq E_{k\in A}) \wedge ((E_{i\in A} > E_{j\in A})$$
$$\vee (E_{j\in A} > E_{k\in A})) \Rightarrow E_{i\in A} > E_{k\in A}).$$

This is automatically satisfied by the definition of E.

Binary independence: E satisfies binary independence iff $\forall\, A', A'' : i, j \in A'$, $A'' : E_{i\in A'}/E_{j\in A'} = E_{i\in A''}/E_{j\in A''}$. The text argues that binary independence is not a property that a seat allocation rule should satisfy.

SOCIAL DECISION RULES

Let us define the set of eligible voters as N, with voters numbered $1 \ldots n$, and the set of alternatives A, numbered $1 \ldots a$. The preference correspondence R is defined over the Cartesian product $N \times A \times A$, with $_{b\in A}R_{ic\in A}$ reading "i prefers alternative b to c or is indifferent between them." For convenience let us define the strict preference relation S, where $_{b\in A}S_{ic\in A}$ reads "i strictly prefers b to c" and $_{b\in A}S_{ic\in A} \Leftrightarrow (_{b\in A}R_{ic\in A}) \wedge \sim(_{c\in A}R_{ib\in A})$.

Let us assume that R is transitive so that

$$((_{b\in A}R_{ic\in A}) \wedge (_{c\in A}R_{id\in A}) \Rightarrow {}_{b\in A}R_{id\in A})$$
$$\wedge ((_{b\in A}R_{ic\in A}) \wedge (_{c\in A}R_{id\in A}) \wedge ((_{b\in A}S_{ic\in A}) \vee (_{c\in A}S_{id\in A})) \Rightarrow {}_{b\in A}S_{id\in A}).$$

Let us define the social preference correspondence R_S over the Cartesian product $A \times A$, with $_{b\in A}R_{Sc\in A}$ reading "society prefers alternative b to c or is indifferent between them." Let S_S be the related strict preference relation. Let the social preference function U map individual preferences onto social preferences: $U : R \rightarrow R_S$.

Decisiveness: R_S is decisive iff $\forall\, b, c \in A : {}_{b\in A}R_{Sc\in A} \vee {}_{c\in A}R_{Sb\in A}$.

Nonnegative (positive) responsiveness: Let U', U'' be preference profiles over $N \times A \times A$. Let U'' be identical to U', except that at least one person has either switched from preferring b to preferring c, has switched from indifference to preferring c, or has switched from preferring b to indifference. Formally:

$(\forall\, i \in N : {}_cS_i(U')_b \Rightarrow {}_cS_i(U'')_b; {}_cR_i(U')_b \Rightarrow {}_cR_i(U'')_b)$

$\wedge\, (\exists\, i \in N : ({}_bS_i(U')_c \wedge {}_cR_i(U'')_b) \vee ({}_bR_i(U')_c \wedge {}_cS_i(U'')_b))$

$\wedge\, (\forall\, i \in N, \forall\, d, e \in A_{/b,c} : {}_dR_i(U')_e \Leftrightarrow {}_dR_i(U'')_e).$

Correspondence R^S is positively responsive iff ${}_bR_i(U')_c \Rightarrow {}_bS_i(U'')_c$, and R^S is non-negatively responsive iff $({}_bR_i(U')_c \Rightarrow {}_bR_i(U'')_c) \wedge ({}_bS_i(U')_c \Rightarrow {}_bS_i(U'')_c)$.

Transitivity: R_S is transitive iff

$(({}_{b\in A}R_{Sc\in A}) \wedge ({}_{c\in A}R_{Sd\in A}) \Rightarrow {}_{b\in A}R_{Sd\in A})$

$\wedge\, (({}_{b\in A}R_{Sc\in A}) \wedge ({}_{c\in A}R_{Sd\in A}) \wedge (({}_{b\in A}S_{Sc\in A}) \vee ({}_{c\in A}S_{Sd\in A})) \Rightarrow {}_{b\in A}S_{Sd\in A}).$

Binary independence: Let R_S^A be the social preference relation defined over set of alternatives A. Relation R_S is binary independent iff

$\forall\, A', A'' : b, c \in A', A'' : {}_{b\in A'}R_{Sc\in A'}^{A'} \Leftrightarrow {}_{b\in A''}R_{Sc\in A''}^{A''},$

where A' and A'' are two sets of alternatives.

PART 1

POLITICAL EQUALITY

CHAPTER 3

Political Equality in Electoral Systems: Equality Implies Proportionality

This chapter argues that the value of political equality implies proportionality in an electoral system. The literature on electoral systems and democratic theory has been remarkably agnostic about how basic values may be translated into institutions. Dahl (1956) constructs an axiomatic theory of democracy based on the idea of political equality but then declares it has little to say about practical politics because it does not consider representative elections. Much of the empirical literature on electoral systems is essentially instrumental—if you want this value, choose this kind of institution. Proportionality is considered as a value but is not grounded in any more fundamental principle. Social choice theory offers a means of translating values into institutions, but this literature has tended to concentrate on social decision rules rather than electoral systems. Here, by contrast, it is argued that proportionality is logically implied by the basic value of political equality, that is, by the concept of democracy itself. Of course, there are many different ways to implement proportionality, and these will be considered later in this chapter. Nevertheless, the value of political equality implies that proportionality is a basic requirement for an electoral system being democratic. If we wish to defend a system that is not proportional, we have to argue that there are other values that outweigh the value of political equality.

This chapter shows that proportionality follows logically from the liberal conception of political equality defined in the last chapter, that is, from the requirement that all individual voters be treated equally. It is thus very different from the usual arguments that proportional representation (PR) is "fair." Frequently the fairness of proportionality is simply assumed. For example, Lijphart (1994, 140) concludes that for many PR supporters, proportionality is simply a goal in itself, "virtually synonymous with political justice." When proportionality is given justification, this tends to be in terms of fairness to political parties or social groups, or in terms of the desirable instrumental effects of proportional representation. For example, McLean (1991) argues that the case for proportional representation rests on the idea that a legislature should be a microcosm

of the population, as did Black (1958/1971). Similarly, Pitkin (1967) identifies the case for PR in terms of "descriptive representation" (the fair
representation of every salient group), while Still (1981) uses the similar
concept of "group representation." The political electoral reform discourse frequently emphasizes the unfairness of nonproportional representation to certain political parties, who win far fewer seats than their
vote share would entitle them to under proportionality. This argument
can be rephrased in individual terms as the demand that the same number of voters for each party be needed to elect a representative (for example, Beetham 1992; Jenkins 1998). Of course, arguments for PR in
terms of fairness to political parties or social groups may be convincing to
a considerable number of people. However, the point here is that they are
not the only arguments, nor I think the most fundamental.

Arguments against proportional representation are often based on
the idea that some other value (such as stability, economic performance,
or accountability) outweighs the fairness of PR (to be considered in
chapters 6 and 8). However, it is sometimes argued that the case for proportional representation rests on one particular kind of fairness or
equality (numerical fairness to parties or social groups), and that other
forms of fairness (e.g., the winner-take-all principle or the constituency
principle) would lead to different conclusions (see, for example, Beitz
1989 and various contributors to Jenkins 1998). This argument is a direct
result of thinking about equality and fairness in group terms. If we consider equality or fairness in terms of groups, it is possible to divide society into groups in many ways, and it is possible to find various principles
to arbitrate between their claims. For example, if we consider equality
between social groups, we get descriptive representation and a justification for PR; whereas if we consider equality between geographical areas,
we get the constituency principle and an argument for single-member
district systems.

It should be noted that the argument made in favor of the fairness
of first-past-the-post elections rests on conceptions of fairness to groups
or political parties every bit as much as the usual arguments in favor of
PR. For example, the winner-take-all principle considers fairness in
terms of parties or candidates, not voters. First-past-the-post is fair, it is
argued, because the party that wins a fair contest gets the prize. Similarly,
the constituency principle is based on fairness to geographically defined
groups of people. Of course, advocates of these principles prefer to
phrase them in individualist terms (the rights of individual residents of a
constituency, or of voters of the plurality party), just as advocates of PR
do. However, as with the usual argument for PR, these arguments are
still group-based in that they conceive individual voters in terms of a pre-

conceived group identity, instead of conceiving them as individuals per se in the liberal sense.

By basing the argument on a liberal conception of equality—that is, the idea that all individual voters should be treated equally—we avoid this relativism. We no longer have to decide which groups deserve special consideration but merely have to make the system fair to individuals. Individuals can then decide which group identities are salient to them when they vote. As a result, it is possible to come to a determinate conclusion—political equality implies proportional representation. The previous chapter has justified why we should prefer the liberal conception of equality over group-based conceptions—it can be justified either in terms of doctrinal liberalism (the rights of individuals have precedence over the rights of groups those individuals make up) or in terms of individual equality providing the only democratic means to arbitrate between the claims of various cross-cutting groups.

Whereas our analysis starts with basic normative principles, such as political equality, and sees what this logically requires in an electoral system, the empirical electoral system literature starts with existing electoral systems and studies their effects. Much of the electoral system literature has focused on the effect of electoral rules on party systems. Duverger (1954/1963) found that first-past-the-post elections tended to produce two-party systems, while proportional representation produced multipartism. Rae (1967) systematically compared district magnitude (the number of candidates elected from each district) and electoral rules to explain cross-national differences in proportionality, large-party advantage, and the number of parties. More recent works in this tradition include Taagepera and Shugart (1989) and Lijphart (1994).

When it deals with normative questions of democracy, the electoral systems literature tends to operate in instrumental terms, as typified by the title of Powell's (2000) book *Elections as Instruments of Democracy.* Various conceptions of democracy are set out, and different electoral systems are evaluated in terms of how far they produce results compatible with these conceptions. Thus in Powell's account majoritarian conceptions of democracy stress the direct accountability of government to the electorate, as operationalized by how likely a change in popular support is to produce a change in government; while proportional conceptions of democracy see democracy as a multistage process requiring "authorized representation," measured in terms of what proportion of the voters voted for a government party, and the degree to which policy outcomes match the preferences of the median voter. Plurality systems do well on the first set of criteria, while proportional systems do well on the second. Similarly Lijphart (1994) contrasts the value of proportionality maximized by proportional systems with the accountability provided by plurality elections. Katz (1997) goes even further, providing a long list of conceptions of democracy (including less credible variants such as "guided democracy," socialist "people's democracy," and Calhounian veto-group "democracy") and tracing the type of election systems required by each. For the most part there is a studied impartiality between plurality and proportional election systems, although there are exceptions. (Lijphart [1999] links proportional election systems with favorable outcomes in terms of factors such as economic equality, quality of life, and environmental protection, while providing similar outcomes in terms of economic growth and stability. Dummett [1997], while being very critical of first-past-the-post and single transferable vote, allows that the choice of replacement depends on competing principles, although he does propose a new system based on a modified Borda procedure. Farrell [2001], while accepting that there is a trade-off between the accountability provided by plurality systems and the accurate representation provided by PR, argues that PR is preferable because the main argument against PR—that it produces unstable government—is empirically untrue.)

The social choice literature studies the axiomatic properties of voting procedures. It thus provides a means for taking values from the normative literature and translating them into rigorous requirements that can be applied to empirical electoral systems. However, the social choice literature has concentrated on social decision rules (where a decision is to be made among competing alternatives) as opposed to seat allocation rules (where political representation is distributed). Most previous technical work on proportional representation has tended to concentrate on the mechanics of seat allocation rules rather than the axiomatic justification of the principle of proportionality (see, for example, Balinski and Young 1982/2001; Taagepera and Shugart 1989).

There is, however, some axiomatic work dealing with the desiderata of electoral systems. Dodgson (1884/1995) advocates a PR system primarily on grounds of individual fairness. The first two desiderata of an electoral system he gives are that every voter has the same chance of being represented and that every represented voter be represented by the same fraction of a member. Ward (1995) uses computer simulations of one-dimensional party competition to argue that proportional representation is the electoral system most likely to produce policy choices close to those of the median voter. Feld and Grofman (1986) consider how a representative system can replicate the preferences of a population as a whole, while Benoît and Kornhauser (1994) show that distributed representation can lead to Pareto-inferior results. Monroe (1995) and Chamberlin and Courant (1983) propose new electoral systems based on maximizing representation. Deemen (1993) shows that certain voting paradoxes apply to list PR systems. Rogowski (1981) suggests that anonymity implies proportionality, but he provides no proof. Hout, Swart, and Veer (2002) show that anonymity, neutrality, consistency, faithfulness, and topsonlyness imply the plurality ranking property; the results presented here draw on this insight. Hout and McGann (2004) show that anonymity, neutrality, and positive responsiveness imply a result equivalent to pure list proportional representation.

This chapter is divided into two sections. The first section sets out the main theoretical result, that political equality implies proportionality in single-vote electoral systems. It also shows that this result can be extended to multiple-vote electoral systems, in that political equality requires that these systems produce proportional results if the preferences of voters correspond to electoral lists. Although the exposition is intuitive (formal proofs are reserved for the appendix) this section is somewhat technical. The second section considers electoral systems in practice. After laying out a typology of electoral systems, it considers how well each system conforms to the ideal of proportionality. It then briefly lays out other considerations that may be significant when comparing electoral systems. This discussion of other effects of electoral systems is continued in parts 2 and 3 of the book, particularly in chapter 6.

1. Theory: Political Equality Implies Proportionality

Political equality logically entails proportional representation, based on the proofs in Hout and McGann (2004). This section relies on the liberal conception of political equality defined in the last chapter. If we consider political equality in terms of individual voters, then equality and impartiality become equivalent. Thus we can proceed negatively, defining equality in a seat allocation rule as not being biased—that is, not taking into account inappropriate considerations. In this way we can axiomatize political equality as the qualities of anonymity and neutrality. That is to say, a seat allocation rule satisfies political equality if it does not discriminate between voters on the basis of their identities (it is *anonymous*) and does not discriminate between alternatives (candidates, lists, or parties) on the basis of their identities (it is *neutral*). As argued in the previous chapter, it is necessary to apply anonymity and neutrality not just to individual alternatives but also to coalitions of alternatives, as decisions in a legislature will sometimes depend on the relative size of coalitions. Formal axiomatizations are given in the appendix.

We also need to define what is meant by *proportional representation*. This may seem unnecessary. However, we will see that the concept of proportional representation and its implementation differ significantly. In particular, the concept of proportionality does not require that we think in terms of fairness to political parties. Indeed, given that our conception of liberal political equality is based on the equality of individuals, it is important that we be able to define proportional representation in a way that does not depend on parties.

The Concept of Proportional Representation

We define pure proportional representation as a seat allocation rule that assigns seat share to alternatives in proportion to their vote totals (as before, alternatives can be candidates, lists, or parties). The concept of pure PR is of course an abstraction. No existent electoral system meets this criterion, although some come close. It would be theoretically possible to allocate legislative weight to alternatives in direct proportion to vote share in the manner suggested by Chamberlin and Courant (1983). However, if we insist that the votes of all legislators have equal weight, the fact that seats are not infinitely divisible means that there is always some divergence from proportionality, although in principle this could be overcome.[1] Other features of many existing PR systems, such as thresholds and small districts, also reduce proportionality. Nevertheless, although there are no empirical examples of pure PR, it serves a purpose here as a counterfactual ideal, and there are existing systems that approximate it quite well.

It should be noted that although it is often assumed that proportional representation must be based on political parties and party lists, this is not the case. Some existing PR systems are based on lists of citizen candidates (who may or may not be affiliated with a party), and it is even possible to define a PR system in terms of individual candidates. Dodgson (1884/1995) proposes such a system. Each voter casts one vote in a large electoral district. Every candidate who received a quota, that is, total votes cast / (number of seats + 1), is elected. Candidates are then able to distribute any surplus votes they may have received in any way they wish. The intuition is that the votes a candidate receives are their property to dispose of at will. Dodgson defends this in terms of the concept of representation. If I am willing to choose someone to make legislative decisions on my behalf, I surely trust this person enough to choose their own deputies to carry out this legislative task.

List proportional representation can be seen as a set of restrictions on the system proposed by Dodgson. Suppose that we require candidates to state in advance how they would distribute their surplus votes. Then we have a rudimentary system of list PR. Of course, all existing list PR systems place considerably more constraints on candidates. Generally, candidates are only allowed to have their names on one list, and all candidates on the list are required to distribute their excess votes in the same way defined by the list. In practice most systems of list PR force candidates to compete as mutually exclusive teams.

This, however, does not force candidates to be organized as political parties. A party is not just a slate of candidates but rather a sociological organization that combines a slate of candidates with an organizational structure, usually a parliamentary fraction, and sometimes affiliated social organizations. Some list PR systems, such as that in Germany, require that lists be affiliated with registered political parties, and thus can be referred to as party-list PR systems. However, other systems, such as that in the Netherlands, afford parties very little in the way of special treatment. Rather, elections are organized in terms of lists of candidates, which any group of citizens can propose. It is true that most lists are affiliated with political parties. However, it is also true that virtually all members of Parliament under the plurality system in the United Kingdom are also affiliated with one of the main parties. Modern politics creates strong incentives for candidates to join parties (see Aldrich 1995), regardless of the electoral system. What is important from a liberal point of view is that while the list PR systems in countries such as the Netherlands accommodate political parties, they do not mandate them. Indeed, hastily assembled citizen lists have won considerable vote share in some recent elections in the Netherlands.

Results

Political equality (operationalized as the axioms of anonymity and neutrality) implies a single-vote seat allocation rule essentially equivalent to pure proportional representation. First, it is shown that any single-vote seat share allocation rule that is positively responsive, neutral, and anonymous satisfies the strong plurality ranking property (alternatives that win more votes get more seats). This result applies to coalitions as well as alternatives (if the seat allocation rule is anonymous and neutral, coalitions whose members win more votes must get more seats in aggregate). In parliaments, governments are typically chosen by majority rule, the vote of investiture usually requiring a coalition. Therefore the outcome depends on the coalition formation game defined by the election and the seat share allocation rule. It is shown that any seat share allocation rule that is anonymous and neutral (and thus satisfies the strong plurality ranking property) defines a coalition game identical to that defined by pure list proportional representation. We show similar results when the seat share allocation rule is assumed to be nonnegatively instead of positively responsive.

First it is necessary to show that anonymity, neutrality, and positive responsiveness imply the strong plurality ranking property—if alternative A wins more votes than alternative B, then it must receive a greater seat share. If we only require nonnegative responsiveness, then anonymity and neutrality imply the weak plurality ranking property (alternatives that get more votes must win at least the same number of seats).

> PROPOSITION 1: *Any seat share allocation rule that is anonymous, neutral, and positively (nonnegatively) responsive satisfies the strong (weak) plurality ranking property.* (Proof in appendix.)

The intuition here is straightforward. If two alternatives have the same number of votes, then by anonymity and neutrality, they must have the same seat share. If in this case one alternative receives more seats, then either the vote allocation system is inherently biased in its favor (violating neutrality) or some voters' votes count for more than others (violating anonymity). If one alternative then increases its vote at the expense of the other or by gaining the votes of people who previously abstained, by positive responsiveness it must receive a greater seat share than the other alternative. Therefore, if one alternative receives more votes than another it must receive more seats (the strong plurality ranking property). If we only assume nonnegative responsiveness, then when an alternative gains votes, it must at least not lose seats. This implies that an alternative that wins more votes than another must get at least an equal seat share (the weak plurality ranking property).

Proposition 1 can be extended to apply not only to seat allocation for individual alternatives, but to seat allocation for coalitions of alternatives. Strictly speaking we define a seat share allocation rule as anonymous, neutral, and positively responsive to coalitions if the allocation of seats to coalitions also satisfies anonymity, neutrality, and positive responsiveness, however we partition the alternatives into coalitions.

> PROPOSITION 2: *Any seat share allocation rule that is anonymous, neutral, and positively (nonnegatively) responsive for coalitions satisfies the strong (weak) plurality ranking property for coalitions.* (Proof in appendix.)

The proof of this proposition is essentially identical to that of Proposition 1. If one coalition of alternatives receives more votes than another, it must receive a greater total seat share if we assume positive responsiveness, and at least an equal total seat share if we only assume nonnegative responsiveness.

In representative bodies, governments are typically formed by a process of majority-rule coalition formation. Which coalition forms is a result of a bargaining process. However, the bargaining situation is defined in terms of which coalitions have sufficient seats to win a majority-rule vote of investiture (or confidence) and form a government. It can be shown that any seat allocation function that satisfies the coalitional strong plurality ranking property defines a coalition formation game identical to that defined by pure PR. Therefore anonymity, neutrality, and positive responsiveness imply a single-vote seat share allocation that produces a parliamentary outcome to all intents and purposes identical to that produced by pure PR.

> PROPOSITION 3: *Any seat share allocation function that is anonymous, neutral, and positively (nonnegatively) responsive for coalitions defines a majority rule coalition game with a set of winning coalitions that is identical to (a subset of) that defined by seat share allocation by pure proportional representation.* (Proof in appendix.)

The intuition behind the proof comes from the fact that under majority rule a coalition is winning if it has a greater seat share than all the alternatives excluded from it. By Proposition 2, anonymity, neutrality, and positive responsiveness require that if a coalition has more votes than another coalition, it must receive a greater seat share. Therefore the set of winning coalitions must be the set of coalitions whose members have more votes than all the alternatives excluded by them. This is exactly the same as the set of winning coalitions under pure PR.

If we only assume nonnegative responsiveness, it is possible for a coalition to win a majority of the votes but only to receive exactly half the seats, and thus be a blocking but not winning coalition. However, it is impossible to have a "manufactured majority" (a situation where an alternative or coalition with a minority of the vote gets a majority of the seats) without violating anonymity or neutrality. The intuition behind this is similar to the case assuming positive responsiveness. By Proposition 2, anonymity, neutrality, and nonnegative responsiveness require that if a coalition has more votes than another coalition, it must receive at least an equal seat share. It is possible for a coalition to have an equal number of seats to its complement, so it is possible for a coalition to win a majority of the vote, but to only receive exactly half the seats. Any winning coalition under our seat share allocation rule is a winning coalition under proportionality but not vice versa.

Extension to Multiple-Vote Systems

The formal results apply to single-vote electoral systems. However, the principle of proportionality is still relevant when considering electoral systems that ask voters for several choices. We can classify multiple-vote electoral systems into two groups. First there are so-called mixed-member systems (Shugart and Wattenberg 2001). These typically give voters a vote for a candidate to represent their district and a vote for a party, but only ask for the voter's first choice in each category. We will argue that these systems can easily be accommodated within our framework. Second there are ordinal rules that ask voters to rank alternatives, such as single transferable vote (STV) and the Borda procedure. It is more difficult to define what we mean by proportionality when voters order candidates instead of casting a single vote. However, in the special case where voter preferences truly correspond to electoral lists, then liberal equality still implies proportionality, as per our result. Thus, to satisfy the condition of political equality a multivote electoral system has to be compatible with proportionality, if all voters choose to vote for a straight list.

Mixed-member systems can be understood as a combination of two single-vote seat share allocation rules. These systems can be divided into two groups — mixed-member plurality and mixed-member proportional (Shugart andWattenberg 2001). An ideal-type mixed-member plurality system typically allocates a certain number of seats to district elections and a certain number to proportional election, with no compensation between the two. The proportional part of the election largely respects the principles of anonymity and neutrality, while the district election typically does not. Consequently, the overall result will violate the principles of political equality we have defined. An ideal-type mixed-member proportional system, on the other hand, distributes seats from the proportional part of the election in a compensatory manner, so that overall seat totals of each party from both stages approximate proportionality. As a result, these systems essentially function as list PR and thus approximately respect political equality.[2]

We can show that ordinal voting systems that respect political equality must be compatible with proportionality when voters have list preferences. Voters have list preferences if they all rank the candidates on one electoral list in the order of the list, and are indifferent between all the candidates not on that list. If this is the case, the preferences of every voter can be summarized by a voting correspondence (voter x supports list y). If this is so, we can apply the theorems of the last subsection and show that liberal equality implies proportionality in this case. Of course, the fact that there is an ordinal voting system gives the voters many options other than voting a straight list. However, if they choose to vote in this way, liberal equality implies that the result should be proportional. The idea of list voting here is intended as a thought experiment. However, it may not be that far from reality in many countries. For example, in the Netherlands over 90 percent of voters routinely vote for the national leader of their preferred party, in spite of having the option of voting for anyone on the party list (see Gladdish 1991).

It should be noted that the normative case for considering voters' entire preference schedule is questionable. It has frequently been stated as obvious that a good election rule should do this (Black 1958/1971, 95; Dummett 1997). However, we can make a normative case for considering only the first preference of voters in allocating seats in legislatures. Under a pure proportional system (an abstraction, of course, given that seats are not divisible in reality), everyone gets a representative of the list they choose, however small. In a sense there is no need to consider second-place preferences because everyone gets their first preference (see Dodgson 1884/1995 for an early statement of this position). Furthermore, it can be argued that the fact that my preferred representative is your very least preferred is irrelevant—their job is to represent me, not you. While this argument is plausible, it requires a stronger theory of representation, such as Powell's (2000) concept of authorized representation. The necessary assumptions are far more demanding than the minimum of liberal equality required in the last section.

We can discuss the use of the most commonly studied ordinal vote mechanisms as seat allocation rules. Both single transferable vote[3] and the Borda count[4] are anonymous and neutral in terms of individual candidates but only if applied to a single district. If voters have list preferences, single transferable vote produces results compatible with proportionality. However, in practice single transferable vote is usually applied to many, rather small districts (in Ireland, the size varies between 3 and 5), rather than a single national district. For this reason, Farrell (2001) finds that single transferable vote in Ireland does not produce strict proportionality, but that it is far closer to it than plurality elections. It is possible to apply single transferable vote to national elections, but this would result in ballots with hundreds, if not thousands of candidates. One solution to the resulting problem of unwieldiness would be to allow voters to vote a straight party ticket. However, if most voters act in this way, the results will be virtually identical to list PR.

The Borda count in general does not satisfy proportionality if voters have list preference, and it has some other features that make it extremely problematic as a seat allocation rule. This is not surprising, as it was originally proposed as a rule for ranking candidates, not for distributing

Voter	1	2	3	4
	a	a	b	b
	b	b	a	a

Fig. 3.1. Configuration of voters under Borda count

Voter	1	2	3	4
	a	a'	b	b
	a'	a	a'	a
	b	b	a	a'

Fig. 3.2. Configuration of voters under Borda count with new party

representatives. Suppose we have two parties a and b, each of which has two voters who favor it, as shown in figure 3.1. Parties a and b both receive a Borda count of 2 and thus receive an equal allocation of seats.

However, now let us assume that a faction breaks away from party a to form party a', giving us the preference distribution shown in figure 3.2. Party a, party a', and party b now all get a Borda count of 4, so all get equal representation. However, this means that the combined representation of parties a' and a is now double that of b. By dividing in two, the original party a has increased its representation at the expense of b. This property of the Borda procedure makes sense when we are ranking candidates—if a new candidate enters the race who is almost identical to a, that candidate should score almost identically to a. However, it is not a desirable quality when distributing seats, because it does not take into account the similarity of candidates or parties. This leads to some potentially undesirable consequences, such as encouraging party fragmentation and possibly excluding minority representation. Apart from these consequences, the results will be arbitrary as they depend as much on the number of candidates of each type running as on the preferences of the voters.

To mitigate these problems, Dummett (1997) suggests a hybrid "quota Borda system" that combines a Borda procedure with a provision that candidates who receive a certain quota of first-place votes are automatically elected. This is essentially a combination of single nontransferable vote with the Borda count, with single nontransferable vote electing candidates receiving a quota of first-place votes and Borda electing the rest. As such it is likely to inherit the problems of SNTV, such as a high premium placed on a party's supporters distributing their votes between candidates optimally (see Cox 1997; Bowler and Grofman 2000). In addition, it does not address the problem of the results being arbitrary in that they are dependent on the number of each type of candidate running.

Other seat allocation rules have been proposed that are technically variations of the Borda count but have quite different effects and goals. Chamberlin and Courant (1983) propose a system based on a Borda-type procedure to maximize the "representativeness" of a committee, in the sense of maximizing the number of people who have a highly ranked candidate on the committee. This would lead to candidates with relatively few votes being overrepresented, so to compensate for this, voting in the committee would be weighted by the number of votes received, so the voting strength in the committee would be identical to ordinary proportional representation. Monroe (1995) proposes a generalization of proportional representation that he refers to as "fully proportional representation." The ordinal implementation of this is technically related to the Borda count. The procedure considers every possible partition of the voters into equally sized groups and assigns each group its Borda winner as its representative. The partition for which the elected representatives best fit the groups is then selected. Monroe claims that the procedure is not practical due to the ease with which it could be manipulated by strategic voting. However, the procedure may prove to be theoretically important in that it may provide a limiting case for proportional representation with candidates rather than lists (the Chamberlin and Courant 1983 procedure may have a similar utility).

So, although our technical results only refer to single-vote seat allocation rules, they can be applied to multiple-vote rules. If voters have list preferences, then liberal equality still implies that the seat allocation rule be proportional. Essentially, political equality requires that an ordinal seat allocation rule be compatible with proportionality, if voters vote in terms of lists rather than candidates. Some ordinal voting systems are compatible with this kind of proportionality, such as single transferable vote and the Borda-type procedures proposed by Chamberlin and Courant (1983) and Monroe (1995), although the Borda count itself is not. It should be noted that it is far from obvious that rules that consider a voter's entire preference profile are normatively superior to rules that only consider first preferences.

2. Electoral Systems in Practice

The previous section showed that the principle of political equality implies proportionality in single-vote electoral systems. It also showed that multiple-vote electoral systems that respect political equality either produce results very similar to proportional systems or are problematic for other reasons. However, proportionality is only a principle: We need to consider how this principle can be translated into institutional practice, given that no existing electoral system is perfectly proportional. This section proceeds by first laying out a typology of electoral systems. It then considers how well they approximate the ideal of proportionality. Finally, other effects of electoral systems are considered.

Typology of Electoral Systems

There is a well-developed literature classifying electoral systems that we can draw upon (see, among others, Rae 1967; Taagepera and Shugart 1989; Lijphart 1994; Katz 1997; Farrell 2001). We can begin by classifying pure electoral systems (systems that use one procedure to assign seats, as opposed to mixed electoral systems that use a mixture of procedures). Following Rae (1967) we can classify these along two dimensions, district magnitude and electoral formula.[5] District magnitude is simply the number of seats distributed in each electoral district. This can range from 1 in a country like the United States with single-member district elections to 150 in the Netherlands, which has a single nationwide district.[6] The electoral formula is the rule used to allocate seats (plurality, proportional representation, single transferable vote, etc.). Table 3.1 summarizes the various combinations.

The simplest formula is plurality, where the candidates are simply ranked according to how many votes they receive. If there is only one seat to be distributed, this gives us single-member district plurality (first-past-the-post) elections where the highest vote-getter is elected, regardless of whether that candidate receives an absolute majority of the vote. A variant of plurality in a single-member district is plurality runoff, sometimes (mistakenly) called "majority-rule runoff."[7] Under this rule, the candidates are ranked by plurality, and all but the top two candidates are eliminated. Another vote is then taken to determine the winner. If

TABLE 3.1.   Typology of Pure Electoral Systems

	District Magnitude	
Formula	**Single Member**	**Multimember**
Plurality	Single-member district plurality (first-past-the-post)	Single nontransferable vote
		Multiple vote
	Plurality runoff	
Proportional	—	List proportional representation
Ordinal vote	Single transferable vote	Single transferable vote
	Borda	Borda

we apply plurality to multimember districts, we get single nontransfer-able vote or multiple vote, depending on how many votes each voter gets. If there are three seats to be distributed, under single nontransfer-able vote, each voter gets 1 vote, and the three candidates with the most votes are elected. Multiple vote works the same way, with the exception that each voter may get 2 or 3 votes.[8]

Under list proportional representation a list of candidates receives seats in proportion to the number of votes it receives, so if a list wins three seats, the first three names on its list are elected. (In some systems the lists have to be associated with political parties, but this is not always the case.) This only makes sense with multimember districts. However, various or-dinal formulas, such as single transferable vote and the Borda count, make sense with either single- or multimember districts (see section 1 for definition of these ordinal rules).

Proportional representation actually refers to a variety of formulas that approximate proportionality. No formula can be exactly propor-tional unless it divides seats. For example, if we have a 5-seat district and a list wins 30 percent of the vote, it can either win 1 seat (20 percent of the total) or 2 seats (40 percent), but not 1.5 seats. This is less of a prob-lem if we have a large district magnitude, as it is possible to get very close to proportionality. With relatively small district magnitudes, however, the choice of formula can have a considerable effect. There are two families of formulas, quota and divisor.[9] With quota methods, first the quota needed to elect a candidate is determined. The list with the most votes is awarded a seat. A quota's worth of votes is then subtracted from its total. This is repeated until all seats are allocated. Different quotas may be used, as summarized in table 3.2. Generally the Hare quota gives less of an advantage to the list with most votes than the Droop quota, which in turn has less large-list bias than the Imperiali quota (Taagepera and Shugart 1989). With divisor methods, there is a series of divisors. The largest list is awarded a seat, and then its vote is divided by the first divi-sor. Each time a list wins a seat, its vote is divided by the next divisor.

TABLE 3.2.   Proportional Representation Formulas

Type of mechanism		
Quota	Hare	Quota = voters/seats
	Droop	Quota = (voters/(seats + 1)) + 1
	Imperiali	Quota = voters/(seats + 2)
Divisor	D'Hondt	Divisors: 1, 2, 3, 4, . . .
	Sainte-Laguë	Divisors: 1, 3, 5, 7, . . .
	Modified Sainte-Laguë	Divisors: 1.4, 3, 5, 7, . . .

This is repeated until all seats are filled. Of the divisor methods, D'Hondt has the greatest large-list bias, followed by modified Sainte-Laguë and Sainte-Laguë (Taagepera and Shugart 1989).

Two other features of proportional representation mechanisms are particularly notable: whether the list is open or closed, and whether there is a minimum threshold required for a list to win any seats. With closed-list proportional representation, the list determines the order in which candidates are elected. With open-list PR the voters are able to determine the order of candidates on the list. For example, in Italy prior to 1994 voters had two votes, one for the party and one for their preferred candidate. The party vote determined how many seats the party received, while the individual preference vote determined who filled those seats. There are also many systems that can be described as semi-closed, in that it is theoretically possible for voters to change the list order but very difficult in practice. The Netherlands is an example of this.[10] Many proportional representation systems have electoral thresholds, so that if a list does not exceed this threshold it receives no seats, even though it would be entitled to some seats by proportionality. For example, in Turkey a party that wins 9.9 percent of the vote receives no seats, whereas it would receive 55 seats if it made the 10 percent threshold.

In addition to pure electoral systems, where one mechanism is used to distribute seats, there are mixed-member systems, where different mechanisms are used to distribute different seats. Typically the election is divided into local and either regional or national seats (or in some cases both). In nearly all cases the national seats are distributed by some form of proportional representation. According to Shugart and Wattenberg (2001), the key variable is whether the national seats are compensatory or not. If the national seats are compensatory, then they are distributed so as to restore proportionality to the overall result. Thus if a party wins a disproportionate number of local tier seats, it receives fewer of the national seats to restore proportionality. However, if the system is not compensatory, the party is allowed to keep all the local tier seats it won, and it wins a number of upper tier seats proportionate to its vote. A second variable is whether the lower tier seats are distributed from single-member districts or multimember constituencies. The various combinations are summarized in table 3.3. If we have single-member district elections to the lower tier and compensatory proportional representation at the upper tier, then we have a mixed-member proportional system, to use Shugart and Wattenberg's (2001) term. Germany is the most noted example of this. Each voter has two votes, one for a single-member district candidate and the other for a party. Seats at the regional (Land) level are distributed so that the overall number of seats each party receives is proportional to the number of party votes. If we have single-member district elections for the lower tier, and noncompensatory proportional representation for the upper tier, we have mixed-member plurality (or what Shugart and Wattenberg refer to as mixed-member majoritarian).[11] An example of this would be the Italian lower house where three-quarters of the seats are chosen by single-member district elections and one-quarter are chosen by proportional representation.

It should be noted that many existing proportional representation systems are actually multiple-tier systems, something that Lijphart (1994) particularly emphasizes. List proportional representation is used for the lowest tier. However, because the districts at this level are quite small, considerable disproportionality can result. To counter this there are regional and/or national seats that are allocated to correct this. Typically such systems give the voter only a single vote, so their local tier vote is tied to their national vote, although it would be theoretically possible to implement such a system with a separate vote for each tier. Countries with such a system include Austria, Belgium, Denmark, Norway, and Sweden. It would also be possible to use other multiple-member district systems for the lower tier, such as single nontransferable vote. Another possibility would be to combine list proportional representation at the lower and upper tiers in a noncompensatory manner, although it is not clear what would be achieved by this.

Thus we have a typology of existing electoral systems. While most of the variation can be captured in the simple dichotomy between plurality and proportional representation, we will see that the institutional details, particularly between different implementations of proportional representation, have considerable effects.

TABLE 3.3. Typology of Mixed-Member Systems

	District Magnitude, Lower Level	
Mechanism	**Single Member**	**Multimember**
Compensatory	Mixed-member proportional	Multitier proportional representation
Not compensatory	Mixed-member plurality (Mixed-member majoritarian in Shugart and Wattenberg 2001)	— (but theoretically possible)

Proportionality in Practice

It is common knowledge that proportional representation produces results that are approximately proportional, while plurality (whether single-member district, runoff, or single nontransferable vote) can produce considerable large-party bias. However, the details are considerably more complex. For example, small-district proportional representation (for example, as in Spain) can also produce a considerable large-party advantage, while national district PR in the Netherlands produces results as close to proportionality as is possible without dividing seats. In India, single-member district plurality elections produce results that are approximately proportional, because there are many regionally concentrated parties. Furthermore, if the goal is to produce proportionality, this can be done with many mixed-member systems, as well as with pure proportional representation.

First it is necessary to define what we mean by *proportionality*. The quality of proportionality used in the theoretical portion of this chapter applies to the electoral mechanism, not to the outcome. An electoral system is proportional if it translates x percent of the vote into x percent of the seats for *any* party, real or hypothetical. This is not the same as the definition used in much of the empirical literature. Instead this literature considers how proportional the results are, comparing the number of seats won by actual parties with the share of the votes won. This relationship is either plotted to form a proportionality profile (Taagepera and Shugart 1989) or the differences are combined to produce a single measure of disproportionality (see Lijphart 1994; Taagepera and Shugart 1989 for discussions of the various indices). It is possible for an extremely disproportional system to produce proportional results. For example, in the United States, plurality elections to the House of Representatives typically produce results that are quite close to proportionality, because parties that would be severely underrepresented either do not run or people do not vote for them. Similarly, in India regional concentration produces approximately proportional results. However, we would not consider the electoral system in India proportional, because a small to medium-sized party with a geographically dispersed following would be severely underrepresented. Nevertheless, providing we proceed with caution, we can draw on the empirical electoral systems literature to discuss the relative proportionality of various electoral rules.

The two main variables to be considered are the electoral formula and the district magnitude, as in the previous section. In terms of the electoral formula, there is obviously a large difference in proportionality between proportional representation and plurality rules. However, which proportional representation rule is used makes little difference (Katz 1997). This is because all the proportional representation formulas tend toward proportional outcomes as the district magnitude gets large. It is only with small district magnitudes that the difference between the various rules makes a difference. Lijphart (1994) finds that the various proportional formulas can be ranked in order of proportionality as follows: (1) Hare, Sainte-Laguë; (2) Droop, Modified Sainte-Laguë; (3) D'Hondt, Imperiali. Single transferable vote is hard to classify as it applies to individual candidates, not parties. However, assuming that people vote party line, Lijphart (1994) finds that single transferable vote is roughly as proportional as Droop and modified Sainte-Laguë. This contrasts to some of the empirical literature, which suggests that STV is not very proportional (see Farrell 2001). This, however, is largely due to the fact that STV is typically implemented with small district magnitudes (3–5 in Ireland), which reduces proportionality.

District magnitude has a strong effect on proportionality, as has been noted since Rae (1967). Indeed Taagepera and Shugart (1989) suggest it is the decisive factor in determining proportionality in that it explains most of the variance in proportionality and other outcomes, such as the number of parties and fractionalization of the party system, especially between countries with PR formulas. Katz (1997), however, finds that higher district magnitude does not lead to more proportionality under a plurality formula (that is, as we move from single-member district to single nontransferable vote with higher magnitudes), although the number of cases is small. Electoral thresholds clearly depress proportionality, as they lead to parties below the threshold being unrepresented, with other parties overrepresented as a result. Taagepera and Shugart argue that it is possible to combine the effect of district magnitude with that of thresholds to produce a single measure (adjusted district magnitude) that characterizes the effect of the electoral system.

Mixed-member systems can produce highly proportional results providing that they are compensatory and there are enough upper tier seats to compensate for any disproportionality resulting from the lower tier allocation. Noncompensatory mixed-member systems will preserve whatever disproportionality exists in the lower tier, and thus can produce results that vary considerably from proportionality, unless most of the seats are in the proportional upper tier, as in the Polish lower chamber. Multitier PR systems are likely to be extremely proportional, as the lower tier allocation by small district PR typically produces only slight deviations from proportionality that can be easily corrected by the upper tier, even if the number of upper tier seats is small.

Given that proportional formulas and large district magnitudes produce proportional outcomes, if the goal is to ensure proportionality, the most obvious electoral system is national list PR. However, there are other systems (mixed-member, multitier PR) that can produce results almost as proportional. Thus, to choose between competing electoral systems that satisfy proportionality, it is necessary to consider other factors. Although much of this discussion will take place in later chapters, the next section briefly summarizes some of these considerations. I will argue that a strong case can be made for national list PR against mixed systems, although the conclusion will be tentative and rest on subjective value weightings.

Other Effects of Electoral Systems

Although there are many procedures that can satisfy proportionality other than national list PR, these systems produce results that are quite different in other respects. Later chapters will consider these arguments in more depth (particularly section 3 of chapter 6, on representation). Nevertheless we can summarize these considerations. National list PR (or failing that, large district magnitude PR) gives the strongest incentives for representatives to pursue a broadly defined public good, while small district magnitudes provide incentives for particularism and even pork barrel politics. Of course, the flip side of this is that small districts give more incentive for representatives to actively pursue local interests. Furthermore, large districts increase the probability that representation will be descriptively accurate, in terms of categories such as gender and ethnicity. It is frequently argued that plurality elections provide more accountability and responsiveness to shifts in public opinion. In chapter 6 we show that this claim is fundamentally flawed. Finally, district magnitude affects the number of parties and the ease with which new parties can enter the system. Larger district magnitude leads to higher party system fractionalization and a higher effective number of parties (Rae 1967; Taagepera and Shugart 1989).[12] A larger district magnitude also means that the vote that a party needs to gain representation is lower, providing there is not a legal threshold. Thus large effective magnitude systems are more competitive than systems with low effective magnitude, in the sense that there are fewer barriers to entry for new parties.

Summary

This chapter has shown that the basic value of political equality implies that an electoral system must be proportional. More precisely, we have shown that any single-vote seat share allocation rule that satisfies anonymity, neutrality, and positive responsiveness must produce results that are to all intents and purposes identical to those produced by proportionality. We obtain similar results assuming nonnegative instead of positive responsiveness. Furthermore, political equality implies that multiple-vote systems must be compatible with proportionality, if voters' preferences correspond to electoral lists. This has notable consequences for the theory of democracy. Much of the previous empirical literature on electoral systems has been extremely agnostic as to ends, the argument being stated in the form "If you desire *x*, then choose electoral system *y*." Similarly, Dahl (1956) argues that the axiomatic approach has little to say about the practice of democracy because it does not deal with representative systems. In contrast, the results of this chapter show that the basic axiom of political equality places strict requirements on electoral systems, namely, that they satisfy proportionality.

Of course, there are many electoral systems that can satisfy proportionality. The most obvious is, of course, list PR. However, mixed-member systems with compensatory seats and multitier PR will also produce proportional results, as will single transferable vote and the Borda-type systems devised by Chamberlin and Courant (1983) and Monroe (1995), provided they are applied to national districts. To choose between these different systems requires other considerations be taken into account, such as the type of representation, accountability, and deliberation desired. This will be considered in chapter 6. For now let us note that the value of political equality implies proportionality, which eliminates many existing electoral systems, including some of the less proportional forms of PR. If such systems are to be justified, a case has to be made in terms of other values that on balance are argued to be more important than political equality. Parts 2 and 3 of this book will consider other such values.

APPENDIX: PROOFS

All proofs in this chapter are based on Hout and McGann (2004).

Let us define the set of eligible voters as N, with voters numbered $1 \ldots n$, and the set of alternatives A, numbered $1 \ldots a$. The voting correspondence V is defined over the Cartesian product $N \times A$, with $_{i \in N} V_{j \in A}$ reading "i votes for alternative j." Assigning the value 1 for true and 0 for false, $\forall\ i \in N \sum_{j \in A} V_j \leq 1$. (Each individual either votes for one alternative or does not vote.) The function T maps the voting correspondence into the total vote for each alternative: $T : V \rightarrow [0,n]^A$. The function E maps the voting correspondence into the seat share for each alternative: $E : V \rightarrow [0,1]^A$. We will assume that seats are infinitely divisible, to abstract from rounding problems.

We can define the following properties of the seat share function E.

Anonymity: Let σ be a function that permutes N. Then E is anonymous if $E(V) = E(\sigma V)$.

Neutrality: Let π be a function that permutes A. Then E is neutral if $\pi E(V) = E(\pi V)$.

Cancellation property: If $T_j = T_k$, then $E_j = E_k$. (If the vote share for two alternatives is the same, then their seat shares must be the same.)

Nonnegative (positive) responsiveness: Let V' be a vote pattern over $N \times A$. Let $V'' = V'$, except that some voters or abstainers have switched to alternative j:

$$(_iV'_j \Rightarrow {_iV''_j}; \exists\, i \in N : {_iV''_j} \wedge \sim{_iV'_j}; \forall\, i \in N : \sim{_iV''_j}, \forall\, k \in A, {_iV'_k} \Leftrightarrow {_iV''_k}).$$

Function E is nonnegatively responsive iff

$$\forall\ (j,k \in A : k \neq j)\ E_j(V') = E_i(V') \Rightarrow E_j(V'') \geq E_i(V''),$$

and E is positive responsive iff $\forall\ (j,k \in A : k \neq j)\ E_j(V') = E_i(V') \Rightarrow E_j(V'') > E_i(V'')$.

Weak plurality ranking property: $T_{j \in A} > T_{k \in A} \Rightarrow E_j \geq E_k$. (If alternative j wins more votes than alternative k, alternative j receives a seat share greater than or equal to alternative k.)

Strong plurality ranking property: $T_{j \in A} > T_{k \in A} \Rightarrow E_j > E_k$. (If alternative j wins more votes than alternative k, alternative j receives a greater seat share than alternative k.)

LEMMA 1: *Any anonymous and neutral seat share allocation function satisfies the cancellation property.*

PROOF: The proof is isomorphic to the proof of Lemma 2 in Hout, Swart, and Veer (2002). We need to show that

$$E_{j \in A} = E_{k \in A} \quad \text{for all } i, k \in P \quad \text{when } T_j = T_k \quad \text{and anonymity and}$$

neutrality hold.

If $T_j = T_k$, we can permute all voters so that the voters of alternatives j and k change places. We will call the permutation function σ'. By anonymity, the seat shares stay the same: $E_j(\sigma'V) = E_j(V), E_k(\sigma'V) = E_k(V)$. We can permute the parties so that alternatives j and k change places. We call this permutation function π'. By neutrality, the seat share again remains the same: $E_j(\pi'\sigma'V) = E_k(\sigma'V)$. However, by construction $\pi'\sigma'V = V$. (We have swapped the supporters of alternatives j and k, and then swapped the names of the parties, so we are back to the original situation.) Therefore, $E_j(\pi'\sigma'V) = E_j(V) = E_k(\sigma'V) = E_k(V)$.   QED

PROPOSITION 1: *Any seat share allocation rule that is anonymous, neutral, and positively (nonnegatively) responsive satisfies the strong (weak) plurality ranking property.*

PROOF: The proof is isomorphic to the proof of Theorem 2 in Hout, Swart, and Veer (2002). For the positively responsive case, we need to show that neutrality, anonymity, and positive responsiveness imply $T_{j \in A} > T_{k \in A} \Rightarrow E_j > E_k$. For the negatively responsive case, we need to show that neutrality, anonymity, and positive responsiveness imply $T_{j \in A} > T_{k \in A} \Rightarrow E_j \geq E_k$.

By Lemma 1, anonymity and neutrality imply the cancellation property:

$$T_j = T_k \Rightarrow E_j = E_k.$$

Let V'' be a vote pattern where $T_j > T_k$. Then we can derive a vote pattern V' where $T_j = T_k$ by having an appropriate number of voters for alternative j abstain, so that the votes for alternatives j and k are equal.

By the cancellation property, $E_j(V') = E_k(V')$.

By positive responsiveness, $E_j(V') = E_k(V') \Rightarrow E_j(V'') > E_k(V'')$.

By nonnegative responsiveness, $E_j(V') = E_k(V') \Rightarrow E_j(V'') \geq E_k(V'')$.   QED

EXTENSION TO COALITIONS

We may arbitrarily partition the set of alternatives A into m nonoverlapping coalitions, $c_1 \ldots c_m$, where $1 \leq m \leq a$. Let us define the set of coalitions resulting from such a partition as C, where

$$C = \{c_1, \ldots, c_m\} : c_i \subseteq A; \quad (\forall i, j : i \neq j) \, c_i \cap c_j = \varnothing; \quad \bigcup_m c_i = A.$$

Let us define the coalition vote correspondence K on $N \times C$, in terms of the vote correspondence for alternatives, V. Let $_{i \in N}K_{c \in C}$ read "i votes for an alternative in coalition c." Thus $_{i \in N}K_{c_k \in C} \Leftrightarrow {}_{i \in N}V_{j \in c_k}$.

Let us define the coalition vote total function for partition C as the sum of the votes received by each alternative in the coalition. Thus

$$U : K \rightarrow [0,n]^m; \qquad U_k = \sum_{i \in N} K_k = \sum_{j \in c_k} \sum_{i \in N} V_j, \quad \text{where } k = 1 \ldots m.$$

Let us define the coalition seat share function for partition C as the sum of the seats allocated to each alternative in the coalition. Thus

$$F : K \rightarrow [0,1]^m; \qquad F_k = \sum_{j \in c_k} E_j(V), \quad \text{where } k = 1 \ldots m.$$

We can redefine the properties used in Proposition 1 for use with coalitions: A seat allocation function E is anonymous (neutral, positively responsive, nonnegatively responsive, canceling, weakly plurality ranking, strongly plurality ranking) for coalitions iff, for all partitions C, the coalition seat allocation function F derived from it is anonymous (neutral, positively responsive, nonnegatively responsive, canceling, weakly plurality ranking, strongly plurality ranking).

Anonymity: A coalition seat allocation function F is anonymous iff $F(K) = F(\sigma K)$, where σ is a function that permutes N.

Neutrality: A coalition seat allocation function F is neutral iff $\tau F(K) = F(\tau K)$, where τ is a function that permutes C.

Cancellation property: A coalition seat share allocation function is cancelling iff $U_{j \in P} = U_{k \in P} \Rightarrow F_j = F_k$. (If the vote totals for two coalitions are the same, then their seat shares must be the same.)

Nonnegative (positive) responsiveness in coalition seat share allocation function F can be defined as follows: Let K' be a vote pattern over $N \times C$. Let $K'' = K'$, except that some voters have switched to parties in coalition j:

$$({}_iK'_j \Rightarrow {}_iK''_j; \exists\, i \in N : {}_iK''_j \wedge \sim {}_iK'_j; \forall\, i \in N : \sim {}_iK''_j, \forall\, k \in C, {}_iK'_k \Leftrightarrow {}_iK''_k).$$

Function F is nonnegatively responsive iff $\forall\, (j, k \in C : k \neq j)\, F_j(K') = F_k(K') \Rightarrow F_j(K'') \geq F_k(K'')$, and F is positively responsive iff $\forall\, (j, k \in C : k \neq j)\, F_j(K') = F_k(K') \Rightarrow F_j(K'') > F_k(K'')$.

Weak (strong) plurality ranking property: F satisfies the weak plurality ranking property iff $U_{j \in A} > U_{k \in A} \Rightarrow F_j \geq F_k$. (If the alternatives in coalition j win more votes than the alternatives in coalition k, coalition j receives an aggregate seat share greater than or equal to coalition k.) Function F satisfies the strong plurality ranking property iff $U_{j \in A} > U_{k \in A} \Rightarrow F_j > F_k$. (If the alternatives in coalition j win more votes than the alternatives in coalition k, coalition j receives a greater aggregate seat share than coalition k.)

LEMMA 2: *Any anonymous and neutral coalition seat share allocation function satisfies the cancellation property.*

PROOF: Isomorphic to Lemma 1.

LEMMA 3: *Any coalition seat share allocation rule that is anonymous, neutral, and positively (nonnegatively) responsive satisfies the strong (weak) plurality ranking property.*

PROOF: Isomorphic to Proposition 1.

PROPOSITION 2: *Any seat share allocation rule that is anonymous, neutral, and positively (nonnegatively) responsive for coalitions satisfies the strong (weak) plurality ranking property for coalitions.*

PROOF: If seat share allocation function E is anonymous, neutral, and positively (nonnegatively) responsive for coalitions, then, for any partition C, by definition the coalition seat share function F derived from it must be anonymous, neutral, and positively (nonnegatively) responsive.

By Lemma 3, if F is anonymous, neutral, and positively (nonnegatively) responsive, it must satisfy the strong (weak) plurality ranking property. If, for any parition C, F satisfies the strong (weak) plurality ranking property, then by definition E satisfies the strong (weak) plurality ranking property for coalitions.   QED

MAJORITY RULE COALITION FORMATION

Let us define pure list proportion representation as a seat share allocation function that allocates a seat share (a real number in [0,1] to each alternative that is equal to the share of the total vote that alternative won).

Coalition games can be defined in terms of the set of winning coalitions W $\subseteq C$. Under majority rule, a coalition is winning iff it has a majority of seat share: $c \in W$ iff $F_c > F_{A-c}$. Under pure list proportional representation, a coalition wins a majority of seat share iff it has more than 50 percent of the vote: $c \in W$ iff $U_c > U_{A-c}$.

PROPOSITION 3: *Any seat share allocation function that is anonymous, neutral, and positively (nonnegatively) responsive for coalitions defines a majority rule coalition game with a set of winning coalitions that is identical to (a subset of) that defined by seat share allocation by pure proportional representation.*

PROOF:

Nonnegative responsiveness: Given that the set of majority rule winning coalitions is defined as $\{c \in C : F_c > F_{A-c}\}$, and under pure list proportional representation the set of coalitions with a majority of seat share is $\{c \in C : U_c > U_{A-c}\}$, we need to show that if seat allocation function E is anonymous, neutral, and nonnegatively responsive for coalitions, then

$$\forall \quad c \in C : U_c > U_{A-c} \Leftarrow F_c > F_{A-c}.$$

If the seat allocation function E is anonymous, neutral, and nonnegatively responsive for coalitions, then by Proposition 2 it satisfies the weak plurality ranking property for coalitions, and thus the coalition seat share allocation F derived from it must satisfy the weak plurality ranking property, $U_{j \in A} > U_{k \in A} \Rightarrow F_j \geq F_k$.

Suppose $F_c > F_{A-c}$ but $U_c \leq U_{A-c}$. If $U_c < U_{A-c}$ then by the weak plurality ranking property, $F_c \leq F_{A-c}$. Contradiction. If E is anonymous and neutral for coalitions, then F must be anonymous and neutral and thus by Lemma 2 must satisfy the cancellation property. If $U_c = U_{A-c}$, then by the cancellation property $F_c = F_{A-c}$. Contradiction.   QED

Positive responsiveness: We need to show that if seat allocation function E is anonymous, neutral, and positively responsive for coalitions, then $\forall$ $(c \in C)$ $U_c > U_{A-c} \Leftrightarrow F_c > F_{A-c}$.

Given that positive responsiveness implies nonnegative responsiveness, we have already shown that $\forall$ $(c \in C)$ $U_c > U_{A-c} \Leftarrow F_c > F_{A-c}$. All that remains is to show that $\forall$ $(c \in C)$ $U_c > U_{A-c} \Rightarrow F_c > F_{A-c}$. This is simply the strong plurality ranking property for F. If the seat allocation function E is anonymous, neutral, and positively responsive for coalitions, then by Proposition 2 it satisfies the strong plurality ranking property for coalitions, and thus the coalition seat share allocation F derived from it must satisfy the strong plurality ranking property.   QED

CHAPTER 4

Political Equality in Decision Rules: Equality Implies Majority Rule

This chapter provides a justification for majority rule for democratic decision making. This might seem superfluous, arguing something that is obvious or at least unchallenged. Indeed Dahl (1956) begins his chapter on populist democracy with a series of quotes from Aristotle, Locke, Rousseau, Jefferson, Lincoln, and Tocqueville, all arguing that democracy essentially implies majority rule. However, there are three reasons for having to provide a justification for majority rule. First, most countries that are regarded as democracies do not use simple majority rule in their legislative process; rather they have systems of checks and balances or division of powers that effectively require more than a simple majority to pass legislation. Second, the results of social choice theory show that the conventional justification of democracy—that majority rule constitutes, or at least reveals, the "will of the people"—is deeply problematic. Third, as Dahl points out at the end of his chapter on populist democracy, in modern democracies we do not make decisions directly through majority rule but through representatives. This chapter argues that the traditional justification of democracy as posited by traditional democratic theory (but for the most part accepted by social choice theory, as was argued in chapter 2) needs to be replaced. Instead of viewing democracy as a process that takes the preferences of individuals and produces the popular will, democracy needs to be seen as a deliberative process structured by a social decision rule. The social decision rule is democratic insofar as it is procedurally fair, that is, conforming to the principle of political equality.

After a representative body has been chosen using a seat allocation rule, this body legislates using a social decision rule. This chapter considers what social decision rules respect the value of political equality. If we limit ourselves to parliamentary amendment procedures, then political equality implies simple majority rule as the decision-making rule. This excludes not only weighted voting and supermajority rule, but also division of powers, presidentialism, and systems with checks and balances that are effectively supermajoritarian. However, this advantage comes at a cost. Majority rule is not transitive. That is, it allows cycling—situations where alternative *a* beats *b*, *b* beats *c*, but *c* beats *a*.

This result has led some to the skeptical conclusion that democracy can only be justified in the most minimal terms. Riker's *Liberalism Against Populism* (1982) is the most prominent statement of this view. However, although social choice does undermine a Rousseauian populist justification of democracy based on the existence of a unique general will, it does not lead to the skeptical conclusion of Riker that the only viable form of democratic justification is a minimal liberalism. If we abandon the constitutive/epistemic framework (that is, that democracy has to provide us with "the" will of the people), then there remain other justifications for democratic processes. It is possible to justify democratic institutions in terms of procedural fairness, which we consider in this chapter. It is also possible to give a deliberative-pragmatic justification, arguing that democratic institutions are justified by the fact that they encourage rational deliberation and social inquiry (see chapter 6). Social choice provides us with sharp tools for determining which institutions meet the criteria of procedural fairness. Indeed, although social choice undermines a populist justification of democracy, it actually recommends the rule preferred by populists—majority rule—as the only fair decision rule.

Following Cohen (1986) we can classify procedural justifications of democracy using Rawls's (1971/1999, 74–75, 176, 318) typology of procedural justice. One option is imperfect procedural justice. There still exists a general will, but we only have an imperfect procedure to find this, as elections only provide a fallible estimate of what the general will is. Cohen argues that the "epistemic populism" advocated by Coleman and Ferejohn (1986) is of this type. I will argue that the continuing existence of an objective general will in such circumstances is implausible. However, there are other possibilities. We can justify democracy on pure procedural grounds—there is no objectively correct answer, but the procedure for making the decision is procedurally fair. Alternatively we can provide a quasi-pure justification—the procedure selects one outcome from the set of outcomes that are normatively acceptable. I will argue that a plausible case can be made for both the pure and quasi-pure procedural lines of justification. I will also briefly consider pragmatist and deliberative justifications of democracy, to which I will return in chapter 6. First, however, we turn to the impact of the social choice results and Riker's interpretation of them.

1. The Impact of Social Choice Theory

Social choice theory gives us two key results relevant to democratic theory. First, making a decision democratically (in the sense of respecting political equality) requires us to use majority rule in practical legislative situations, or at the very least, it eliminates all the commonly used alternatives to majority rule. Second, majority rule does not typically produce a single, best outcome but rather allows cycling. On the basis of this Riker argues that the results of voting are meaningless. This section will lay out these results in intuitive form and show why Riker's conclusion does not hold.

The first result is a consequence of May's (1952) theorem, which proves that majority rule is the only binary social decision rule (i.e., the only social decision rule for deciding between two alternatives) that is anonymous, neutral, decisive, and positively responsive, as defined in chapter 2.[1] Anonymity and neutrality imply that if two alternatives get the same number of votes, the result must be a tie. Adding positive responsiveness to this implies that the alternative that gets more votes must win (i.e., majority rule). The political relevance of May's theorem is that if we diverge from majority rule, then we must either privilege some voters over others, or privilege some alternatives over others. If we use any form of weighted voting, we clearly advantage some voters. If we use a supermajoritarian voting system, we advantage the status quo (and those who like it) because in the event of neither alternative receiving (say) 60 percent of the votes, the status quo is chosen.

It might be argued that positive responsiveness is too strong a requirement. For example, Nurmi (1987, 67) argues that while positive responsiveness is a desirable quality, nonnegative responsiveness (if two alternatives are in a draw, and a voter switches to A, A does not lose as a result) is more essential. However, if we substitute nonnegative responsiveness for positive responsiveness, anonymity and neutrality still require a sticky form of majority rule—the alternative that wins the most votes must get at least a draw. Of course in politics draws are typically not possible, and the only way we can break a draw and still respect neutrality is to choose randomly. Contrary to the claim of Coleman and Ferejohn (1986, 18–19), relaxing positive responsiveness does not allow us to use supermajoritarian decision rules as this term is normally understood in politics—if we allow the status quo to stand in a case of a draw, we have violated neutrality, as the status quo is privileged. Rather we are simply allowed to use rules such as one that chooses the alternative that gets more than 60 percent of the vote and otherwise tosses a coin to decide, or indeed a rule that chooses completely at random. These rules are all less responsive to preferences than majority rule. As shown by the results of Rae (1969), Taylor (1969), and Straffin (1977), majority rule is also the rule that maximizes responsiveness to people's preferences.

We argued earlier that binary independence should be required in social decision rules (chapter 2). This was justified by the fact that in a legislative setting it is possible to arbitrarily create new alternatives to manipulate the outcome. If we do not limit ourselves to binary rules, various anonymous and neutral ordinal procedures are possible, including the Borda count, the Copeland rule, and the Kemeny rule. However, even if the case for demanding binary independence is not accepted, this only weakens the argument made here slightly. Instead of political equality implying majority rule, it implies majority rule or some other non-binary rule that satisfies anonymity and neutrality, such as the Borda count, the Copeland rule, or the Kemeny rule. Political equality still rules out weighted voting and supermajoritarian decision rules. Thus the demand of political equality eliminates all of the commonly used alternatives to majority rule.

The second social choice result of relevance to us is that majority rule does not necessarily produce a single best outcome if there are more than two alternatives, but rather allows cycling (a situation where a majority prefers alternative 1 to alternative 2, alternative 2 to alternative 3, but alternative 3 to alternative 1). The possibility of majority-rule cycling has been recognized since Pliny the Younger (see Farquharson 1969; McLean and Urken 1995, 67–70). The phenomenon was rediscovered in modern times and given a rigorous exposition by Condorcet (1788/1995, 113–50) then independently rediscovered by Dodgson (1876/1995) and Black (1948). The simplest example of voting cycling is the familiar Condorcet cycle, as illustrated with the preference profile in table 4.1.

If voter 1 prefers candidate a to candidate b to candidate c, and voters 2 and 3 have the preferences given in the figure, then a majority of the voters prefer candidate a to candidate b, and a majority prefer candidate b to candidate c. However, a majority also prefer candidate c to candidate a, producing a cycle. Arrow's (1951/1963) theorem is essentially a generalization of this. If the rule is nondictatorial and is based only on pairwise comparisons between a and b (satisfies independence of

TABLE 4.1.   The Condorcet Cycle

Voter 1	Voter 2	Voter 3
a	b	c
b	c	a
c	a	b

irrelevant alternatives), then we can find some preference profile that produces cycling.

The Black-Arrow results only show that cycling will exist under some preference profiles. The results of Black and Newing (1951/1998), Plott (1967), McKelvey (1976, 1979), and Schofield (1978) show that if we are dealing with multiple issues or an issue that has more than one dimension, then cycles will nearly always occur. This result has been proved using powerful mathematical tools, although it is possible to present it geometrically, as demonstrated by Enelow and Hinich (1984), Feld and Grofman (1987), and N. Miller, Grofman, and Feld (1989). (See Austen-Smith and Barks 2000 for a comprehensive, technical exposition.) The basic intuition is that there are always overlapping winning coalitions, so any winning coalition can be broken. Consider a three-person divide-the-dollar game where the players decide by majority rule as shown in figure 4.1. Point A represents player A taking the whole dollar, point B represents player 2 taking the whole dollar, and so forth. A point halfway between A and B represents players A and B splitting the dollar between them and giving none to C, while a point in the middle of the triangle represents a three-way split. Suppose the first proposal is a three-way split. Player A can then propose to player B that they split the dollar between just themselves, and both of them will vote for this as they can both get more than with a three-way split. However, player C can then go to player B and propose giving player B 60 cents, while taking the remaining 40 cents himself. Players B and C will both vote for this over the previous split, as they are both better off. However, player A can adopt the same strategy, offering player C 60 cents. This cycle can continue indefinitely. Of course, in practice the players may decide to split the dollar three ways to avoid the negotiation costs involved and the risk of being the one excluded (especially if the game is repeated many times), but this does not reduce the importance of the potential for cycling. If they come to a compromise, it is under the conditions of the threat of cycling. Majority rule does not produce a single outcome that cannot be defeated. In technical language, the core (the set of alternatives that cannot be beaten) is empty. It is always possible to split the winning coalition by offering one of its members a better deal.

This model can be generalized to policy choice. Instead of the players dividing a dollar, they have to decide a policy on two issues, say economic policy (high or low taxes and spending) and abortion (how permissive or restrictive the policy should be). Let us assume that each player has an ideal set of policies and prefers that the eventual outcome be as close to that as possible. This assumption (that preferences are related to a distance function) is actually not required to prove the cycling

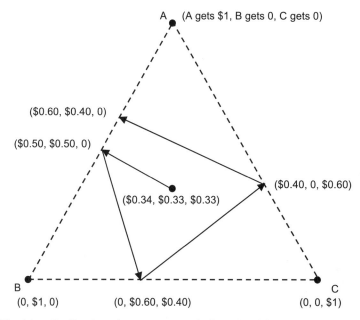

Fig. 4.1.   Cycling in a three-person majority-rule divide-the-dollar game

theorem—all that is required is that preferences be continuous.[2] However, having preferences based on distances allows us to use simple
geometry instead of algebraic topology. Thus in figure 4.2 we assume
player B is left-wing on economic policy and permissive on abortion,
while player C is right-wing on economics, but also permissive on abortion. Player A is moderate on economic policy and restrictive on abortion. In this context, we can construct the same kind of cycling behavior
in policy choice as we found with the divide-the-dollar game. There are
always multiple potential winning coalitions, as any coalition of two players can overturn the current outcome.

Indeed, we can find far more radical cycling. In figure 4.1, the cycling
was limited to the triangle defined by the players (the players distributed
all the money among themselves). However, in figure 4.2, it is possible to
create agendas that can take us beyond the triangle to any alternative we
choose. Suppose we start with alternative 1 in the center of the triangle.
Suppose that alternative 2 is proposed as an alternative. Both players B
and C prefer alternative 2 to alternative 1, as it is (marginally) closer to
their ideal points, so alternative 2 is adopted. Now suppose alternative 3
is proposed against alternative 2. Both players A and B will vote for it, so
it will be adopted. Likewise, alternative 4 will be adopted over alternative

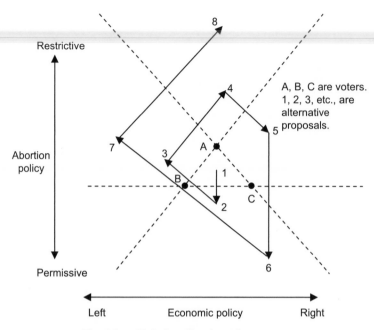

Fig. 4.2.   Global cycling in policy space

3 with the support of players A and C. We can continue like this indefinitely, each time proposing an alternative that two of the players support
over the previous one, but which is farther from the center of the triangle.
This is the essence of the global cycling result. We can construct an agenda
that will get us to any alternative through a series of votes, even alternatives that are ludicrously far from the ideal points of every voter.

A possible objection is that it is unnecessary to consider the two issues together, and that we could avoid cycling if we took separate votes
on each issue. Some writers (D. Miller 1992; Dryzek and List 2003) have
suggested that deliberation may allow us to disaggregate issues in this
way. This objection is misguided. First, as Knight and Johnson (1994)
argue, deliberation may allow us to disaggregate decisions, or it may have
exactly the opposite effect, uncovering new dimensions and interdependencies. Second, and more important, many policy choices are intrinsically multidimensional and interconnected. If we take individual votes
on such issues, the combined outcome may be one that nobody would
support as an overall outcome considered together (see Anscombe 1976;
Saari and Sieberg 2001; Lacy and Niou 2000). Indeed the outcome may
even be logically or practically impossible. It would make no sense to de-

sign an aircraft by taking independent votes on the choice of wing, fuselage, wheel, and so on. Similarly, it makes little sense to talk about policy on education spending, for example, without considering other government programs that might receive the same money. A great deal of policy-making is about the relative weight we give to different objectives. Such problems are by their very nature multidimensional.

A better objection would be that the extreme outcome 8 in figure 4.2 would never occur in practical politics. This is probably the case—cycling is likely to be limited. An alternative far beyond the central triangle of A, B, and C, such as alternative 8, will be unanimously beaten by *any* alternative in the central triangle. In order to move far beyond the central triangle, the agenda setter would have to exclude all central alternatives after the very early rounds. Thus an alternative far from the central triangle would be unlikely to be chosen with a random agenda, as every time a central alternative was proposed it would win and pull us back to the center (see Kramer 1977; Ferejohn, McKelvey, and Packel 1984 for rigorous expositions of this intuition). Neither is it likely that we would get far from the center with an open agenda, as anyone unhappy with the extreme outcome could pull it back by proposing a central alternative. Strategic voting could also prevent the agenda setter's plan—if the players knew that the agenda would eventually lead to a very undesirable outcome, they could vote against every proposal. Thus in practice we are unlikely to find the kind of indeterminacy that drives Riker's argument that the results of majority rule are meaningless. Rather, the results of majority rule are likely to be confined to a limited central area. However, the problem of cycling within this area remains, so social choice still poses significant questions for democratic theory.

Nicholas Miller's (1980) concept of the uncovered set allows us to formalize the conclusion that cycling is likely to occur, but that it will be limited to a small, central set. An alternative is defined as covered if there is another alternative that beats it (by majority rule) and beats every alternative that the first alternative beats. The uncovered set is the set of alternatives that are not covered in this sense. Miller shows that most common majority-rule institutions (open amendment, closed amendment with strategic voting, two-party competition) produce outcomes in the uncovered set and speculates that the uncovered set tends to be small and centrally located. McKelvey (1986) shows that this is indeed the case when preferences are spatial (outcomes are preferred the closer they are to a player's ideal point) and provides limits for the size of the uncovered set. Schofield (1999) provides a more general characterization of the uncovered set.[3] Feld et al. (1987), Feld, Grofman, and N. Miller (1988, 1989), and N. Miller, Grofman, and Feld (1989) provide

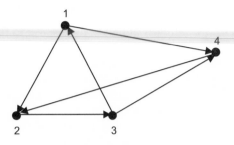

4 is covered by 1. 1, 2, and 3 are uncovered.

Fig. 4.3.   The covering relation

geometric interpretations of the uncovered set, and they show that it becomes small as the number of voters becomes large.

The uncovered set can be seen as the set of alternatives that could be reasonably chosen by a group of people deliberating. Conversely, a covered alternative could never be a reasonable choice. Figure 4.3 illustrates this intuition. Suppose we have four alternatives: 1, 2, 3, and 4. An arrow in the figure means that one alternative is majority-rule preferred to another. Thus alternative 1 is majority-rule preferred to 2 and 4, but 3 is preferred to 1. Alternative 4 is covered. Alternative 1 beats alternative 4, and it also beats everything that alternative 4 beats. Thus there is no good reason to propose alternative 4 as a group choice. True, alternative 4 beats alternative 2, but so does alternative 1, and alternative 1 is preferred to 4. No matter what alternative it is compared to, alternative 1 does at least as well as (and sometimes better than) alternative 4. The same is not true for alternative 2, and alternative 2 could be reasonably proposed in deliberation. Indeed, if alternative 3 was the other alternative under consideration, alternative 2 is the only one that can beat it. With these majority-rule preferences, it is not clear whether alternative 1, 2, or 3 should be chosen, but it is clear that 4 should not be.

It has proven difficult to determine exactly how large the uncovered set will be in practice. However, it appears likely that it will include a nontrivial part of the alternative space even with a large number of voters. Hartley and Kilgour (1987) show that with three voters and Euclidean preferences, the uncovered set is equal to the Pareto set (the set of alternatives that are not unanimously defeated by another alternative) when the voters are equidistant. Epstein (1998) shows that in distributive games, the uncovered set is essentially the Pareto set. Bianco, Jeliazkov, and Sened (2004) calculate the uncovered set for the U.S. House using Poole and Rosenthal's (1995) NOMINATE scores. They find that the uncovered set accounts for a considerable amount of the space between the median Democrat and the median Republican. Thus it appears that while the uncovered set eliminates a great deal of the policy space, there is still a considerable amount of space left for bargaining.

This bargaining is normatively important. The fact that the legislators are forced to bargain can reveal cardinal utility information. That is, it can reveal not only which alternatives legislators prefer but also the intensity of their preferences. As Buchanan and Tullock (1962) argue, legislators can trade their support on issue dimensions they care little about, for support on issues that are of crucial importance to them. These choices reveal information about intensity of preferences. Thus the outcome of a majority-rule bargaining game reveals information unavailable to us if we only considered the legislators' preference orderings. Indeed, this may lead to better outcomes than those produced by a (transitive) social welfare function (the conditions under which this is the case are considered in chapter 6). However, legislative bargaining and vote trading cannot overcome the problem of cycling or Arrow's theorem, as Tullock (in Buchanan and Tullock 1962, 338–39) argues it does. Rather, vote trading typically implies unstable outcomes (see Park 1967; Bernholz 1973; Oppenheimer 1975; N. Miller 1975, 1977a). Instead we can argue in the manner of N. Miller (1983) that cycling may not be such a bad thing after all.

In practice, parliamentary government typically involves electing a government by majority rule and then allowing this government to pass its program on party line votes, subject to the possibility of majority-rule votes of no confidence. This amounts to a comprehensive negotiated outcome, and it satisfies anonymity and neutrality. Instead of thinking of the legislature as making a succession of decisions on individual issues, with legislators trading votes across issues, we have one grand bargain at the beginning of the legislative session that encompasses all issues. (Indeed in many European democracies, the agreement between coalition partners is often a long, exhaustive document taking months to negotiate.) This grand bargain has the added advantage that all costs of the bargain are internalized (see chapter 6). There is no possibility of a series of votes that are individually majority supported but are not supported when considered as a package. Thus the inefficiency associated with the "paradox of vote trading" (Riker and Brams 1973) cannot occur.

Thus we can see that cycling is almost inevitable with majority rule. With any decision of any complexity (that is, any decision that cannot be reduced to a single dimension), there will be multiple, overlapping winning coalitions. However, this cycling does not produce the radical effects claimed by Riker. While there will be some indeterminacy, cycling will be limited to the uncovered set. Thus the results of majority rule are neither arbitrary nor empty, but rather reduce to a centrally located set of alternatives. This conclusion—that cycling is ubiquitous but limited—leads us to the conclusion that democratic theory needs to be rethought, but that the normative value of majority rule can be defended against Riker. The next three sections consider various ways this may be accomplished.

The fact that intransitive social preferences are likely to be pervasive in legislatures, together with the fact that the uncovered set is likely to be nontrivial in size, forces us to rethink how a legislative procedure can be neutral and anonymous. Majority rule produces cycling, but a legislative procedure has to produce one outcome. Therefore the process by which the agenda is set also has to be neutral and anonymous. As Nurmi (1987) points out, an amendment process with a set agenda is not neutral even if it uses majority rule, as there is a bias in favor of outcomes that are not considered until the end (see also N. Miller 1995). Similarly, a process where one player gets to choose the agenda is not anonymous, as that player can manipulate the agenda. However, an open agenda process using majority rule would satisfy anonymity and neutrality. Still, such a decentralized procedure might be extremely unstable, and is rarely used (at least for government-sponsored legislation). A legislative rule where the agenda is set by an agent that is subject to a majority-rule vote of no confidence satisfies anonymity and neutrality, providing any member can propose a no-confidence motion. This is the procedure used in many parliamentary democracies.

Excursus: Convincing a Skeptic that Cycling Exists in Practice

We can show theoretically that the existence of majority-rule cycles (at least in the limited form explained here) is virtually inevitable. Even three self-interested people dividing a dollar by majority rule face one. However, there is widespread skepticism among political scientists that cycles have any relevance for practical politics. This may in part be due to the extremely technical way in which the results have been presented or to the drastic empirical predictions that accompanied early accounts of the results—predictions of chaos and instability that did not seem in line with observed reality. It may also be due in part to fact that the normative claims that were drawn from the results were unpalatable to many, notably Riker's claim that majority-rule cycling undermined traditional democratic theory. I will argue that while the drastic empirical predictions and skeptical normative implications of cycling were generally unjustified, majority-rule cycling is practically significant and forces us to rethink democratic theory. However, we should not expect to observe cycling in chaotic behavior or dramatic Machiavellian manipulation of the public, but rather in mundane phenomena such as coalition negotiations and logrolling.

What empirical evidence is there for majority-rule cycling? The answer is that we observe the effects of cycling in pervasive phenomena such as legislative logrolling and coalition negotiation, which are difficult—if not impossible—to explain without cyclical or at least intransitive social preferences. We cannot directly observe cyclical social preferences, because we cannot make windows into people's souls to observe their complete preference orderings. On the other hand, neither can we directly observe an electron; we can only observe effects that cannot be explained without the existence of such a particle.

One place we can observe the effects of cycling is in coalition negotiations. Indeed, the best way to think about cycling is as the existence of multiple overlapping winning coalitions. Whichever coalition currently makes up the winning majority, there is always the potential for some of the minority to join with some members of the current majority coalition to create a new majority, just like in the three-person divide-the-dollar game in figure 4.1. Thus any majority coalition can be replaced. This is typically the case in countries with multiparty parliamentary government, such as the Netherlands or Norway. In fact, in the Netherlands, most combinations of the main parties have been tried in the last fifty years (Christian-Socialist, Christian-Liberal, Socialist-Liberal). Note that government in such countries is typically not unstable. However, the threat of cycling has profound effects on political behavior and outcomes, in that there is always an alternative government coalition waiting in the wings.

Another place we can observe the effects of cycling is in legislative logrolling (a situation where legislators support measures they do not like as part of a deal to get measures they do like passed). Indeed, Oppenheimer (1975) shows that logrolling is logically related to the phenomenon described in Downs (1957) where a "coalition of minorities" can defeat issue-by-issue majorities. Bernholz (1973) and N. Miller (1975, 1977a) show that logrolling logically implies the presence of cycling or at least intransitive social preferences (roughly speaking, an intransitivity can be thought of as a cycle that includes some ties).[4]

As far as I am aware, no legislative specialist has disputed the importance of logrolling in legislatures where a single, cohesive party does not control a majority. It may take a decentralized form in candidate-centered legislatures such as the U.S. Congress, or it may take the form of a single, grand coalition agreement by parties at the beginning of the

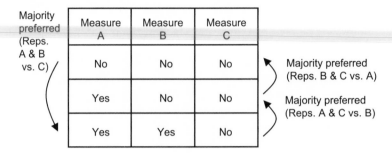

Fig. 4.4.   Logrolling implies intransitivity.

legislative term, as is common in Europe. In both cases, normal politics could not go on without some form of logrolling, and thus without some form of cycling or intransitivity. As N. Miller (1975, 110) puts it: "We may note in conclusion that there is some irony in the fact that students of the American political process, on the one hand, have very typically emphasized the importance of logrolling and coalition formation, but, on the other hand, have very typically dismissed the 'Arrow paradox' as little more than a mathematical curiosity or have ignored it entirely. We see that the two phenomena are logically bound together."

The intuition behind the argument that logrolling implies cycling (or at least intransitivity) can be demonstrated simply using the example in figure 4.4. Let us assume the simplest possible example of majority-rule logrolling. Let us assume a three-person legislature, with representatives A, B, and C. Each wishes to pass a measure bearing his or her name. Representative A's measure would benefit A's constituents greatly, but not the constituents of B and C, while it would be paid for by everyone. Similarly the measures proposed by B and C exclusively benefit their constituents. Let us also assume that the three proposed measures are efficient—the total social benefits exceed the costs. Although all three measures are socially beneficial, each will fail in a majority-rule vote, because they only benefit the constituents of one representative, while they impose costs on two. However, if representatives A and B come to a deal, they can pass both their measures and are both better off. Thus passing A and B is majority-preferred to passing nothing. However, representatives A and C could then come to an agreement to repeal measure B. This would make them both better off. If this happens, B and C can then get together and pass a measure to repeal measure A, and we are back where we started. Now any two representatives can make a deal to pass their measures, and the cycle starts over again. (It would be possible to

have a unanimous vote to pass A, B, and C, but then any two representatives would be able to cut a deal to cut out the third.)

We should note that the structure of this problem is similar to that
in the divide-the-dollar game in figure 4.1. Any two players can join to
claim all the gains, but the third player can split this coalition by offering
one of the members even more, and so on. Bernholz (1973) and N. Miller
(1975, 1977a) show that any example of logrolling implies the presence
of this kind of intransitivity. Therefore, to the extent that logrolling and
coalition negotiation are central to politics, so is cycling.

It has been argued that it is possible to create logrolling situations
without cycles (Bernholz 1975). However, this relies on agents having a
very particular kind of nonseparable preferences (without knowing the
outcomes of other issues, people cannot say whether they like or dislike a
measure), so the situations defined are not actually logrolling as defined
by N. Miller (1975, 1977a) or indeed Bernholz (1973).[5] Furthermore, this
should offer little comfort to advocates of a populist conception of
democracy. In fact the widespread existence of nonseparable preferences
is every bit as problematic for populist democratic theory as cycling. If
preferences are in general nonseparable, then a vote on an issue cannot
reveal the will of the people about that issue. Rather, the most it can reveal is the will of the people conditional on the way every other issue is
resolved. Furthermore, the votes on which the first vote is conditional are
themselves conditional on all the other votes. Thus even though there
may be a single outcome (that is, a collection of decisions) that is majority-preferred to all others, we will never know if we have found it. The
only way to know this is to compare every conceivable combination of
outcomes, something that is clearly practically impossible in a legislative
setting. If preferences are nonseparable, it may still be possible to defend
democracy as a reasonable way of negotiating our way through all the in-
dependencies between issues (this is compatible with the case made in
section 4 of this chapter). However, it is not possible to argue that the collection of votes taken reveal an unconditional popular will.

If we are only seeking situations of intransitivity, as opposed to strict
cycling, then it can be shown that this can be produced by a simple col-
lective-action problem. Suppose the familiar Prisoner's Dilemma game
in figure 4.5. Let us label the four possible outcomes [A], [B], [C], and
[D]. Clearly outcome [D] is majority-preferred to outcome [A]. However, when we compare [A] to [B], the result is a draw, with one player
preferring each outcome. When we compare [B] with [D], again we get a
draw. However, this violates transitivity, because by transitivity, if [D] is
preferred to [A], and we are indifferent between [A] and [B], then we
must prefer [D] to [B]. Therefore if collective action problems exist (and

		Player 2			
		Defect		Cooperate	
Player 1	Defect	0, 0	[A]	−5, 10	[C]
	Cooperate	10, −5	[B]	5, 5	[D]

[D] → [A] ~ [B] ~ [D]

Fig. 4.5.   A Prisoner's Dilemma game (player 1's payoffs first)

I am unaware of anyone who claims they do not), then we should also expect problems of intransitive social preferences.

There is a recent body of literature that, while accepting that cycling may theoretically occur, argues that it is unlikely to happen in practice, or at least will not have normatively troubling results (Regenwetter et al. forthcoming; Mackie 2003; Dryzek and List 2003). Although many of the claims made by these authors are convincing, they do not refute the basic point that cycling is pervasive in legislative situations. All three authors challenge Riker's (1982) democratic skepticism. However, from a normative point of view, I believe that they all give too much ground to Riker, in that they accept that the widespread existence of cycling would undermine democracy. Rather than challenging the significance of cycling, I believe a more fruitful strategy is to show that cycling does not undermine the case for democratic institutions such as majority rule, but instead is an essential part of democracy.

Regenwetter et al.'s *Foundations of Behavioral Social Choice Research* (forthcoming) argues that cycles are unlikely to be encountered in elections with a finite, limited number of candidates, as is the case with virtually all candidate elections. The authors argue that previous estimates of the probability of cycling based on the assumption of an "impartial culture" (the assumption that all preference profiles are equally likely) are misleading. If we make more realistic assumptions about preferences, the probability of cycling rapidly falls. Using a Bayesian procedure, the authors also estimate the probability of cycling in actual elections using survey and electoral data, and find it small. As a result, the authors conclude that electoral procedures producing misleading outcomes (failing to select a Condorcet winner—an alternative that beats every other alternative in a head-to-head race) is far more likely to be a problem than cycling.

Regenwetter et al., however, only cover candidate elections, as opposed to legislative bargaining. (It should be noted that justifying populist democracy is not the main goal of Regenwetter et al.'s book, although they argue that their findings should counter the pessimism of scholars such as Riker [1982] and should allow the conclusion that democratic decision making is possible.) It should not surprise us that cycling is unlikely in candidate elections. It is not possible to order candidates tailor-made to exploit cycling opportunities or to beat certain other candidates. Furthermore, parties may well have a monopoly over candidates of a certain ideological type and restrict their competition (see Aldrich 1995). However, in a legislative setting, it is possible to create new alternatives at will. As argued earlier, it is here that we would expect to observe cycling. Indeed, it is in legislatures that we see the clearest empirical evidence of cyclical social preferences in the form of logrolling and coalition negotiation behavior.

Mackie's *Democracy Defended* (2003) deals with Riker's interpretation of social choice head-on. The goal of the work is explicitly normative, challenging what the author describes as Riker's (1982) "antipopulist" agenda. After arguing that the results of social choice theory do not imply that democratic choice is meaningless, Mackie challenges many of the examples Riker gives of cycling and agenda manipulation, such as the Powell and Depew amendments, the Wilmot Proviso, and the 1860 U.S. presidential election. Many of these examples concern manipulation by an agenda setter strategically contriving cycles, rather than the type of cycling I have discussed. Of course, it is not possible for Mackie to conclusively disprove Riker's interpretation of these events, because it is not possible to know for sure the complete preferences of the agents. (Mackie 2003, 37–38, criticizes Riker on precisely this point.) What Mackie provides is a series of alternative interpretations that do not involve Rikerian manipulation. On the basis of this, he argues that Riker's claim that democratic outcomes are essentially the result of arbitrary manipulation by elites is false.

Once again, this does not refute the claim that cycling is pervasive in legislatures, or make a populist conception of democracy viable. Mackie may well be right that agenda manipulation is far harder to accomplish and less common than Riker (1982) would have us believe; and he is certainly correct in arguing that it is likely to be extremely difficult to manipulate majority-rule procedures to produce outcomes far away from the central group of voters. However a populist conception of democracy demands that a determinate "will of the people" be revealed. In legislatures we observe the effects of cycling in phenomena such as logrolling and coalition negotiation. Given that a different logrolling agreement or a different coalition could have been equally well negotiated, we cannot argue that the outcome that happened was the "will of the people." Rather it was just the agreement that was made. It may well be the case that the degree of indeterminacy in these negotiations exists within fairly narrow bounds (as argued earlier), but this indeterminacy is normatively important. Indeed it will be argued that it is normatively desirable, allowing minorities to retain some influence and forcing majorities to be reasonable.

Dryzek and List (2003) argue that deliberation can overcome the consequence of cycling. This argument is dealt with in detail in chapter 6. In brief, I argue that deliberation cannot overcome the phenomenon of cycling, but rather that cycling creates the context in which democratic deliberation is likely to take place.

Thus we find evidence for majority-rule cycling in commonplace phenomena such as coalition negotiations, logrolling, and collective action problems. This, however, does not imply dramatic empirical consequences, such as chaos and instability. Neither does the presence of cycling imply Riker's (1982) conclusion that elections have no value except to restrain elites somewhat by throwing the rascals out periodically. It is to Riker's use of the cycling results that we turn next.

2. Riker and His Critics—Majority Rule as Imperfect Procedural Justice

Cohen (1986) argues that Riker's rejection of populism is actually a rejection of populism as pure procedural justice, to use Rawls's terminology. That is, the populism that Riker refutes assumes that the outcome of majority rule itself constitutes the popular will. Cohen argues against Riker that it is possible to defend populism as a form of imperfect procedural justice—there is an objective, correct outcome, but there is no infallible procedure to find it. The "epistemic populism" proposed by Coleman and Ferejohn (1986) is an argument of this type. I will argue in the two sections that follow this that majority rule can better be justified as pure or quasi-pure procedural justice—that is, as a fair procedure or as a procedure that selects one out of the set of acceptable outcomes. This section deals with Riker's critique and the populist response to it.

Riker's interpretation of the social choice results leads to two logically separate conclusions. The first concerns justifications for democracy, and states that populism is untenable as a justification for democracy. The second concerns institutions, and states that the failure of populism implies that majority rule is not normatively privileged over any other institution that occasionally removes governments, even "unfair voting methods" (Riker 1982, 246). Riker conflates the two conclusions because he identifies populism with the argument that majority rule is privileged. However, the two arguments are logically separate.

This gives us two possible responses to Riker. First, Riker can be challenged on the level of justification—the conclusion that populism is untenable can be questioned. This is the route taken by the epistemic populists. Second, regardless of whether we accept Riker's argument about populism being untenable, we can challenge the conclusion that this implies that majority rule does not have normative priority. This is the route I take in the following two sections.

Riker (1982, 238) defines populism as the propositions that government policy should be what the people want and that the people are free when their wishes are law. Populism is rejected by Riker because the social choice results show that majority rule cannot tell us what the will of the people is. Thus Riker (239) does not challenge the normative content of populism—that the government ought to do what the people want—but rather argues that we cannot know what the people want because different voting systems produce different outcomes and the same voting system may produce different outcomes at different times. Riker (241) then proceeds with the crucial assumption that liberalism and populism exhaust all the possibilities for democratic theory. Thus liberalism, defined as the doctrine that voting does no more than provide a means to remove elected officials and prevent tyranny, is the only remaining option. Riker argues that liberalism survives the social choice results because it demands far less of voting, asking only that elections periodically remove officials—possibly in a perverse or random manner. Riker (14) identifies the idea that majority rule has normative value with populism, so when populism falls, so does the normative priority of majority rule. Liberalism does not privilege majority rule, and indeed Riker (250) argues that it prefers institutions (such as division of powers and checks and balances) that restrain majority rule.

Thus Riker provides an argument for both a liberal interpretation of democracy and for liberal (i.e., nonmajority-rule) institutions. However, there are several key assumptions that can be challenged. First, Riker assumes that liberalism and populism are the exclusive alternatives for democratic theory. Nowhere does Riker defend this assumption; it is simply asserted as if self-evident (1982, 241). This assumption is crucial to the practical side of Riker's argument. If there are other alternatives, the failure of populism would not imply rejection of the normative priority of majority rule. There might be other ways to justify majority rule, and I will argue that this indeed is the case. As Knight and Johnson (1994) put it, Rousseau and Schumpeter do not exhaust the possibilities of democratic theory.

Second, Riker's interpretation of the social choice results is questionable. Riker argues from the global cycling result that the results of majority rule are arbitrary. However, the social choice results summarized in the previous section (many of which, to be fair, are more recent than Riker's book) do not indicate this. It is true that majority rule does not produce a single determinate outcome, but the result is likely to be drawn from a small, central set of alternatives. Thus majority rule does provide a great deal of information about which alternatives are reasonable choices. This opens the door both to a revised form of populism (such as the epistemic populism of Coleman and Ferejohn) and to procedural justifications of democracy that do not depend on the concept of a popular will.

Finally, if we accept Riker's reading of the social choice results, it can be questioned whether liberalism actually survives any better than populism. This is the critique provided by Coleman and Ferejohn (1986, 21–23). They argue that Riker's interpretation of the cycling results is as fatal to Riker's instrumental justification of liberalism as it is to populism. Riker argues that the only justification elections can have, given the social choice results, is the instrumental liberal one of checking the oppressive tendencies of government. However, if the results of majority rule are completely arbitrary, voting cannot fulfill this function. If removal from office is completely random (like being struck by lightning), then elections will have no effect on the behavior of government. For elections to check the behavior of governments, they need to remove bad governments more often than good governments.[6] However, if they do this, then they provide some information as to whether the government is in line with the public will or not. This allows for a weaker (epistemic) form of populism. However, Przeworski (1999) provides an answer to this objection, giving a convincing justification of the value of minimalist democracy, even if the results of elections are essentially random.[7]

Coleman and Ferejohn give a social choice–informed alternative to Riker, but, as Knight and Johnson (1994, 281) argue, they retain Riker's definition of the problem. That is, they accept that the key question is whether government decisions can be determined by the popular will. Riker argues that populism is untenable because majority rule cannot tell us what the popular will is. Coleman and Ferejohn (1986, 15–19) challenge the assumption that indeterminacy in voting results means that voting cannot reveal the popular will. They put forward a modified version of populism—epistemic populism—in which the popular will is assumed to exist, but is imperfectly known. Voting does not define the popular will but only provides information about what it is—hence the qualifier epistemic. Voting is privileged as the best source of information about what the popular will is. This assumes that the results of voting are not completely arbitrary. Ferejohn and Coleman refer to the social choice results outlined in section 1 to argue that this is the case. Voting produces results that are to some degree indeterminate, but cycling is confined within certain bounds, so voting can still inform us about the popular will.

There are problems with epistemic populism, however. Most notable is the failure to provide any justification for the existence of a popular will independent of the results of voting. Coleman and Ferejohn indeed do not even attempt to defend the existence of a popular will but merely state it as an assumption that there needs to be an objectively correct policy. This is especially problematic as we do not simply need objectively correct principles but actual policies. We need to argue that there are objectively correct policies on (say) tax exemptions for colleges. By comparison, by the time we get to this level of detail, Rawls (1971/1999, 176, 318) has long since abandoned imperfect procedural justice, arguing that we can only select one alternative from the set of policies that are roughly compatible with the principles of justice.

A second problem is the need for votes to be interpreted as judgments and not expressions of interests. For democracy to have epistemic value, votes have to represent considered judgments of what the correct policy is. However, political philosophers do not get to tell voters how to use their votes. The need for votes to be disinterested judgments thus severely limits the applicability of epistemic populism.

A final reason for abandoning epistemic populism is that we can get the same practical results without the unnecessary metaphysical weight of an objectively correct set of policies. The practical implications of epistemic populism are virtually identical with those of the procedural justifications of majority rule laid out in the next two sections. Epistemic populism gives majority rule normative priority as the best means of finding the correct policies, although it acknowledges that this method is fallible. Justifications of majority rule as pure or quasi-pure procedural justice do not claim to produce an objectively correct policy, but still give normative priority to majority rule either as a fair procedure or as a procedure that produces reasonable outcomes. Thus we get the same practical results—majority rule is justified but by no means infallible. The advantage of the pure and quasi-pure justifications is that they may be convincing to people who are not willing to accept the metaphysical assumptions demanded by epistemic populism.

Thus Riker's argument that the results of social choice theory force us to accept minimal liberalism and constitutionally restrained democracy can be challenged without accepting a populist justification of democracy. First, the results of majority rule are far less indeterminate than Riker argued, a point made far more clear by research published since Riker's book. Second, the assumption that populism and minimal liberalism are the only logically possible alternatives is untenable. Riker makes no argument for this assumption, but without it Riker's normative argument crumbles. Strangely, many of Riker's critics do not challenge this assumption but try instead to justify some form of populism. However, if other alternatives are possible, we can abandon populism without being reduced to minimal liberalism. Most significant, we can abandon a populist justification for democracy, while still arguing for the institution that populists favor—majority rule. Thus majority-rule democracy can be defended, but not in populist terms. Rather than defending democracy as revealing the will of the people, we can defend it in procedural terms as a fair procedure for reaching reasonable agreements. The next two sections provide such arguments.

3. Majority Rule as Pure Procedural Justice

Given that the results of majority rule are not completely arbitrary, we can provide a pure procedural justification for majority rule based on its intrinsic fairness. Rawls defines pure procedural justice as a situation where justice is defined purely in terms of the fairness of the institution and not in terms of the outcome. An example of this would be a fair lottery. There is no reason why anyone deserves to win more than anyone else, but we can say that if the lottery is fair, then it satisfies the requirements of pure procedural justice. We can provide a similar justification for majority rule. Even if we remain agnostic about what the correct outcomes are, we can still demand that the procedure be fair. One way of thinking of this is in terms of distributive justice. We could argue that influence over collective decisions is a good that is desirable for everyone and demand that it be distributed fairly. Of course, the degree of influence a person exercises depends on things like skill and personality that we cannot distribute. However, we can insist that political resources be distributed fairly. Distributing political resources fairly clearly requires that votes are distributed equally. However, it also requires that the procedures for turning votes into decisions are not systematically biased in favor of certain voters or certain alternatives.

Social choice theory gives us very strict prescriptions for which institutions are fair, at least if we define fairness in terms of political equality. As stated earlier, May's (1952) theorem shows that the only determinate procedure for choosing between two alternatives that satisfies political equality is majority rule. This eliminates all the commonly used alternatives to majority rule, as any other nonrandom binary procedure privileges either some voters or some alternative (and thus the voters who like it). Random procedures (such as a pure lottery) may also satisfy political equality, but majority rule is the procedure that is most responsive to voters' preferences and thus makes most use of the information we have about what people want. Thus if we have representative democracy, political equality implies that these representatives use majority rule to produce collective decisions. In terms of the rule to elect representatives, chapter 3 showed that the only single-vote electoral system that satisfies political equality is proportional representation.

It should be noted that Rawls does not consider majority rule as an example of pure procedural justice, as it sometimes produces unjust outcomes. Rawls, of course, is assuming that justice has an independent definition in the form of the two principles he has deduced. Chapter 2 has already provided arguments why the value of political equality needs to be applied directly to political institutions and not to a hypothetical choice situation.

If we are to treat democratic justice as a form of distributive justice, it is necessary that political resources be a desirable good. Political resources are a desirable good if they make a difference to the outcome.[8] If it were the case, as Riker asserts, that the results of majority rule were arbitrary, it would not matter whether I am fairly represented or whether the procedure is biased against me. The results would simply depend on the guile of agenda-manipulating politicians. Questions of procedural fairness would be moot. Therefore, first it is necessary to show that the results of majority rule are not completely arbitrary, but that preferences actually affect outcomes. This follows in a straightforward manner from the social choice results summarized in section 1. The outcomes under majority rule will fall in the uncovered set, which is typically a small, centrally located set of alternatives. The location and size of the uncovered set depends on which outcomes are majority-rule preferred to others, and thus depends on the preferences of voters.

Second, it is necessary to show that if the voting procedure is biased against me, my interests suffer. It seems obvious that if the voting procedure is biased against me so that my vote and the votes of people like me do not get full weight, then the outcome is less likely to be favorable to me. This is indeed the case. If the votes of my group are underweighted enough, then the number of coalitions we can form with other players that can change the outcome falls. We are less able to form coalitions to overturn outcomes that we do not like. Furthermore our bargaining power falls. The number of coalitions where we make the difference between winning and losing decreases (and of course falls to zero if our votes are completely discounted).[9] We cannot be better off, and may well be worse off.[10] The procedure can be biased against us in other ways. If the procedure is biased in favor of some outcome, this may disadvantage me if I do not like this outcome. All supermajoritarian voting systems are biased in that they favor the status quo, as will be demonstrated at length in the next chapter. Therefore we have an interest in making sure we get our fair share of voting weight, and that the procedure is not biased in favor of an outcome we find undesirable.

Thus I have every reason to believe that if I do not receive my fair share of political resources—if my vote is underweighted or if the voting procedure is biased against me—then my interests are likely to be harmed. Therefore we can apply the principles of distributive justice to political institutions, arguing that justice consists of distributing political resources equally. We can thus justify majority rule as the only decision rule that treats every voter and every alternative equally.

4. Majority Rule as Quasi-Pure Procedural Justice

The justification of majority rule as pure procedural justice in the last section makes no reference to the qualities of the outcomes produced by majority rule. Indeed this is why I refer to the justification as being pure in terms of the procedure. Majority rule is democratic because the outcome is the result of a fair game in which no voter and no alternative is unduly advantaged. While this can justify majority rule as being democratic in the narrow sense of satisfying political equality, it should leave us slightly uneasy. It does not justify majority rule as a way of reaching reasonable collective decisions.

However, majority rule can be justified as producing reasonable outcomes. We have seen that majority rule produces outcomes in the uncovered set. This set of alternatives is the set that could be reached by reasonable deliberation. Put another way, any alternative that is covered cannot be reasonably defended. If alternative a covers alternative b, then a is preferred to b, and to everything b is preferred to. There is no good reason to propose b in discussion, because a could be substituted for it and would do at least as well, no matter what it is compared to. Furthermore, the uncovered set is typically a small, centrally located set of alternatives, so majority rule is an effective means of eliminating most conceivable alternatives.

Using Rawls's terminology, we may label this a quasi-pure procedural justification of majority rule. The procedure picks one outcome out of the set of reasonable outcomes, thus producing one outcome within the acceptable range. Rawls also justifies majority rule as quasi-pure procedural justice, but his argument is rather different from that presented here. For Rawls (1971/1999, 318), the acceptable range of outcomes is defined independently by the two principles of justice, which he derives from hypothetical deliberation behind a veil of ignorance. Thus a law is just "if the law actually voted is, so far as one can ascertain, within the range of those that could reasonably be favored by rational legislators conscientiously trying to follow the principles of justice." By contrast, I define the acceptable range of reasonable outcomes in terms of the outcome of an actual deliberative procedure. An outcome is reasonable because it is possible to make a case for it, and there is not another outcome that is unambiguously preferable to it (that is, it is not covered).

Majority-rule deliberation serves as an effective means for identifying a selection from the uncovered set. Calculating the entire uncovered set is actually extremely difficult. To do this, we would need to know everyone's preference over every conceivable alternative. While we can map the uncovered set in highly simplified hypothetical examples, the amount of information required to calculate it in practice with real preferences is prohibitive. However, we know that the outcome of majority-rule deliberation will lie within the uncovered set. Thus majority rule gives us a practical way to identify an acceptable outcome.

Thus although majority rule cannot give us a single "best" outcome, it gives us a great deal of information about which alternatives are reasonable choices and which are not. Thus Riker is correct to argue that a Rousseauian populism that requires the identification of "the" general will—a single alternative unambiguously preferred by the population—is not viable in light of the social choice results. However, it is incorrect to claim on this basis that the outcome of majority rule is arbitrary or meaningless. Majority rule, after all, gives us a social preference between any two alternatives. While we do not have a single social preference, we do have a mass of preference relations.[11] From this information we can distinguish which alternatives may be reasonable choices, and which can never be.

5. Other Justifications for Majority Rule

The two justifications of majority rule that I have just given are not exhaustive. If we abandon the constitutive/epistemic framework (the idea that majority rule reveals the general will in a populist fashion), it is also possible to defend majority rule in a pragmatist or deliberative manner. That is to say, majority rule is justified in that it produces reasonable discussion that constructs an outcome that represents the public interest. I believe that this line of justification is viable. However, the level of proof is far higher than that required for the procedural argument. That is, it is necessary to argue empirically that majority rule produces reasonable deliberation and defensible outcomes. Furthermore, I believe that the defense of democracy in terms of political equality has value, even if the pragmatist/deliberative justification is accepted. As argued in chapter 2, political equality is a sine qua non for democracy—a procedurally un-equal system is not democratic, no matter how reasonable the outcomes it produces are. However, it should be noted that the procedural justifi-cation is generally compatible with the pragmatist/deliberative justifica-tion. Indeed, the pragmatist and deliberative justifications require a pro-cedural argument. Pragmatism requires unforced social inquiry (Dewey 1927/1946; Knight and Johnson 1996, 1999), and deliberative democracy requires unforced agreement. This, in turn, requires procedural fairness. I take this argument up again in chapters 6 and 7.

Conclusion

This chapter has provided an alternative justification for majority rule as a democratically defensible decision rule. It is true that the results of social choice theory force us to rethink democratic theory. Riker is cor-rect that a theory of democracy that relies on the discovery of the one true "will of the people" is no longer viable. Given cyclical social pref-erences, no reasonable procedure can logically exist that can always give us a single outcome that is preferred to all others. However, this does not imply that the results of majority rule are arbitrary, or that all we can expect of democracy is periodic alternation of governments. Rather, majority rule is the only decision rule that is procedurally fair in terms of treating all voters and alternatives equally. It also provides a great deal of information about which alternatives are popularly acceptable, and rejects most of them. It may also be possible to justify majority rule on pragmatist or deliberative grounds, a possibility we will consider fur-ther in chapter 6. While social choice theory may undermine the "pop-ulist" theory of democracy—the idea that democracy is legitimated by its ability to find "the" will of the people—it does not undermine the case for the political procedure populists typically favor—majority rule.

It is important to recognize that majority rule is treated here as a rule that structures a deliberative process, not a procedure that produces the correct democratic outcome directly from legislators' preferences. Rather, majority rule defines a game in which legislators bargain, nego-tiate, deliberate, persuade, and trade, subject to the requirement that the final agreement receive the support of a majority. Majority rule is justified normatively because it is procedurally fair, and because we have reason to expect that the game carried out subject to majority rule will produce reasonable outcomes. Of course, for a majority-rule game to satisfy political equality, the agenda-setting procedure must also be democratic. If the agenda is fixed, then some alternatives are advantaged. Similarly, if some player controls the agenda, that player is advantaged. An open agenda procedure satisfies political equality but may well be chaotic. A procedure that combines political equality and stability is used in most parliamentary democracies. Following election to the legislature, the legislators negotiate a governing coalition and a coalition program. This is then passed by a series of party line votes. However, the government is always subject to threat of a vote of no confidence, which can be proposed by any legislator. Essentially the vote of investiture for the government and the negotiation about the governing program represents a grand bargain covering all policy areas.

Furthermore cycling actually strengthens the case for majority rule. Since Riker, cycling has been viewed as being corrosive to democracy, a problem to be solved. For example, Coleman and Ferejohn (1986) argue that it is still possible to talk about the general will in spite of cycling, while Dryzek and List (2003) argue that deliberation may be able to prevent cycling. Mackie (2003) and Regenwetter et al. (forthcoming) argue that while cycles are logically possible, they are uncommon and thus unlikely to cause problems. However, following the argument of N. Miller (1983), it is rather the case that cycling is what makes democracy as we know it possible. Cycling simply means that there are multiple, overlapping potential winning coalitions. This means that the current winning coalition can be replaced. As will be argued in chapter 5, this allows minorities to protect themselves while still respecting majority rule, without giving out vetoes that can be abused to protect unjust privileges and extort advantages. Furthermore, the existence of multiple potential winning coalitions creates strong incentives for coalition building and the deliberation that goes with it (see chapter 6). Far from being a problem to be solved, cycling is rather an integral part of the way democracy operates. This may be the most significant consequence the social choice literature has for democratic theory.

PART 2

MINORITY PROTECTION

CHAPTER 5

Minority Protection, Rights, and Supermajoritarianism

The only practical decision rule for legislatures that fully respects political equality is majority rule, as argued in the previous chapter. However, there are other values that we need to take into account besides political equality, notably the protection of minorities and the respect for rights. Thus it is commonly argued that there is a trade-off between political equality (maximized by majority rule) and minority protection (better provided by systems with external checks and balances, which require more than a simple majority to enact legislation). This chapter argues that this trade-off does not exist and that actually majority rule provides most protection to minorities. Furthermore it does so precisely because of the instability inherent in majority rule.

As we have seen, majority rule is the only legislative decision rule that completely satisfies political equality. May (1952) shows that majority rule is the only positively responsive, decisive, binary voting rule that satisfies anonymity (voters are treated the same regardless of their names) and neutrality (alternatives are not discriminated between on the basis of their names). If we use a system other than majority rule, then we lose either anonymity or neutrality. That is to say, either some voters must be privileged over others, or some alternative must be privileged over others. With supermajority voting, the status quo is privileged—if there is no alternative for which a supermajority votes, the status quo is maintained. Following Rae's (1975) argument, given that the status quo is more desirable to some voters than to others, some voters are effectively privileged. It is certainly the case that supermajority rules can privilege (protect, if you prefer) some voters. Unfortunately, it is not possible to privilege every group over every other group. If supermajority rules create a privileged group, there must be a corresponding underprivileged group.

Nevertheless, supermajoritarian decision rules are widespread, both explicitly and implicitly. For example, in the United States explicitly supermajoritarian rules exist in the form of the 60 percent cloture requirement to end a filibuster in the Senate, the two-thirds requirement to override a presidential veto, and the need for a supermajority to amend the Constitution (see Krehbiel 1998). Implicitly, the existence of two legislative chambers with different bases of representation is supermajoritarian, in that more than 50 percent of the popular support is likely to be needed to ensure a majority in both chambers, a fact recognized long ago by Condorcet (1787/1986). The committee system has a similar effect, to the extent that committees are able to act as gatekeepers, able to hold up consideration of legislation. For similar reasons, presidentialism is effectively supermajoritarian, to the extent that the consent of both the president and legislature is required to pass and implement laws. Outcomes decided by judicial review also rest on a supermajoritarian basis, in that constitutional amendments require a supermajority. The number of democracies with simple majority-rule legislatures with few external checks is actually quite small, limited mostly to the small countries of Europe.

Such supermajoritarian decision-making rules have been justified in terms of the need to protect minorities from "the tyranny of the majority." In the United States, this argument is associated with James Madison (quite inappropriately, I will argue) and John C. Calhoun. Buchanan and Tullock (1962) provide a formalization of this line of thought, arguing that the unanimity rule maximizes the protection of individual rights and economic efficiency, and that supermajoritarian rules are a second-best approximation to unanimity. Guinier (1994) also argues that supermajoritarian voting can protect minorities. It is notable that the idea of minority protection is often conflated with the idea of rights protection, as though the two are synonymous. The two concepts, however, are logically quite distinct. The protection of rights from the regular political process may serve to protect minorities from overbearing majorities, or it may serve to entrench established oppressions. (Consider the relationship between states' rights and segregation in the United States.) Nevertheless any democratic regime that privileges certain rights over the decisions of the regular political process is necessarily supermajoritarian, in the sense that a simple majority is unable to make a binding decision, as will be argued in section 6.

In contrast to the argument that supermajoritarianism protects minorities, this chapter shows formally that as we move from majority rule toward unanimity, the ability of minorities to defend themselves by overturning unfavorable outcomes is diminished. Therefore majority rule offers most protection. The proof assumes that people do not know how they will fare under the status quo in the future, and in particular whether their interests are more likely to be threatened by government action or by some other force or event that requires government action to protect against. In cases where we are exceptionally sure that the status quo is just and protective of all minorities (perhaps juries or the fundamental rights required for democracy to function), it can be argued that supermajoritarian decision-making rules may provide more protection, although even here the argument is not obvious.[1] However, in the case of "continuing politics," such as regular legislation and policy-making, it will be argued that we cannot know what the status quo will be in the future, and that therefore our argument that majority rule provides most protection for minorities applies.

The first section of this chapter reviews the literature on supermajoritarian decision making. The second illustrates how supermajoritarianism can produce perverse results. The third section formally analyzes the logic of supermajoritarian decision making. The fourth provides the proof that majority rule offers the greatest protection to minorities. The fifth considers the effect of uncertainty about the future on these considerations. Section 6 considers the relationship between minority protection, rights, and constitutionalism, while section 7 deals with the instability of majority rule resulting from cycling, and why this is essential to the protection of minorities.

1. Supermajority Rule and Democracy

The theory that checks and balances are needed to restrain majority rule (thus producing a system that is effectively supermajoritarian) is frequently ascribed to James Madison. However, as Rae (1975) and Kernell (2003) argue, ascribing such a view to Madison is problematic, given that Madison sought a strong national government, capable of decisive action and able to overcome the immobilism of the Articles of Confederation.[2] As we are all familiar with from Federalist 10, Madison identifies the problems of minority and majority tyranny. The republican principle (i.e., majority rule) protects against minority tyranny. However, the only solution to majority tyranny given in Federalist 10 is to have a large "extended republic" where a single cohesive majority would not exist, a solution completely compatible with majority rule.[3] It is not until Federalist 51 that Madison advocates external checks and balances, in the context of a president elected independently of Congress. It is notable that Madison did not support an independently elected president at the Constitutional Convention until mid-July 1787, immediately after he had lost the argument about equal representation for the states in the Senate. Indeed, the original Virginia plan presented to the convention, authored primarily by Madison, was essentially a majority-rule parliamentary system with the executive chosen by the legislature. At the Constitutional Convention,

Madison argued against many of the constitutional features we now consider "checks and balances."[4] Furthermore Madison clearly opposed the principle of supermajoritarianism (arguing that it reversed the principle of free government and equaled minority rule), as the following section from Federalist 58[5] demonstrates.

> It has been said that more than a majority ought to be required for a quorum; and in particular cases, if not all, more than a majority of a quorum for a decision. That some advantages might have resulted from such a precaution cannot be denied. It might have been an additional shield to some particular interests, and another obstacle generally to hasty and partial measures. But these considerations are outweighed by the inconveniences in the opposite scale. In all cases where justice or the general good might require new laws to be passed, the fundamental principle of free government would be reversed. It would no longer be the majority that would rule: the power would be transferred to the minority. Were the defensive privilege limited to particular cases, an interested minority might take advantage of it to screen themselves from equitable sacrifices to the common weal, or, in particular emergencies, to extort unreasonable indulgences. (Hamilton, Madison, and Jay 1788/1961, 361)

Madison gives us, at best, an ambiguous justification for restraining majority rule with checks and balances; according to Rae (1975), it is John C. Calhoun (1842/1982, 1850/1943) who gives us an unequivocal theory. Society is made up of various classes of people, any of which may wish to intrude on the rights of others. A system of "concurrent majorities," whereby the approval of a majority of each class is required for action, can prevent this from happening. Calhoun argues that various features of the U.S. Constitution (most notably equal representation for the states in the Senate) embody this principle. Indeed more recent scholars, such as Weingast (1998) and Aldrich (1995) have analyzed the way in which institutions such as North-South parity in the Senate and the norm of ticket balancing by the parties essentially provided the Southern states with a veto until the 1850s.

Dahl (1956) is critical of what he terms the "Madisonian" theory of democracy (essentially the view that checks and balances are required to restrain majority rule). Madison relies on majority rule to protect against minority tyranny. Dahl argues that in cases where positive government action is required to protect rights, restraining majority rule with checks and balances undermines this protection. (Ironically this echoes the argument made in the section from Federalist 58 cited previously.) Furthermore Dahl argues that there is no empirical evidence that rights are better protected by the American political system than by European constitutions with far fewer constitutional checks, and that institutions such as the filibuster, equal representation in the Senate, and judicial review have been used far more frequently to frustrate the extension of fundamental rights than to protect them, most notably in the case of civil rights in the South.

Buchanan and Tullock (1962) provide a different justification for supermajoritarianism. Given a predetermined allocation of rights and property,[6] the decision-making rule that best protects this allocation is naturally unanimity. Furthermore unanimity is the only rule that guarantees that the outcome will be economically efficient in the sense of being Pareto superior (it is not possible to make anyone better off without making someone else worse off) to the status quo. If unanimity is impossible because of decision-making costs, supermajoritarian rules may be the second-best solution, in that they provide more protection than majority rule against costs imposed by society on individuals.

Rae (1975) critiques Buchanan and Tullock on several grounds. Unanimity only minimizes the costs society imposes on individuals if we make the strong assumption that an unwanted policy imposes a far greater cost on individuals than not getting a policy that is needed. Rae (1969) shows that if we assume these costs are equal, majority rule is optimal. Furthermore, Rae (1975) criticizes the concept of Pareto optimality as essentially locking in the status quo and being blind to distributional considerations.[7] Most significant, Rae shows that universal consent is logically impossible when a decision (even if it is to take no action) has to be taken. If there is disagreement and a decision has to be taken, some decision has to be imposed against someone's will.

From a rather different political perspective, Guinier (1994) also argues that supermajoritarian voting may protect minority rights. This is somewhat ironic given that supermajoritarian rules, such as the filibuster in the Senate, have been historically employed to obstruct civil rights legislation. While Guinier is certainly correct to point out that supermajoritarian decision rules are widespread, it is not clear that the exclusion of minorities Guinier seeks to remedy results from majority rule, as much as from certain winner-take-all institutions such as single-member district elections. (Guinier is supportive of proportional representation.) Miller (1996) provides a social choice theoretic analysis of Guinier's claims.

Although it is tangential to our concerns here, there is some literature on the effect of supermajoritarian rules on economic outcomes. As noted, Buchanan and Tullock (1962) argue that only unanimity guarantees economic efficiency. Barry (1965/1990), however, argues that the use of the "offensive veto" may lead to economic inefficiency—groups with veto power may try to use that veto to extort privileges, which may lead to worthwhile projects not being undertaken. Moe (1989) argues that supermajoritarian institutions in Congress lead to inefficient bureaucracies, in that bureaucratic structures are designed not to maximize the performance of an agency but to lock in the gains of the winning coalition and prevent future congressional majorities and administrations from being able to change the goals of the agency. Similarly, Scharpf (1988) argues that the supermajoritarian nature of German cooperative federalism produces inefficient policy.

2. Pathologies of Supermajority Rule

Using some simple examples, we can illustrate some of the problems that supermajoritarian rules can produce. Such rules can lead to the complete exclusion of minorities, to immobilism where the status quo is impossible to challenge, to situations where ideologically concentrated minorities are advantaged over more dispersed majorities, and even to situations where points at the very extremes are strategically defended by blocking coalitions.

Consider the situation depicted in figure 5.1. There are eight voters with simple spatial utility functions (they each prefer outcomes closer to their ideal point). Three have ideal points at position a, three at position b, and two at position c. Under majority rule five votes are required to defeat a proposal, and thus there is no core (a proposal or set of proposals that cannot be defeated). For any proposal it is possible to find a counterproposal that at least five voters prefer. However, the voters at positions a, b, c have equal bargaining power in determining the outcome. When we move from majority rule to supermajority rule, this changes. If we adopt a supermajoritarian quota of six to pass a proposal, the solid line between positions a and b becomes the core. It is impossible to find a counterproposal that six voters prefer to a point on the line between a and b. As a result, the voters at c lose all bargaining power and influence over the outcome. If we increase the quota from six to seven, then any point in the triangle abc will be a core point. We may characterize this situation as a "tyranny of the status quo." As long as the status quo is within abc, it cannot be changed. Whoever had influence when the status quo came to pass has their way. Thus we can show that it is at least possible that adopting supermajoritarian rules may severely harm the interests of minorities, compared to their position under majority rule.

Of course, supermajoritarian rules can advantage certain minorities. A very high quota will definitely advantage minorities that are fa-

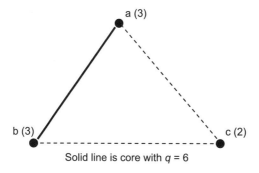

Solid line is core with $q = 6$

Fig. 5.1.   Configuration of eight voters

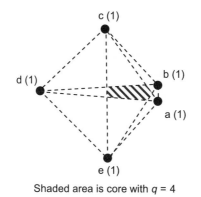

Shaded area is core with $q = 4$

Fig. 5.2.   Configuration of five voters

vorable toward the status quo. Furthermore, supermajoritarian rules may advantage ideologically concentrated minorities. Consider figure 5.2. Here there are five voters, at positions a, b, c, d, and e. Under majority rule ($q = 3$) there is no core. In terms of bargaining power, the voters at a and b might have an advantage, in that they can join with any other voter to form a majority, but they are not able to impose their will on the others. However, if we increase the quota to 4, then the shaded area becomes the core. The influence of one minority (the two voters at positions a and b) has increased, but at the expense of the smaller minority positions (c, d, and e). Thus we would expect supermajoritarian rules to benefit minorities who are large and concentrated enough to form blocking coalitions at the expense of smaller and less concentrated minorities.

Figure 5.3 (based on Laing and Slotznick 1987) illustrates an even more problematic situation that can arise under supermajoritarian rules.

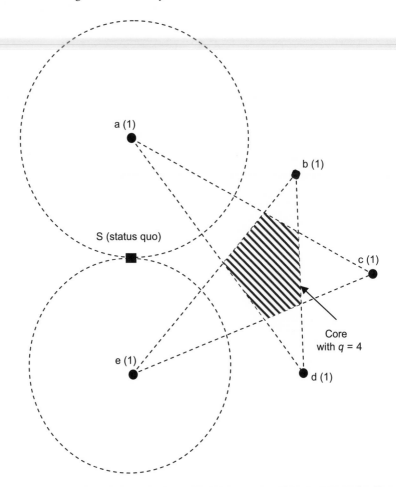

Fig. 5.3.   Configuration of five voters with $q = 4$ and status quo point S

Here status quo point S may be impossible to overturn with a voting quota of four, even though it is not in the core.[8] If we have a supermajoritarian rule with a quota of four, then the shaded area in the figure is the core. If a point in the core is the status quo, it will be impossible to overturn it. However, if we start from status quo point S, it may be that we never get to the core. This is because voters a and e form a blocking coalition. There are points that four voters would prefer to point S. However, there is no point in the core that either voter a or e prefers to the status quo, as can be seen from the fact that the iso-utility curves of a and e do not intersect the core. As a result it may be strategically rational for a and e to block any attempt to move from the status quo. Although there are points that they prefer to the status quo, if these are adopted, this may lead to the adoption in the next round or later of core points that voters a and e do not prefer to the status quo S. In an experimental setting, Laing and Slotznick (1987) confirm the existence of this phenomenon. The situation here may appear familiar. A blocking coalition defends a status quo that some of its members might like to change, because it fears that if it allows change, this will open the floodgates to further changes that it views as undesirable.

3. Analyzing Supermajority Rule

Supermajoritarian rule can have some problematic effects, as we have seen. This section will show why supermajority rule is inherently less democratic than majority rule in that it uses less of the information we have about the preferences of society. When we move from majority to supermajority rule, we effectively throw away the preference information we have about pairs of alternatives wherever a supermajority does not prefer either alternative to the other. In place of using preference information to decide between the two alternatives, we have to decide on some other ground. Usually, the alternative that is the status quo prevails. Thus the decision rule is biased in favor of one of the alternatives, or in the language of May's theorem, is not neutral. We have replaced a democratic decision with an imposed one, a decision based on preferences with a decision based on precedent.

Of course, as we move from majority to supermajority rule, we reduce the instability in outcomes associated with majority rule. This is precisely because we are deciding between fewer pairs of alternatives using society's preferences. Instability under majority rule results from the fact that social preferences may involve cycles (a is preferred to b is preferred to c is preferred to a). As we stop relying on preferences and rely more on which alternative is the status quo, the probability of such cycles diminishes. However, in the next section, I will show that it is precisely this instability that offers protection to minorities under majority rule.

We will analyze majority rule and supermajoritarian decision rules using the graph-theoretic framework from Miller (1980). Consider figure 5.4(a). A line from point 1 to point 2 means that alternative 1 is majority-rule preferred to alternative 2. Let us assume that there are an odd number of voters and that the preferences of all voters over possible alternatives are a linear ordering. That is, if 1 and 2 are alternatives, then every voter has a preference over 1 and 2, and every voter's preferences

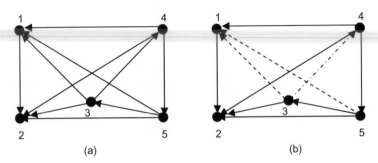

Fig. 5.4. Society's preferences over alternatives under majority and supermajority rule

are transitive (if a voter prefers 1 to 2, and 2 to 3, then the voter prefers
1 to 3). Then Miller (1980) shows that society's preferences under majority rule can be expressed as a tournament (technically, a complete asym-
metric directed graph). That is to say, if we take any two alternatives,
then society strictly prefers one to the other, and thus all points in the
graph are connected. However, although individual preferences are transitive, society's preferences are not—alternatives 3, 4, and 5 form a cycle.

    Let us consider what happens when we go from majority to super-
majoritarian rule, by raising the voting quota required for one alternative to beat another from 50 percent + 1 to some higher value. As the
voting quota is raised, some of society's preference relations are erased.
If the voting quota is q, and the proportion of the population that prefers
alternative 3 to 4 is greater than 50 percent, but less than q, then the decision rule no longer gives a social preference between alternatives 3 and
4. Thus we go from the situation depicted in figure 5.4(a), where the decision rule ranks all pairs of alternatives, to that in figure 5.4(b), where
the dotted line represents preference relations that have been erased. As
we further increase the voting quota q, preference relations cannot be replaced. If q people do not prefer alternative 3 to 4, or 4 to 3, then a higher
quota q^* clearly cannot prefer 3 to 4 or vice versa.

    However, as Rae (1975) argues, it may well be necessary to make a
decision between two alternatives, even though our decision rule does not
rank them. In this case some other criterion, outside of the population's
preferences, has to be used. Generally in the case of supermajoritarian
systems, the status quo is privileged. The alternative that is the status quo
is maintained unless some other alternative is preferred by quota q of the
population. This, of course, violates neutrality and privileges people who
favor the status quo.

    Similarly, we can see why increasing the voting quota reduces the instability associated with majority rule. Saari (1997) shows that as we increase the voting quota, then the set of alternatives that are not defeated by any other alternative (the core) must expand monotonically. That is, the core under voting quota q^* must be a subset of the core under quota q^{**}, if $q^{**} \geq q^*$. Considering figure 5.4, we can see why this must be the case. As we raise the quota from q^* to q^{**}, we erase the lines representing the preference relations between any two alternatives where the majority in favor of one over the other is less than q^{**}, but greater than q^*. However, no new social preference relations are added—if the social preference between two alternatives is undefined under quota q^*, it will still be undefined under the higher quota q^{**}. As a result, the set of alternatives that are undefeated will not shrink as some social preference relations are deleted, and it may expand.

Thus we can see that the effect of going from majority rule to more supermajoritarian quota rules is to ignore more and more preference information and to rely more and more on precedent—whichever alternative is established as the status quo prevails. Naturally, this makes the status quo more stable, at the cost of the outcome being less democratic. However, as I will show in the next section, it is precisely this instability—the ability to overturn undesirable outcomes if necessary—that guarantees protection to minorities.

4. Supermajority Rule and the Protection of Minorities

It has frequently been argued that supermajoritarian decision rules (both explicit and implicit) safeguard minorities. However, we have seen that such processes essentially discard preference information when the majority is less than quota q, and they impose the status quo in these cases. To argue that replacing marginal democratic outcomes with a priori outcomes protects minorities requires some strong assumptions. First, we must believe that minorities are more at threat from a change in the status quo than from a failure to change the status quo, either in response to an existing injustice or some new threat. Second, we must be able to say what the status quo is and will be. In other words, we require certainty (or at least a high degree of confidence) about what the status quo will actually be in the future. The next section will argue that this assumption of certainty is unrealistic over the time span of constitutional arrangements. This section will show that if we do not have prior knowledge of our interests, majority rule provides most protection to the worst-off minority.

Suppose we are choosing a voting system not knowing our interests or what the status quo will be, a situation somewhat akin to Rawls's (1971/1999) "veil of ignorance." We wish to choose the system that guarantees us the best outcome in the case that we turn out to be the worst-off minority. The worst outcome we could find ourselves in would be to be faced with a very unfavorable outcome that we are unable to overturn by joining with a coalition of other voters. Considering different voting quotas, we can show that the higher the quota, the lower the utility floor we are guaranteed, and thus that the system that guarantees us the highest utility floor is majority rule.

> PROPOSITION 1: *Given a voting rule with quota q, let $m_i(q)$ be the utility associated with the least preferred position for agent i that, if enacted, no coalition including i could overturn given sincere voting. Then $m_i(q) \geq m_i(q+1)$.* (Proof in appendix)

The intuition behind the proof is straightforward. Let us define the $_iCore$ (the core for voter i) as the set of alternatives that voter i cannot overturn by joining with a coalition of other voters of size q or greater and replacing it with another alternative. The worst thing that can happen to voter i is the outcome in the $_iCore$ that is least favorable to voter i. As the quota q increases from q^* to q^{**}, the size of the $_iCore$ monotonically increases, as some social preference relations are deleted and none are added, so some alternatives that voter i previously could have overturned become invulnerable. As the $_iCore$ under quota q^* must be a subset of the $_iCore$ under quota q^{**} ($q^{**} > q^*$), the worst outcome for voter i in the $_iCore$ under quota q^{**} must be at least as bad as the worst outcome under quota q^*, and possibly worse. Thus a higher quota exposes voter i to potentially worse outcomes that cannot be overturned through a coalition with other voters. Majority rule is the decision with the lowest voting quota that does not result in indeterminate outcomes. (A quota of less than 50 percent can result in situations where alternative 1 is socially preferred to alternative 2 and alternative 2 is socially preferred to alternative 1.) Thus majority rule offers maximum protection against the imposition of an outcome that a voter is unable to bargain to overturn.

Simple majority rule gives us the most protection against having unfavorable outcomes imposed on us. Indeed, provided that preferences are distributed in at least two dimensions and do not meet some very stringent symmetry conditions (Black and Newing 1951/1998; Plott 1967; McKelvey 1976, 1979; Schofield 1978), each agent can find a coalition to overturn any outcome except their own ideal point. The problem is that any other agent can do the same. Whether this forces agents to engage in reasonable negotiation or whether this leads to chaos is a behavioral question, which will be addressed in subsequent chapters. Nevertheless, majority rule offers greater protection against an imposed outcome than any other system, and therefore the system that offers most protection for minority rights is, ironically, majority rule.

5. Supermajority Rule and Uncertainty

To argue that it is prudent to privilege the status quo over an alternative that is majority preferred, it is necessary to be able to say what the status quo is. Furthermore, the greater the degree of uncertainty about the status quo, the more reasonable it is to use the assumption of ignorance as a device for arguing about justice. I will argue here that over the time frames relevant to constitutional choice, the status quo may be quite indeterminate.

The analysis here builds on the work of Brunel-Petron (1998)[9] concerning the theory of rights. Brunel-Petron argues that we have to consider rights as claims on outcomes. The mapping, however, between the law and the rights we possess in practice is problematic. This mapping may change over time, in particular in response to changes in technology and social mores. Thus although the law may not change, if there is a significant change in technology or mores, this law may represent a very different outcome. This argument is similar to that made by Rae (1975) with regard to "utility drift": Even though law stays the same, the outcome changes because the subjects of that law change their behavior in ways that harm each other.[10]

This idea can be applied to our consideration of the status quo. Indeed between the set of possible status quo positions and the set of possible payoffs, there are several mappings. Supermajoritarian rule privileges the status quo by making it hard to change the law. The status quo that is protected, however, is not an outcome or payoff, but rather a set of legal formalisms. If the way in which these legal formalisms are translated into outcomes or payoffs changes, then the substantive status quo will change, although the formal status quo is untouched. Figure 5.5 illustrates the mappings from the set of possible laws to the set of possible payoffs.

First the written law produced by legislation has to be translated into government action or policy. The interpretation of law by the executive and the courts can, of course, change over time, which will substantively change policy. This kind of slippage is particularly significant in supermajoritarian systems. Under simple majority rule, it is relatively easy for the legislature to "correct" changes in interpretation by the executive or judiciary by simply passing new legislation. If the decision rule is supermajoritarian, however, the executive and judiciary may

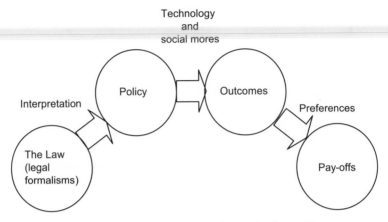

Fig. 5.5.   Mappings from the law to final payoffs

have far more discretion. As such, supermajoritarian rule may amount in practice to a form of concealed guardianship, if the interpretation is performed by an unelected body. Indeed Dahl (1956) criticizes the U.S. Supreme Court in this role. Moe and Howell (1999) argue that supermajoritarian rules effectively empower the U.S. president because he has some unilateral power to determine how laws are implemented. Likewise it can be argued that the power of the European Commission (the executive of the European Union) is enhanced by the fact that the Council of Ministers proceeds on the basis of unanimity or qualified majority voting and thus has a hard time overturning commission rulings.

Even if government policy remains constant over time, the outcomes that this policy represents may change because of changes in technology, behavior, social mores, or the environment in general. For example, slow government response may be tolerable or even desirable in normal conditions, but disastrous in time of national emergency. (This is why Federalist 22 is so hostile to supermajoritarianism.) Technology may also affect the effective consequences of laws. The right to keep weapons may have very different consequences depending on the development of military technology. The development of efficient computers has surely changed the impact of data privacy laws (or lack thereof). Similarly, social mores change the consequences of laws. A law banning public nudity would have no effect if nobody wished to behave in this way, or if nobody minded. Neither would the lack of such a law.

In addition to the direct effect on the relationship between policy and outcomes that a change in technology, behavior, or mores may have, there may be indirect effects mediated through economic processes. Changes in technology change production functions. As a result, demand for factors of production changes, as does their relative value. The factors that are crucial to people's livelihood and welfare, and the relationship between them, also change. A type of economic regulation that appeared equitable may no longer be so. In an agrarian society, we would not expect people to even conceptualize the need for organized labor. It is only with the advent of an industrial society that disputes over the right to organize or not to be organized become salient, as industrial labor is now a key factor of production. Similarly, in a postindustrial economy, intellectual capital may become the crucial factor of production. Laws concerning intellectual property that seemed reasonable when employees were expected to work for a firm for life may be extremely problematic in a society where frequent job shifts are commonplace. Suddenly, the distribution of intellectual property rights between employer and employee becomes a crucial concern.

Finally, even if outcomes remain constant over time, society's preferences over these outcomes may change. Thus the eventual payoffs to the various actors would be different, and our considerations of justice would have to adapt to this. One particular instance in which society's preferences may be exceptional is during a time of crisis. It is possible that legislation may be passed hastily under crisis conditions despite supermajoritarian rules, because all parties may want action of some type to be taken quickly. However, these hastily made decisions may prove extremely difficult to change when time allows more detailed consideration.

It is very difficult to argue that we can know what the status quo will be in the medium term, let alone that it will be a satisfactory outcome. Thus attempts to engineer specific outcomes using constitutional mechanisms appear hubristic. Furthermore, we have not yet considered one further change we would expect to occur over time: The agents themselves will change, as some die and others are born. Supermajoritarian rule privileges the status quo, and for this reason it privileges the choices of one generation over those of the succeeding one. In this sense supermajoritarian rule can be thought of as a mechanism by which a dominant group today protects itself against the majority of the next generation, bequeathing to their children a world that not only did they not create, but that they may not even be able to revise.

6. Minority Protection and the Constitutional Protection of Rights

The ideas of minority protection and the protection of rights are often conflated. This is not surprising, as the equivalence of the two ideas follows naturally from the traditional justification of constitutional democracy. It is argued that minorities need to be protected from the "tyranny of the majority" and that the constitutional protection of rights accomplishes this. However, minority protection and rights protection are quite distinct concepts. Granting many constitutional rights may help minorities in some cases, but it may also harm them (the role of states' rights in perpetuating segregation in the United States is an obvious example). Furthermore, the constitutional protection of rights implies supermajoritarianism—constitutional rights mean little or nothing if the constitution can be amended by a simple majority. Given that a constitution that can be amended by majority rule clearly cannot protect against majority tyranny, the only alternatives are for constitutional amendment to be supermajoritarian, or for the constitution to be regulated undemocratically by a minority. Thus our critique of supermajoritarianism as a device for rights protection can also be leveled at systems of constitutional rights.

We continue to use the same definition of rights as in the previous section. Rights are privileged claims over outcomes. How we define outcome sets is complex (see, for example, Pattanaik and Suzumura 1994; Sugden 1985; Hees 1998, 2003; Sen 1976; Nozick 1974), but this is not our concern here. Rather we are concerned with how the implementation of rights claims is arbitrated, and under what circumstances this trumps regular politics. When we say that rights are privileged claims, the word *privileged* can mean two distinct things. First, rights claims can be morally privileged. It is hard to dispute that certain claims should be morally privileged in a democratic system. As Dahl (1988) argues, certain rights are implicit in a democratic system, such as freedom of expression and organization. Other rights are essential to a functioning democracy, such as a minimal level of economic independence. If a democratic system fails to respect such rights, it essentially abolishes itself. However, there is a second sense in which a rights claim can be privileged. A claim can be privileged in the sense that it is held to overrule a regular political decision. This is the position typically taken by advocates of constitutionalism. Certain rights (typically speech, person, and property) are so fundamental that they should typically be constitutionally protected against majority rule.

Privileging constitutional rights, however, is problematic for a number of reasons. *First, constitutions cannot protect rights.* Put simply, constitutions cannot protect rights because constitutions cannot act. Having rights guaranteed in a constitution provides no guarantee that these rights will be respected in reality. Indeed, many totalitarian regimes, such as the former Soviet Union, had very impressive batteries of rights written into their constitutions. These, however, were only paper rights as the enforcement of these rights was in the hands of the Communist Party, which also held political power. The German Weimar Republic also had an extremely elaborate system of checks and balances, but these failed to prevent the rise of Hitler. Indeed they may have even contributed to it by making it easy for antidemocratic parties (Nazis and Communists) to create gridlock while still in a minority. For rights to be protected in any substantive sense it is necessary for there to be a method of enforcement. In the terms of Nino (1996), we need a "constitution of power," as well as a "constitution of rights."

Second, protecting rights requires action. For example, for the right to free speech to be respected, it is not enough for the government to do nothing. Rather it is necessary for the government to actively protect people from those who may commit acts of violence or intimidation if they speak freely. Put another way, it is necessary to dispense with the libertarian fallacy that governments are the only threat to rights and to recognize that both governments and nongovernmental actors can be equally destructive of rights. Thus rights should be seen as an outcome of government action. Government action (or inaction) in period t ensures that rights are respected. This means that democratic choice is possible in period $t + 1$. Rather than viewing rights as something that has to be guaranteed prior to a democratic decision, rights can rather be viewed as a dynamic part of the democratic process, both an outcome and a prerequisite of democracy.

Third, rights are not free. Rights are privileged claims. Therefore if we grant one person a claim over an outcome, we necessarily impose a restriction, duty, or cost on someone else (except in the trivial case where we grant someone a right to do something that no one would want to stop them doing anyway). To put it starkly, one man's right to property in the antebellum South was another man's slavery. Later the right of states to self-governance conflicted with individual civil rights. Any rights claim that requires resources to fulfill necessarily imposes a duty on society. If we decide an individual has a right to receive health care in an emergency room, society has to pay for it, either through taxes or through higher premiums. If we grant a right to one person, we necessarily take a right from someone else. One person's right to health care conflicts with another's right to keep their income untaxed; one person's right to play metal guitar in their apartment conflicts with another's right to quiet. In this context, it makes little sense to talk about maximizing rights, even subject to the requirement that these rights are universal (Rawls 1971/1999).[11] Given that all rights granted involve taking rights from others, a case needs to be made not for why rights should be trumps (to use Dworkin's 1978 phrase), but for why some rights should trump others.

In politics there are very particular costs to granting rights. If rights are taken as claims that take precedence over ordinary democratic decisions, then there is a trade-off between the level of constitutionally protected rights and the level of democracy. At the extreme, if someone or another has a constitutionally protected rights claim over every decision, there is no room left for democracy, as every decision has already been taken. Furthermore, as Glendon (1991) argues, rights claims tend to be absolute, which makes reasonable political compromise harder. Of course, as Dahl (1988, 182) argues, it is natural for everyone to want their most cherished interests to be given special protection (i.e., for their interests to be privileged over others'). However, as already argued, it is logically impossible for everyone to be privileged over everyone else.

Fourth, too many rights may make everyone worse off. If we give individuals absolute control over certain decisions, and they act without regard for the interests of others, we may end up with an outcome that nobody likes, even though it is the result of individual choices. Amartya Sen (1970b) first demonstrated the pervasiveness of this problem (referring to it as the "Impossibility of a Paretian Liberal"). The illustration he gave, however, does not capture the importance of the problem for us.[12] Aldrich (1977) recognized that the problem highlighted by Sen was essentially a collective action problem. (See Miller 1977b for a discussion of the differences between Aldrich's game-theoretic and Sen's social choice–theoretic interpretations.) The problem can be illustrated in the game shown in table 5.1.

Suppose we have two neighbors in an apartment. One plays electric guitar, the other trombone. They both like to practice. However, if they both practice whenever they like, they inflict significant costs on each other. This gives each a payoff of zero. However, if they coordinate their practice times (perhaps practicing when the other was out of the building), they would both be better off, receiving a payoff of 5 each. However, if each has an unconditional right to practice whenever he or she would like, this may not happen. Whatever the trombonist does the guitarist is better off practicing whenever she likes, and whatever the guitarist does,

TABLE 5.1.   A Prisoner's Dilemma Game (trombonist's payoff first)

| | | Guitarist | |
		Show restraint	Play loud, anytime
Trombonist	Show restraint	5, 5 [A]	−5, 10 [C]
	Play loud, anytime	10, −5 [B]	0, 0 [D]

[A] → [D] ~ [B] ~ [A]

the trombonist is better off practicing whenever he likes. Thus we have the familiar Prisoner's Dilemma situation. If we were just dealing with two apartment dwellers, we would hope that they could negotiate an amicable solution, although Glendon's (1991) tales of litigation on matters like this caution us against too much optimism. However, if we are dealing with a situation where there are many agents, this is less likely. The usual solution to a collective action with many players is to have some type of central enforcement. We do not rely on people to pay taxes or provide national defense voluntarily but have the government enforce this obligation. But this is precisely the solution we foreclose when we give the players unconditional rights to choose their own behavior.

The consequence for us of Sen's paradox is that assigning rights inappropriately may make everyone worse off. It is clear that assigning rights may make some people better off at the expense of others. However, it is possible for some rights assignments to harm everyone. This is typically the case when the actions of the players not only affect the players themselves but also affect other people or groups. As Saari (2001) shows, this is an inevitable result of decentralized decision making where the aggregate consequences of decisions are not internalized by the players. (For reasons explained in chapter 4, we should also note that this implies a majority-rule intransitivity—outcome [A] is unanimously preferred to [D], we are indifferent between [D] and [B], but [A] is not majority-rule preferred to [B].) This problem clearly applies to environmental issues—if we grant an unconditional right to emit, we are likely to end up with a level of pollution no one would choose. If we grant an unconditional right for landowners to do as they choose on their land, we may well see land use patterns that the landowners collectively would not choose. The same framework would apply also to questions of federalism (Sen 1976). If we grant different subnational units unconditional control over certain actions that affect other states (such as pollution control or interstate commerce) we may end up with highly suboptimal outcomes.

Clearly, decentralizing decision making has benefits—where the decision does not have strong effects on other people or units, it makes little sense not to delegate the decision. Delegation both increases freedom and may well increase the quality of the decision, given that decisions can be tailored to local or individual tastes and circumstances. However, if the choices of individual units have strong effects on other units, then delegation can lead to outcomes nobody would want. The problem is to decide which decisions should be delegated, or, to put it another way, when to give decision-making rights to decentralized units as opposed to when to make the decision collectively. A democratic solution would be to allow the people collectively to decide this question via majority rule. After all, the principle of popular sovereignty is that the people should be decisive over every decision, *should they choose to be*. This, however, brings us back to straightforward majority-rule democracy, not constitutionalism, where some decision-making rights are delegated regardless of the opinion of the majority.

This brings us full circle to the basic problem of constitutionalism. If certain rights are to be protected, even against the majority, some group has to decide which rights these are to be, and it also has to have the power to overrule the majority in cases *where this group decides that rights have been violated*. The group with this power then has the ability to use it to protect entrenched privileges or oppressions. As Dahl (1956) argues, a constitution cannot decide whether its provisions are being used to defend legitimate rights or unjust privileges. If the majority is not sovereign, then a minority must have the power to overrule the majority. If the right to overrule the majority belongs to a group subject to no higher power (at least earthly), then you have a form of judicial guardianship. (The Iranian Council of Guardians, which has a veto over all legislation, would be an example of this.) If the right to overrule the majority belongs to a constitutional court, the degree of guardianship is less, as it is possible to change the constitution. Amending constitutions, however, typically requires more than a simple majority. Thus constitutionalism is essentially a form of supermajoritarian rule, albeit one that gives an unelected body of judicial guardians considerable discretionary power.

In terms of empirical evidence, there is no evidence I am aware of that constitutional rights protection regimes protect basic rights better than simple majority rule. As Dahl (2001) argues, the problem is that all advanced industrial democracies for the most part respect the basic rights necessary for democratic governance, such as freedom of speech, the press, and organization. If we consider cross-national assessments of basic liberal rights, such as those compiled by Freedom House (2004), we find very little variation among industrial democracies—the United States, with its constitutionalist rights regime, receives a virtually perfect score, as does the Netherlands, which has virtually no formal checks on a parliamentary majority. Furthermore, even within the United States, it is not clear that judicial review is responsible for the high level of respect of basic rights—Dahl (1956, 1988) argues that there is not a single case of the Supreme Court overturning an act of Congress that would have taken away a basic right.[13] Thus it seems that high-income democracies respect basic rights regardless of whether there are constitutional protections such as judicial review. However, if we move away from basic rights and consider the protection of the interests of minorities, it is here we would expect majority rule regimes to provide more protection than superma-joritarian ones. We would expect to see differences in the status of ethnic minorities, the poor, and also some majority groups (such as women). We turn to the evidence for this in chapter 8.

7. Cycling and Minority Protection under Majority Rule

I have argued that majority rule provides the most protection for minori-ties and that supermajoritarian rule merely replaces the possibility of domination by a majority with domination by a privileged minority. We can now relate this argument to the discussion of majority-rule cycling in the last chapter. It is precisely the presence of multiple, cycling majori-ties that provides the possibility of a check on majorities without artifi-cially empowering a minority. We see this at work in many of the small countries of Europe (Austria, Denmark, Finland, Norway, the Nether-lands, Sweden) that have coalition government but very few constitu-tional checks and balances.

Majority-rule cycling can protect minorities in two ways. First, as Miller (1983) argues, it can ensure that there are no permanent losers. A group out of power can always expect to be able to defeat the incumbents in the future and thus have an incentive to keep playing the game, which enhances the stability of the system. Second, the need to build and main-tain majority coalitions provides protection to minorities. Because any winning coalition can be split, the minority always has a means of retali-ation. Furthermore, it is not in the interest of members of the winning coalition to try to drive the losers to the wall. If the winning coalition is too harsh to the other players, then these players may approach part of the winning coalition and sell their support for a very low price. They may give their support on all other issues in exchange for votes on the one issue that they view as crucial to their identity. For example, if a coalition of liberals and socialists in the Netherlands tried to prevent state funding of parochial schools, the confessional parties could go to the socialists and offer them support for any economic program they prefer, in exchange for abandoning the schools proposal. The socialists, being more con-cerned with economics than parochial schools, would accept this, thus breaking the coalition with the liberals. The liberals, anticipating this out-come, would not try to end support for parochial schools. Far from being a problem for democracy, majority-rule cycling actually provides a way to reconcile the demands of majority rule and minority protection.

Interestingly, although Buchanan and Tullock have been among the foremost advocates of unanimity rule, the following quotation from *The*

Calculus of Consent (1962, 132) provides an argument very similar to the one I have just made.

> Applying the strict Pareto rules for determining whether one social situation represents an improvement over another, almost any system that allows some such exchange to take place would be superior to that system which weights all preferences equally on each issue. By way of illustration, it is conceivable that a proposal to prohibit Southern Democrats from having access to free radio time might be passed by simple majority vote in a national referendum should the issue be raised in this way. Such a measure, however, would not have the slightest chance of being adopted by the decision-making process actually prevailing in the United States. The measure would never pass the Congress because the supporters of the minority threatened with the damage would, if the issue arose, be willing to promise support on other measures in return for votes against such discriminatory legislation.

Summary

The previous chapter argued that majority rule uniquely embodies the values of popular sovereignty and political equality. However, these are not the only values we are concerned with in matters of constitutional choice. This chapter has considered minority protection and rights. It is commonly argued that there is a trade-off between political equality (best served by majority rule) on one hand and minority protection (best served by external checks and balances) on the other. This chapter has argued that this trade-off is illusory and that majority rule provides more protection for the worst-off minority than any other decision rule.

Majority rule offers the most protection to minorities because it makes it easiest for a minority to form a coalition that can overturn an unacceptable outcome. Supermajority rules can certainly protect (or rather privilege) some minorities, but only at the expense of others. It is not logically possible for every minority to be privileged over every other minority. Supermajority rules make the status quo hard to overturn and thus privilege minorities who favor the status quo over those who favor changing it. Arguments in favor of supermajoritarian institutions have tended to be built on the assumption that the threat to minorities from government action or a change in the law is greater than the threat from government inaction or the maintenance of current laws. Given the history of the United States this assumption is problematic, especially given the use of supermajoritarian institutions to impede the extension of civil rights. Furthermore, given uncertainty about legal interpretation, technology, social mores, and preferences over the timescale involved in constitutional choice, any assumptions about where the threats to rights are likely to lie are inevitably heroic.

The protection of minorities under majority rule is a direct result of the instability and cycling phenomena outlined in the last chapter. The defense against a "tyranny of the majority" is that any majority can be split and defeated. Indeed, under such circumstances it would be very foolish for the current majority to try to drive those excluded from it to the wall by attacking their most vital interests. This would provoke members of the minority to try to buy off some members of the majority coalition, trading their support on other issues for concessions on the one issue they consider vital. (Chapter 8 argues that this is precisely the dynamic at work in the so-called consensual democracies of Europe.) There is no "tyranny of the majority" because there is no single, cohesive majority ready to dominate everyone else. This, of course, is essentially the "extended republic" argument made by James Madison at the Constitutional Convention of 1787 and in Federalist 10.

APPENDIX: PROOFS

> LEMMA 1: *Let the $_iCore$ be the "core for agent i," that is, the set of points that a coalition C including agent i cannot overturn. The $_iCore$ with quota q will be a subset of the $_iCore$ with quota q + 1. The $_iCore$ must contain at least the ideal point of agent i.*

The $_iCore$ can be thought of as the set of points that agent i cannot block by proposing a point that i and $q - 1$ other voters prefer. Let $L(C)$ be the set of points that coalition C cannot overturn—that is, the set of points for which there does not exist another point that coalition C unanimously prefers. Then the $_iCore$ for quota q is

$$\bigcap_{C \subseteq N: |C| \geq q, i \in C} L(C) = \left(\bigcup_{C \subseteq N: |C| \geq q, i \in C} (L(C))' \right)'.$$

It is clear that for $\bar{C}$ such that $|C| = q$, $L(\bar{C}) \subseteq L(\bar{C} + i)$, where $i \notin \bar{C}$. If there is a point x such that coalition $\bar{C}$ cannot find another point that it unanimously prefers, then there cannot be a point that the larger coalition ($\bar{C} + i$) unanimously prefers to x. Therefore

$$\left(L(\bar{C}:|C| = q)\right)' \supseteq \left(L(\bar{C} + i)\right)'$$

$$\Rightarrow \bigcup_{C \subseteq N:|C| \geq q, i \in C}(L(C))' \supseteq \bigcup_{C \subseteq N:|C| \geq q+1, i \in C}(L(C))' \Rightarrow \left(\bigcup_{C \subseteq N:|C| \geq q, i \in C}(L(C))'\right)'$$

$$\subseteq \left(\bigcup_{C \subseteq N:|C| \geq q+1, i \in C}(L(C))'\right)' \Rightarrow \bigcap_{C \subseteq N:|C| \geq q, i \in C}L(C) \subseteq \bigcap_{C \subseteq N:|C| \geq q+1, i \in C}L(C)$$

$$\Rightarrow {}_iCore(q) \subseteq {}_iCore(q + 1).$$

Given that a coalition containing i cannot overturn i's ideal point, and the $_iCore$ is defined as those points that a coalition containing i cannot overturn, then the $_iCore$ must at least contain i's ideal point.   QED

PROPOSITION 1: *Given a voting rule with quota q, let $m_i(q)$ be the utility associated with the least preferred position for agent i that, if enacted, no coalition including i could overturn given sincere voting. Then $m_i(q) \geq m_i(q + 1)$.*

Formally $m_i(q) = \min_{x \in {}_iCore(q)} u_i(x)$. It is obvious that $\min_{x \in X} u_i(x) \geq \min_{x \in Y:Y \supseteq X} u_i(x)$, given $X, Y \neq \emptyset$. Given Lemma 1 that $_iCore(q) \subseteq {}_iCore(q + 1)$, it can be seen that $\min_{x \in {}_iCore(q)} u_i(x) \geq \min_{x \in {}_iCore(q+1)} u_i(x)$, and thus $m_i(q) \geq m_i(q + 1)$.   QED

PART 3

DELIBERATION

CHAPTER 6

Deliberation, Rationality, and Representation

This chapter considers the relationship between the value of deliberation and the value of political equality. Deliberative democracy has probably been the dominant theme in the literature on democratic theory over the last fifteen to twenty years. Essentially it is argued that democracy has to be conceptualized not simply as a procedure for aggregating preferences but as a process whereby people interact, discuss, and find mutually satisfactory solutions. This conception of democracy is quite complementary to the theory of democracy developed so far in this book. After all, social decision rules are conceptualized in chapter 2 as the ground rules for legislative deliberation. Although the conclusions reached here differ from those of some deliberative democrats, the starting assumptions are similar. To summarize, it will be argued that the same institutions that satisfy political equality—proportional representation and majority rule—are those that are most likely to produce the kind of deliberation that deliberative democrats favor. Furthermore, deliberative democracy allows us to redefine social reason in a way that is defensible in a plural society.

Much is claimed for the value of deliberation in the literature. For example, in addition to more obvious and plausible claims that deliberation leads to better-informed decisions and can produce a better quality of reasoning, it is claimed that deliberative democracy can overcome the problems posed by social choice (D. Miller 1992; Dryzek and List 2003); that it can reconcile the freedom of the ancients with the freedom of the moderns (Cohen 1996); that it can reconcile procedural democracy (i.e., majority rule) with constitutional democracy with checks and balances (Gutmann and Thompson 1996); and (exaggerating slightly) that it can transcend all the contradictions of the philosophy of consciousness from Kant through Heidegger (Habermas 1984). There appears to be little that cannot be achieved with deliberation.

While accepting that deliberation is central to the theory and practice of democracy, it is necessary to be skeptical of many of these claims. For example, as argued in the previous chapter, it is logically impossible to reconcile majority rule with constitutional democracy based on checks and balances, as the latter is effectively supermajoritarian. It will be argued in this chapter that deliberation does not offer an escape route from the problems posed by social choice theory; and in the next that the consensual basis on which a great deal of the deliberative democracy literature rests is logically flawed. Furthermore, it will be argued that there is a hard trade-off between the value of deliberation (which requires small group interaction) and the value of participation—a trade-off some deliberative democrats simply ignore, promoting both values simultaneously. However, it is important not to minimize the importance of deliberation in democratic theory because of the exuberance of some of its advocates.

I will argue that the institutions that satisfy political equality—proportional elections to the legislature and majority rule in it—are the institutions most likely to bring about reasonable deliberation. Partially this conclusion is tautological. Since Habermas (1984), rationality in deliberation has been defined in terms of the conclusions that people acting in good faith would reach if they deliberated under ideal conditions. Political inequality would violate such ideal conditions. However, the conclusion is also partly based on the incentives institutions provide for people to be open to changing their preferences. As Nino (1996) argues, the more people who need to be convinced in order to carry a decision, the more rational (in the sense of being universalistic and impartial) the arguments will need to be. Political inequality reduces the incentives to be reasonable, because it is possible for some people to get their way without having to persuade so many people.

Deliberative democracy can also give us a more suitable standard for social reason in a plural society. Social rationality has been understood as transitivity not only in social choice theory but also in traditional democratic theory. However, the demand for a transitive social welfare function is a preposterous one in a plural society, as argued in chapter 2. If we take value pluralism seriously, then the best we can achieve is a compromise between different values, and there may be many acceptable compromises. The concepts of communicative rationality (Habermas 1984) and public reason (Rawls 1993/1996) define a reasonable outcome as what could be agreed upon under fair conditions. The works of Dewey (1927/1946), Lindblom (1965), and Nino (1996) provide examples of communicative conceptions of reasonable decision making within the context of majority rule. Thus deliberative democracy can provide us with an attainable ideal for democratic choice.

While deliberative democracy has much to contribute to the theory of democracy, it is necessary for it to take account of social choice theory. Some deliberative democrats (Dryzek 1990; Cohen 1998) have argued that voting is only a small part of democracy, and that the overall consensus-building process in society is more important. This argument was refuted on the grounds that voting is necessary if consensus is not reached, and even if it is, the anticipated voting outcome would influence what would be agreed (chapter 2). Democratic deliberation is deliberation oriented toward decision making by voting. As such social choice theory is relevant. As Knight and Johnson (1999, 570, 572) argue, formal theory can be a primary tool both for examining the incentives people face under different institutions and for examining the intrinsic, normative characteristics of such institutions.

This chapter will also consider representation. Given that a great deal of the deliberation that happens in a modern democracy is among elected representatives, it is necessary to consider the relationship between these representatives and those they represent. Indeed, since Burke (1777/1963) the connection between the question of representation and the mode of deliberation has been recognized. Thus deliberation will be related to both social decision rules and electoral systems.

Section 1 lays out the main claims about the value of deliberation and, in particular, the concept of social reason. It also considers the empirical and logical limits on what deliberative democracy can achieve, arguing that there is a trade-off between deliberation, participation, and political equality. Finally, it refutes the suggestion that deliberative democracy offers an escape from the problem of cycling. Section 2 considers the relationship between political equality and the value of deliberation in social decision rules, arguing that majority rule is likely to maximize both. It also considers the conditions under which this is most likely to produce reasonable outcomes. Section 3 considers the relationship between deliberative rationality and accountability in electoral systems, analyzing different conceptions of representation.

1. The Value of Deliberation and Social Reason

The idea that deliberation is valuable in democratic decision making is hard to object to. It would seem perverse to argue that we can make better decisions by avoiding discussion of the issues in question. However, the relevant question is not whether deliberation is valuable, but rather how it should be valued against competing values, and indeed whether there are trade-offs between deliberation and other things we find valuable. Thus, after laying out why deliberation is valuable, we consider the trade-off between it and the values of political equality and participation.

Three main reasons are given by the proponents of deliberative democracy as to why deliberation should improve the quality of democratic decisions. First, deliberation can make people better informed and thus able to come to better decisions. Second, deliberation can cause people to change their preferences (or at least their positions) and frame their arguments in more public-spirited ways. Third, deliberation may itself constitute social reason. That is to say, there are certain kinds of questions where the only measure of what counts as a reasonable resolution may be in terms of what can be defended deliberatively. This is particularly likely to be the case when we have competing reasonable claims. In addition to the claim that deliberation leads to better decisions, it is also argued by some that deliberation is valuable regardless of the outcome, because it has edifying effects on the participants. This argument will be considered in the next subsection, in the context of the relationship between participation and deliberation.

The first reason why deliberation should produce better decisions is the most obvious. In order to make reasonable decisions, people have to be informed about what they are deciding. This underlies the argument made in favor of deliberative democracy by Fishkin (1995). Members of a mass public have little incentive to inform themselves, because they are likely to have little impact on the outcome. That is to say, there is a strong incentive toward rational ignorance. Thus for Fishkin the measure of a reasonable democratic decision is what the people would decide if they were informed. We can estimate what this outcome would be by taking a representative sample of the people and having them deliberate. Of course, another way of informing people would be compulsory political education. The democratic advantage of deliberation is that it allows open access to the debate and avoids the question of who gets to decide what people are to be informed of.[1] Another advantage of deliberation is that it leads the participants to share information and experience. This can be valuable in that people can become specialists in certain areas and inform others (thus limiting the effects of bounded rationality—see Warren 1996; Fearon 1998) and also in that people are informed of a broad range of perspectives. One objection to the information-sharing argument is that people only have an incentive to share information when it benefits them, leading others to discount what they say as meaningless "cheap talk" (Austen-Smith 1990a,b, 1992). However, there are several responses to this. If people interact repeatedly, they have an incentive to cultivate a reputation for honesty (Mackie 1998). Furthermore, Przeworski (1998) argues that political communication can have an important coordinating function even if the actors are self-interested.[2]

The second claim made for deliberative democracy is that it causes people to change their preferences and to argue in a more public-spirited way. This claim, in fact, defines deliberative democracy for some writers (for example, Dryzek 1990).[3] It is possible that the process of deliberation will lead to people changing their ultimate values, allowing consensus on the matters under question. However, this extreme form of value change, erasing the plurality of values, is not necessary for deliberation to be valuable. Even if a plurality of ultimate values is maintained, people may change their positions; that is to say, they retain their ultimate ends but are persuaded to accept other means to fulfill or pursue them. This may change situations where people take opposing positions into situations where all parties can achieve their objectives — that is, it can produce win-win solutions. Warren (1992) gives a nuanced account of the circumstances where such transformations of preferences are likely to occur and where they are not.

In addition to possibly allowing participants to identify win-win solutions to conflicts, deliberative democrats argue that deliberation forces participants to adopt more reasonable arguments. For example, Habermas (1990a) argues that communication oriented toward finding agreements leads to moral arguments that are universalizable and impartial. That is to say, I do not argue in terms of what is good for me, but in terms of what is justified for anybody. Similarly, Rawls (1993/1996) and Gutmann and Thompson (1996) argue that public deliberation leads to the adoption of norms of reciprocity — I only make arguments that I can justify in the context of other people who are arguing in good faith about what is fair — and publicity — I cannot make arguments that only work if people are unaware of them.

There are two mechanisms by which deliberation may produce the adoption of more reasonable arguments. One is the simple need to convince more people. As Nino (1996) argues, if it is only necessary to convince a small group of people, then it is possible to be successful by appealing to a very narrow sense of self-interest. But as it becomes necessary to build a broader coalition and convince more people (and, equally important, a more diverse group of people), it becomes necessary to frame arguments more broadly. An argument of the form "We should do x because x benefits people like us" is only convincing to people like us. To convince other people, it is necessary to couch the argument in more general terms. Eventually (it is hoped) this leads to arguments based on universal moral principles.

The second mechanism is through negotiation. Political negotiation is typically multilateral. If I wish to achieve my objective, I need to seek allies, and these potential allies can cooperate with me, or they can find other partners. Lindblom (1965) argues that this need to find allies is one of the most important forces toward reasonable decision making in politics. If I am intransigent in my demands, potential allies will shun me and seek cooperation elsewhere. In order to gain allies, I need to take account of their interests and make concessions. Furthermore, it is to my advantage to develop longer-term relationships with allies. This gives an incentive to develop a reputation for fairness and keeping my word. Even though I may be able to gain a temporary advantage by double-crossing an ally, this is not in my long-run interest. This leads to the development of norms whereby my interests and the interests of my allies are accommodated and balanced. In the language of Rawls (1993/1996) we start out with a sense of the rational (our own interests) and end up with a conception of the reasonable (a conception of the balancing of our interests that can be defended to other people seeking a fair way to balance our interests).

The idea of negotiation is looked on with suspicion by some deliberative democrats, as it involves the pursuit of self-interest. However, it is crucial to the understanding of realistic political deliberation. This is recognized by the philosophers who have had the most influence on the deliberative democracy literature, Habermas and Rawls. Of course, a case can be made from *The Theory of Communicative Action* (1984, 286) that Habermas views negotiation as merely strategic and not communicative action, and indeed Johnson (1991) critiques this distinction as being unsustainable.[4] However, Habermas's more recent writings give negotiation a more positive role. For example, Habermas (1996a, 25) argues that compromise makes up the bulk of the political process, and that given value pluralism, bargaining between values is legitimate provided that the conditions under which the bargaining takes place are fair. The negotiation of competing interests is central to Rawls (1993/1996). People are assumed to have different interests, and political justice is considered as a fair equilibration of these interests, although Rawls makes it clear that more is required than a mere modus vivendi between competing interests.[5] For Rawls (1993/1996, 52–54) the rational (the individual pursuit of ends) and the reasonable (the willingness to propose fair terms to balance interests) are complementary. Without individual interests, the reasonable would be empty, as there cannot be a fair balancing of interests if no one has any interests. (Even altruism—putting the interests of others first—is meaningless unless those others have interests.) Likewise, without a sense of the reasonable, social cooperation would be impossible.

The final value of deliberation is that in many circumstances deliberation is constitutive of what is reasonable. That is to say, we can only say what a reasonable decision is after deliberation about it. For example, Dewey (1927/1946, 206–7) argues that the value of democracy is that it leads to debate and discussion in which the public is able to define itself and its interests. Similarly, we can consider the choice of fair terms

Player 2
A   B

		A	B
Player 1	A	4, 2	0, 0
	B	0, 0	2, 4

Fig. 6.1.   An assurance game

of social cooperation as laid out by Rawls on the first page of *A Theory of Justice* (1971/1999). Social cooperation benefits everyone; however, certain terms of cooperation benefit some people more, while other terms benefit others. When a society deliberates over how to cooperate, there is clearly a common interest in agreeing to some form of cooperation; however, there is also a distributive aspect to the problem, in that society has to decide how the gains to cooperation are to be shared among various people. What we are faced with is essentially an assurance game, a two-player example of which is given in figure 6.1. If players 1 and 2 are able to both play strategy A or strategy B, they both are better off than if they play different strategies. However, coordinating on strategy A suits player 1 better, while coordinating on strategy B is better for player 2. (In figure 6.1, player 1's payoff is given first in every cell.)

For problems such as whether to coordinate on outcome A or B, it is hard to see what standards of rationality we can use other than to engage in deliberation. Clearly it is collectively irrational for the players to play different strategies, but there is no objective standard as to which coordinated strategy is better. Of course, if the game is repeated, it may be possible to play A sometimes, and B at others. Indeed there may be an infinite number of ways to divide the gains of cooperation. We could appeal to norms of equality, but this simply poses the question "Equality of what?" Different people may disagree as to what the basis of comparison should be (equality of outcome, equality of desert, equality of opportunity, equal division of the gains from cooperation, all of which may give different outcomes). Furthermore, when deciding the division of the gains from social cooperation, there is no common metric according to which all goods can be judged. Different people will value different goods and outcomes more highly than others, and people will differ in the importance they place on different matters.

Social rationality has been understood as transitivity (the ability to rank-order the alternatives from most to least favored) not only in social choice theory but also in traditional democratic theory. Both Rousseau (1762/1997) and Condorcet (1785/1995) argue that voting should produce a single best outcome that can be referred to as the will of the people. Both Arrow (1951/1963) and Riker (1982), on one hand, and their most vehement critics accept the standard of transitivity.[6] (Witness the literature that attempts to minimize the effects of cycling or provide escape routes from it—Coleman and Ferejohn 1986; Dryzek and List 2003; Mackie 2003.) In this context we can see why transitivity is not a sensible criterion to demand of a social decision.

It is apparent that some outcomes are clearly bad, in that they make everyone worse off than some other outcomes (the Pareto or efficiency criterion). However, we need to make a choice between outcomes that pass this test (are Pareto efficient), and this decision is distributional. Distributional games typically produce cycles (a three-person majority-rule divide-the-dollar game is the simplest example). Some outcomes benefit some groups more than others. Therefore some groups favor some outcomes and other groups others. The eventual outcome is the result of negotiation or accommodation between different interests, not the result of a single interest from which we can expect transitivity. Thus social reason is inherently different from individual rationality. A socially reasonable outcome is one that balances a plurality of different claims, not one that maximizes a single criterion. This conception of reason is very different from the anthropomorphic ideal of collective will formation found in Rousseau and a great deal of traditional democratic theory, as well as social choice theory; however, it is quite compatible with the conceptions of public or communicative reason that take the plurality of values seriously, such as those found in Dewey, Rawls, and Habermas.

Indeed we can reinterpret Arrow's theorem (1951/1963) as a demonstration of the difference between individual and collective rationality. The axiom of independence of irrelevant alternatives implies that the choice between two alternatives can only depend on preferences between those two alternatives, not on preferences for any others. Therefore the choice between two alternatives A and B must depend on the coalition for alternative A versus the coalition for alternative B (it may depend on identity of the members of the coalitions, not just the size). Arrow shows that the only way to maintain transitivity under this condition (and the requirement of universal domain and Pareto optimality) is to have a single unitary winning coalition (i.e., a dictator). If we have multiple winning coalitions (as we must under a democratic decision rule), or even a single winning coalition with multiple members, then transitivity will be violated under some preference profiles. This has been interpreted by many (notably Riker 1982) as showing that there is no democratically satisfactory decision rule, and others (notably Sen 1979) as showing that Arrow's conditions simply eliminate all the information needed to make a social decision. The interpretation here differs from both of these, in that both Riker's and Sen's interpretations accept the reasonableness of requiring transitivity. I argue that democratic decision making with a plurality of values is incompatible with transitivity. In the context of collective decision making, negotiation between competing values is not a second-best solution when consensus fails, but an integral and vital part of social reason.

The advantages claimed for deliberation are, I think, extremely plausible. We would in general expect deliberation to result in people being better informed (although it might also result in the opposite effect if there is enough misinformation, noise, and propaganda in the debate — see Stokes [1998]; Przeworski [1998]); it may well lead to people changing their opinions and coming to reasonable agreement (although as Knight and Johnson 1994 argue the opposite could also result — people discover they have irreconcilable differences they had not previously recognized); and deliberation and compromise may be the only reasonable way to resolve distributional issues. Indeed I would expect to find these effects of deliberation at work in any functioning democracy. The claims of some deliberative democrats, however, go far beyond this. Some argue for a form of deliberative democracy that involves mass participation and present this as an alternative to conventional representative democracy (Barber 1984;[7] Dryzek 1990, 2000). It is argued by others that deliberative democracy can overcome the problems posed to democratic theory by social choice (Miller 1992; Dryzek and List 2003). The following two sections lay out the logical and empirical limits of what deliberative democracy can provide.

The Limits of Deliberative Democracy

We have seen the claims made as to the value of democratic deliberation. This section, however, focuses on the limits on what deliberation can provide us with. Given that people only have a limited amount of time to spend on politics, and given that deliberation requires small group interactions, there is a binding trade-off between the values of deliberation, participation, and political equality. Some of the literature on deliberative democracy conflates deliberation with participation. Indeed some writers frequently classed as "deliberative democrats" (for example, Barber 1984; Dryzek 1990) emphasize participation as much as deliberation. It sometimes seems to be assumed that "all good things go together." (It should be noted that there is a long tradition that views deliberation as a function of representative government — Burke, Madison, and Mill being three notable examples — and that not all modern deliberative democrats share a populist enthusiasm for direct participation.)

However, in large democracies there is a trade-off between the values of direct participation and deliberation. In order to overcome this trade-off, it is necessary to violate another value that many deliberative democrats value—political equality. Thus I will argue that the values of deliberation, direct participation, and political equality form a trilemma. It may be possible to achieve two of these values, but only at the cost of sacrificing the third.

Fishkin (1995) argues that there are four democratic values we should be concerned about: political equality, deliberation, participation, and nontyranny. Furthermore, he argues that there are trade-offs between these values. We have discussed the question of majority tyranny in chapter 5 and concluded that typically it does not conflict with political equality. However, even without considering nontyranny as a separate value, it can still be shown that the other three values cannot be maximized simultaneously. Of course, reasons can be given for valuing all three of them. We have covered the value of political equality and deliberation at length already. As Pateman (1970) points out, there is considerable literature that disputes whether high levels of participation are valuable at all, claiming that this leads to instability. However, Pateman responds (following Mill 1861/1993 and Rousseau 1762/1997) that participation is valuable and edifying in itself. Essentially the argument is that participation in politics leads to moral development—people cease to view matters in terms of narrow self-interest and are forced to consider things in a more civic-minded fashion.

It is important to note that the trade-off here involves *direct* participation, not participation in general. By direct participation I mean involvement in the actual decision process, such as voting on legislation. This does not include indirect participation, such as attempting to influence decision makers. Thus the trade-off does not involve many activities that make up civil society, such as participating in social movements, interest groups, or political parties. The argument made here is *not* that too much citizen participation leads to an overload of demands on democracy by civil society. Rather it is simply the claim that if too many people are directly involved in the legislative process, then this process will either not be very deliberative or not very egalitarian. For example, it is quite possible to argue in the manner of Habermas (1996b) that democracy requires the strong generation of influence from an active civil society, while at the same time insisting that this influence be mediated through representative institutions in order to ensure that decisions satisfy equality and discursive rationality.

Even if we agree that deliberation, direct participation, and political equality are all desirable, it is clear that we cannot achieve all three at the same time, at least not in a large democracy. (Large here includes even the smallest modern nation-states.) There are two constraints that are relevant. First, there is a limit to the amount of time that people are willing to devote to politics. Even if participation in politics is desirable (for either the individual or the society), there are many other ways in which people may want to spend their time. This constraint could in principle be overcome by coercion (people being "forced to be free," to use Rousseau's famous phrase), but this is clearly problematic in a free society.

The second constraint is that posed by complexity. Deliberation requires small group discussion. People have to discuss things in an interactive way. This is simply not possible with millions of people all participating at the same time. As Williamson (1975, 42–43) shows, the number of individual interactions in a peer group network is $n(n-1)/2$, where n is the number of people. Thus with 5 people we have 10 interactions, with 10 people 45 interactions, with 100 people 4,950 interactions, with 1,000 people 499,500 interactions, and so on. Furthermore it is vital for deliberation that people be able to interact. Deliberative theorists emphasize that deliberation is not simply about exchanging information but about exchanging binding commitments and agreements (Habermas 1990a, 58–59). Ideally deliberation produces consensus, but when it does not, compromise is necessary. This requires players to come to binding agreements and deals. The more players the more complex and the harder it is to negotiate a deal including everyone. When we get beyond a fairly small group, the only practical way to negotiate a deal is for groups to delegate the right to negotiate on their behalf—that is, to have representatives. In modern democracy, this process happens at least twice: The people elect representatives, and these representatives choose a party leadership that chooses actual policy or negotiates over it with other parties.

Dryzek (1990) suggests that it is possible to overcome the problem of complexity and have mass participation deliberative democracy by not insisting that everyone take part in every decision. This, however, leads to the violation of political equality. If self-selecting issue-publics deliberate and decide various issues, then other interests are not considered. It may well be that certain groups have resource advantages that may make it easier to participate, such as time and education. If this is the case, we face the prospect of domination by what Elster (1983) called a "self-appointed activist elite." (We should note that this activist elite need not be liberal or progressive—it could be the white, upper-middle-class parents on a school board just as easily as members of left-wing social movements.) Even if it is possible to address inequality in resources, self-selection is still a problem. The people motivated to participate are likely to be those who have a strong personal stake in the particular outcome. Thus the interests of a

small number of people with a lot at stake may be weighted dispropor-
tionately to the interests of a very large group of people each of whom has
less at stake individually. In other words, concentrated interests will be
privileged over diffuse interests. Dividing policy-making into decisions
taken by discrete issue-publics also leads to problems concerning disag-
gregation and Sen's (1970b) theorem (chapter 5, this vol.). The policies
that individual issue-publics make are reasonable when each issue is considered individually, but the overall package may make no sense (indeed
may be unfeasible) when considered collectively. The individual parts effectively make a collective decision that could not be defended deliberatively to the whole population.

Warren (1996) argues that because of the complexity of public decisions, the public can only participate in a small number of them, and
therefore the majority of decisions need to be made authoritatively. The
problem then becomes how to generate a democratically acceptable form
of authority. Warren (1996, 57) argues that such democratic authority can
only result from people deferring when there exists "a set of institution-
alized protections and securities within which the generative force of discursive challenge is possible." Although most decisions are taken authoritatively, challenge is always possible, so society's discursive resources are
channeled into those issues where they are most needed ("contested" issues, as opposed to "settled" ones). I find this account persuasive. It does
not, however, overcome the trilemma even for the limited domain of issues designated "contested." If the final court of appeal is the ability of
self-appointed interest publics to contest, then political equality is violated, as the resources (financial and educational) to participate may be
unevenly distributed. If the final court of appeal is majority-rule democracy, then votes are equally distributed, even if expertise is not. However,
we are no longer dealing with direct participation and control, unless we
opt for direct democracy and give up a high level of deliberation. It is notable that Dewey (1927/1946, 206–8) assigns this role to majority rule: Its
value is that it forces experts to take account of the interests of mass
publics, who although they lack expert knowledge do have the ability to
judge experts.

Fishkin (1995) proposes randomly selected citizens' juries as a solution. However, citizens' juries are simply a form of representation and
thus do not produce mass participation. Instead of using elections to
choose those who deliberate, we instead use the random sampling tech-
niques used in survey research to select a deliberative body that is representative of the population as a whole. This has some advantages, notably that it satisfies political equality (everyone has the same chance of
being selected). However, only a very small minority of the population

would be selected in any given time period, while the remainder of the population would participate even less than under an elected assembly (they do not even get a vote for their representatives). Citizen juries and deliberative polls do not get around the fact that in order to have a small group that can deliberate, it is necessary for the majority of the population to be represented, as opposed to being actually present.

It should be noted that improved communication and information technology do not dissolve the trilemma. The Internet may indeed make it easier for citizens to become involved and to make contact with other citizens. However, it does not overcome the problem of rational ignorance that Fishkin (1995) points to. More important, it does not overcome the problem of network complexity. An online debate may provide a vast range of opinions (indeed there may well be a problem of information overload, as participants try to shout the same views louder and louder). However, it does not make negotiating an agreement between millions of people any easier. As noted earlier, negotiation involves making binding agreements—I concede this, you concede that. The only way to achieve this with a large population is by delegation to representatives.

Figure 6.2 illustrates the trilemma between political equality, deliberation, and direct participation, and relates it to various democratic alternatives (representative democracy, plebiscitarian democracy, and self-selected participatory democracy). For example, representative democracy can satisfy political equality and deliberation, but it is not particularly participatory. If the people elect representatives by proportional representation (chapter 3) and the representatives make decisions by majority rule (chapter 4), then political equality is satisfied. The representative body can be small enough for reasonable deliberation, although this may involve delegation to party leaders or specialist committees. However, most of the population participates only by voting for representatives. It will be argued in chapter 8 that "consensual democracy" (Lijphart 1999), as practiced mainly in the small countries of Europe, fits this pattern in that it is egalitarian, deliberative, but has limited direct participation. It is notable that Lijphart (1977) argues that this type of democracy requires that elites have sufficient independence from their constituents to negotiate mutually beneficial accommodations.

Plebiscitarian democracy satisfies political equality and participation, but not deliberation. Instead of bargains negotiated by representatives, decisions are taken by direct votes by the people. This satisfies political equality, in that everyone's vote counts for the same. It is also highly participatory, in that everyone can participate on every decision. However, it is the antithesis of deliberative democracy. Given that any

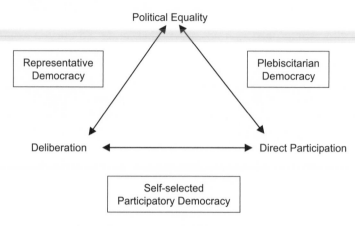

Fig. 6.2.   The trilemma of deliberative democracy

individual will have little impact on the outcome, there are weak incentives for voters to spend time to get informed. More troubling from a deliberative point of view is the fact that it is not possible for the voters to negotiate a reasonable solution. The voters are simply presented with alternatives, and they are expected to vote on them. (Control over the agenda and the wording of the alternatives may be an important source of political power that violates political equality.) Furthermore, direct democracy requires that the public agenda be broken down into discrete issues that are voted on separately. This further undermines reasonable democratic deliberation. Even if voters make reasonable choices about each issue individually, the overall package of policies taken as a whole may make no sense (Anscombe 1976; Saari and Sieberg 2001; Lacy and Niou 2000). Indeed, the overall package may not even be feasible. For example, a people may decide to vote for a wide range of public services but vote against the taxes required to pay for them.

Plebiscitarian democracy involves mass direct participation but does not ask much of each participant. Most significant, each participant is not required to deliberate. Self-selected participatory democracy requires that decision makers participate more fully, such as by attending meetings or participating in deliberation. However, it is difficult in a liberal society to coerce people to deliberate (although not impossible; consider jury service). Furthermore, even if mass deliberative participation could be coerced, the result would be a body far too large to deliberate reasonably. Self-selected participant democracy gets around this by having an open right for anyone who wants to participate. This implicitly relies on the fact that many people will choose not to. The price of this is that political equality is violated. The self-selected group that chooses to participate may well be made up of those with resource advantages (such as time and education) or those who have a disproportionate stake in the issue in question.

This book has argued that the trade-offs that are often claimed between political equality and other political values are largely illusory. However, the conflict between political equality, deliberation, and direct participation is very real. From an analytic point of view, this is where we end. From a normative point of view, I would argue that direct participation is the value that is most dispensable in politics. Once again, it should be emphasized that the trade-off with other values involves direct participation—participation in the final decision-making stage—not indirect forms of participation, such as being active in social movements, interest groups, or political parties. As I have argued at length, political equality is at the heart of what we mean by democracy. Deliberation is clearly necessary to make reasonable political decisions.

However, the case for direct participation is more dubious. Certainly it can be argued that people feel that a decision is more legitimate if they have personally participated in its making. Pateman (1970) argues that political participation is intrinsically edifying, leading to better, more open-minded citizens. However, participation is also a cost—time spent playing politics cannot be spent in other ways. Indeed, mass political participation could be regarded as highly inefficient, as a massive waste of collective time and life energy. As Femia (1996) argues, political participation may be edifying, but no one has made a convincing argument that it is more edifying than a variety of alternative activities, such as playing musical instruments, attending religious services, doing charity work, spending time with one's children, or staring into sunsets. Jon Elster (1983) makes the argument that it makes no sense for participation to be an end in itself. People only engage in politics in order to achieve some other objective, so participation has to be justified instrumentally. Warren (1992), while sympathetic to the idea that democratic participation transforms people's preferences and identities, argues that it cannot be expected to transform them completely. Even if we accept that the self is constructed socially through discourse, this does not imply that discourse and social interaction can arbitrarily transform the self in beneficial ways. Rather, the transformation of preferences is only likely in regard to specific kinds of issues. Finally, if participation is intrinsically desirable, it is possible to participate in activities other than direct political decision making. Participation in these social or indirect political activities can provide the edifying effects of participation without the trade-offs with more fundamental democratic values.

The Failure of Deliberative Democracy as an Escape from Social Choice

Various authors have argued that deliberative democracy offers an escape from the problems posed by social choice theory in general and Arrow (1951/1963) in particular. Thus it is hoped that deliberation can "save" democratic theory from the nihilistic findings of social choice. This line of argument typically accepts Riker's (1982) reading of social choice theory, which argues that Arrow's theorem and the global cycling results undermine traditional democratic theory, leaving a Schumpeterian minimalist democracy as the only viable alternative. (For example, Dryzek [2000] entitles a chapter in his book on deliberative democracy "Minimalist Democracy? The Social Choice Critique.") The results of social choice theory are nowhere near as corrosive to democratic theory as Riker argued, and the "problems" posed by social choice theory (such as cycling) are actually a vital part of the normal working of democracy, as I argued earlier. Thus, using deliberation as an escape route from the social choice results is unnecessary, even if it were viable. The remainder of this section will argue that it is not even viable.

The simplistic version of the argument that deliberative democracy overcomes the problems of social choice (that deliberation can produce consensus, and so voting is not necessary) has already been dealt with. A more sophisticated argument is that democratic deliberation does not necessarily produce consensus, but it restricts people's preferences in such a way that transitive social choice is possible. David Miller (1992) and Dryzek and List (2003) provide arguments of this type. This argument can actually be found in Arrow (1951/1963), following Black (1948), who showed that a sufficient condition for this to be the case under majority rule is for preferences to be single-peaked in one dimension. That is, people may disagree on which alternative is best, but they all line the alternatives up in the same order, implicitly agreeing on how the alternatives are to be compared. Arrow (1951/1963, 83) speculates that other restrictions may produce similar results for mechanisms other than majority rule. The argument of David Miller (1992) and Dryzek and List (2003) is that deliberation will structure people's preferences in such a way. I will argue that even if this is the case, it does not solve the problems posed by social choice theory. I will concentrate on Dryzek and List's version of the argument because it is the most recent and most rigorous.

Arrow's theorem states that there is no transitive social welfare function that satisfies four apparently indispensable conditions—universal domain, independence of irrelevant alternatives, the Pareto condition, and nondictatorship (chapter 2). Riker argues that this absence of a transitive social welfare function means that all democratic outcomes are arbitrary. Dryzek and List (2003, 7) argue that deliberation may allow us to safely dispense with at least one of Arrow's conditions. This would allow for the possibility of finding a transitive social welfare function. They argue, "If *any one* of these conditions is relaxed, there exist social choice procedures satisfying all the others, and such procedures can, in principle, be employed in democratic decision making." This claim is actually too strong—the fact that a procedure satisfies the four conditions does not prove that it is even minimally democratic. More important, Dryzek and List assume that to be democratically acceptable a social choice procedure must be transitive. This rules out majority rule, which almost certainly produces cycles when preferences are not one-dimensional.

Dryzek and List's escape routes from Arrow's result are not convincing. First they argue that deliberation may enable us to dispense with universal domain by introducing more structure in preferences. To escape cycling we need for preferences to be single-peaked in one dimension. However, many issues are intrinsically multidimensional. In particular, any issue that involves spending money involves a budget constraint, so that the amount I want to spend on program A will depend on how much is spent on program B. Deliberation will not reduce this kind of multidimensionality—indeed as people become more informed they may well gain a better appreciation of these interdependencies.

Dryzek and List give four solutions for multidimensional preferences. The first is to decompose the issue into dimensions on which there are single-peaked preferences, and decide these separately. This will produce a transitive social welfare function. However, it is unlikely to produce a sensible decision and may even produce a Pareto inferior one (see Anscombe 1976; Saari and Sieberg 2001; Lacy and Niou 2000). Imagine designing an airplane by taking separate votes on the type of wing, fuselage, engine, and so on. This will produce a transitive ranking, but it is highly unlikely to produce a viable airplane, precisely because it ignores the multidimensionality and interdependence of the problem. Dryzek and List's second solution, lexicographic ordering, faces similar problems. (Even if fuel economy is the most important parameter in my car choice, it would be foolish to make my decision purely on the basis of that.) The third solution is logrolling. In practical terms, this is often how political institutions deal with multidimensionality. Dryzek and List are correct to note that logrolling has some normative value in that it makes use of information about intensity of preferences (this is why Buchanan and Tullock [1962, 131] argued that vote trading protected minorities). However, logrolling is not an escape from Arrow's theorem, because there are typically any number of possible logrolls (see Bernholz 1973; N. Miller 1975,

1977a). Which one occurs depends on the negotiating skills of the participants. This puts us right back in the Rikerian arbitrariness that the authors are seeking to escape. The fourth solution is not a solution at all but simply a statement that it is better to explore the dimensionality of the problem than to decide ahead of time that it is insoluble.

Furthermore, it is far from clear that democratic deliberation will reduce the number of dimensions. As both Mill (1996) and Knight and Johnson (1994) argue, the values of deliberative democrats lead precisely to open institutions and to more people being drawn into the process. This has the potential to increase the number of dimensions and thus generate cycling. By arbitrarily restricting the alternatives available, we can certainly produce a transitive social ordering; however, this process cannot be described as democratic, deliberative or otherwise. Claiming that democratic deliberation will produce unidimensionality seems a lot like trying to have our cake and eat it too. We want the benefits of a restricted set of alternatives, without admitting the unsavory restrictions and exclusions needed to produce it. Of course, whether free deliberation reduces or increases the number of dimensions is an empirical matter. Dryzek and List produce some evidence that it reduces dimensionality, but it is far from clear this evidence is generalizable. Furthermore, to overcome the problem of cycling, it is not enough to reduce the number of dimensions; it is necessary to reduce it to a single dimension — even two dimensions can produce global cycling.

Apart from restricting preferences, Dryzek and List give two other ways that deliberation may provide an escape route from Arrow's theorem. First, deliberation may allow us to dispense with the independence of irrelevant alternatives condition. If deliberation produces consensus about what the alternatives are, we do not have to worry about people disingenuously adding alternatives to manipulate the outcome. The problem here is that deliberation would have to produce complete consensus as to what the relevant alternatives are. The inclusiveness and equality valued by most deliberative democrats require an open agenda, so anything less than unanimity would not help us. Furthermore, many decisions that interest us are continuous. For example, the tax rate can be anything between 0 and 100 percent. It does not make much sense in such cases to argue about there being consensus about there being a finite number of relevant alternatives.

Second, Dryzek and List argue that if deliberation allows us to agree on interpersonal utility comparisons, then we can get a transitive social welfare function while satisfying all of Arrow's conditions. This is certainly true, but it hardly helps us with democratic decision making. This is because in the inevitable absence of consensus about a just way to compare interpersonal utilities, we need a social choice procedure to decide how to aggregate these utilities. This is not to say that utilitarian procedures such as counting quality-adjusted life years to evaluate medical procedures cannot be useful in reaching rational decisions, only that such decisions presuppose a prior decision on values, democratic or otherwise.

We next consider an alternative way to reconcile social choice theory and deliberative democracy. This is to drop the transitivity requirement and accept that social preferences orderings may be cyclical. This allows us to rehabilitate majority rule, the procedure most commonly associated with democratic decision making. Instead of seeking to find escape routes to avoid cycling, we should embrace it. Cycling in social preferences does not imply chaos or radical instability. Cycling simply means that there are multiple alternative majorities, rather than a single, permanent, dominant majority. From the point of view of pluralist and democratic theory, the former is almost certainly preferable.

2. Procedural Justice and Deliberative Democracy in Social Decision Rules

The previous chapters have laid out a procedural theory of democracy based on the principle of political equality and have shown that this implies very specific institutions. We have seen in the previous section that deliberation does not allow us to disregard the results of social choice theory. Therefore we need to ask whether there is a trade-off between political equality and deliberation. I will argue that the requirements of the two values are actually complementary. This section will argue that majority rule is the social decision rule most likely to bring about reasonable deliberation. The next section will argue that proportional representation is the seat allocation rule most likely to lead to reasonable deliberation in legislatures.

Why Majority Rule, Not Consensus, Is Most Likely to Promote Reasonable Deliberation

I have shown that political equality implies majority rule as a social decision rule. However, many deliberative democrats have argued that consensus is the preferred rule for producing reasonable deliberation. It is important to distinguish between consensus as an outcome and consensus as a decision rule. It is hard to deny that an outcome to which everyone freely agrees (consensus as an outcome) is reasonable. However, it is not clear that giving everyone a veto (consensus as a decision rule) is the best way to reach reasonable agreement. I will argue in the next chapter that the consensual basis for deliberative democracy and social contract theory is logically flawed and should be replaced by a theory based on majority rule. Here, however, I argue that majority rule is the decision rule most likely to bring about reasonable deliberation in practice.

Of course, if we consider social reason to be defined as deliberation under fair procedures (as we did in the first section of this chapter), and we define fairness in terms of political equality, then by definition there cannot be a trade-off between political equality and the value of deliberation in this sense. Majority rule is the only decision rule that is fair in the sense of treating all voters and all alternatives equally. Consensus—like all supermajoritarian rules—is biased toward the status quo and those who favor it, as was demonstrated in the last chapter.

We can also consider what kind of decision rules will lead to people deliberating reasonably and to people's preferences being transformed in a public-spirited manner. This is an empirical question, but it is very difficult to study empirically because there is no obvious way to measure the "reasonableness" of deliberation under different rules, or how people's preferences were transformed. In the absence of empirical evidence, we can consider theoretical arguments as to why some rules encourage reasonable deliberation more than others. The problem with the deliberative democracy literature based on consensus is that too often it requires the assumption that people will conduct themselves reasonably. This amounts to assuming away the problem. The point is to find rules that encourage people to behave reasonably or at least do not discourage them by allowing reasonable behavior to be exploited.

Therefore we need to consider the incentives that rules give for reasonable deliberation. If a rule leads to those who deliberate reasonably being systematically exploited by those who are narrowly self-interested, then we would expect over time that people will stop behaving reasonably. Indeed, even if everyone starts out behaving reasonably, such a rule would be morally corrosive in that it creates an incentive to take advantage of others. On the other hand, deliberation will be encouraged by a rule that at the very least does not punish the reasonable, and preferably creates an incentive for people to deliberate reasonably, even if for self-interested motives. If people start to deliberate reasonably for self-interested reasons, then we may hope that the reasonable behavior becomes established, either out of habit or out of the belief that the behavior will be reciprocated. Furthermore, this process may be self-transforming—if I have to convince other people to get what I want, then I have to learn their perspectives, and perhaps take their interests into account.

There are two reasons why we would expect majority rule to be the rule most conducive to reasonable democratic deliberation. First, as Nino (1996) argues, the dynamic that causes preference transformation may be the need to convince other people of one's argument. To convince other people, I cannot make very narrow arguments of the type "This is good for me." If I am trying to convince a small, homogenous group, I may be able to get away with narrow arguments of group self-interest. However, the more people I need to convince, the broader my arguments need to be, perhaps eventually becoming universal moral arguments. Nino (1996) shows that majority rule is the decision rule forcing me to convince the most people in order to win the vote. Consensus may appear at first to require more people to be convinced, but this is only the case for someone advocating taking action or overturning the status quo. With consensus, the vote of one person in favor of the status quo is sufficient to defeat everyone else. Similarly, with a 60 percent supermajority rule, those in favor of the status quo only need to convince 40 percent of the participants to win. With majority rule, 50 percent is necessary to act or to block action. Thus to get one's way, one has to convince half the participants, which is more than is required for victory under any other rule.

The second reason for believing that majority rule is the rule most likely to lead to the reasonable transformation of preferences is its effect on the conduct of negotiation. Under majority rule, intransigence is a very risky strategy, because any proposal can be overturned and replaced by another by majority vote. If a player refuses to compromise, it is always possible to make a coalition around them. Indeed, it can be shown that majority rule is the decision rule with the smallest set of alternatives that cannot be overturned (Saari 1997). Therefore, the only way to protect your interest is to seek allies, which entails taking their interests into account. However, this is not the case under other voting rules. Under supermajoritarian rule or consensus, some outcomes may be locked in—if they become the status quo, it may be impossible to find a supermajoritarian coalition to overturn them. In this instance, players who like the status quo have absolutely no incentive to compromise—they are guaranteed what they want. Indeed, intransigence becomes an extremely prudent strategy—the favorable status quo becomes an asset to be defended. Worse yet, if supermajoritarian rule gives a group an effective veto, it may use this veto on matters on which it is indifferent, in order to extort concessions (or side payments) on other issues, a phenomenon Barry (1965/1990) called "the offensive use of the veto." Chapter 5 has already considered the pathologies of supermajority rule in detail, so it is not necessary to repeat the analysis, except to say that supermajority rule creates many incentives for obstructionism and extortion, as opposed to reasonable deliberation.

We can also consider how reasonable the terms of social cooperation negotiated under different decision rules are likely to be in terms of equity and efficiency. The previous chapter has shown that consensus (and supermajoritarian rules in general) tend to lock in existing injustices and thus are unlikely to be equitable. By contrast, majority rule is the most egalitarian social decision rule. The conservative bias intrinsic to consensus is somewhat ironic, given the left-wing leanings of many deliberative democrats. In terms of efficiency, we would expect consensus to produce efficient decisions in theory, in the sense that if it was possible to make everyone better off and nobody worse off, everyone would agree to it. However, in practice, consensus and highly supermajoritarian rules are likely to be extremely inefficient due to transaction costs. Under consensus a proposal beneficial to virtually everyone can be held up by one person, who would then need to be compensated. Indeed, as Barry (1965/ 1990) argues, the holdout may not even suffer from the proposal but may be strategically extorting "compensation." For this reason, even Buchanan and Tullock (1962), who are among the most enthusiastic endorsers of unanimity rule, accept that in its pure form it may produce an unacceptable degree of inefficiency due to transaction costs. We would expect majority rule in theory to produce efficient outcomes, as argued in chapter 4. The next subsection considers the conditions under which we should expect efficient outcomes in practice.

Thus there does not appear to be any trade-off between the values of deliberation and political equality with regard to social decision rules. The decision rule dictated by the political equality (majority rule) is that most likely to bring about democratically satisfactory deliberation. In this, I am following Dewey (1927/1946), Barry (1995), and Nino (1996), who all conceived majority rule as the institutional basis of deliberative democracy. However, the outcome of this deliberation does not just depend on the procedural rule under which the deliberation takes place; it also depends on how participants play the game. Social decisions involve negotiation and vote trading. Next we consider the literature on what kind of outcomes these games are likely to produce, and under what conditions these outcomes will be normatively acceptable.

Rationality, Instability, and Deliberation

Two criteria were laid out for an outcome being reasonable, over and above the decision being reached by reasonable procedures (section 1). First, the decision should be efficient. That is, it should not be possible to make some people better off without making others worse off. If there is another outcome that does this, it is clearly better, and it is not reasonable to advocate the first outcome. Put slightly differently, the outcome should make use of all the possible gains from cooperation. The second criterion is that the outcome should be distributionally just. This section considers how well majority-rule bargaining will meet these criteria and under what conditions it will fail.

Let us start with efficiency. Buchanan and Tullock (1962, 131) argue that vote trading in legislatures typically leads to more efficient outcomes, in spite of widespread popular suspicion of the process. Legislators trade influence on issues they care little about for influence on issues that are vital for them and their constituents. This allows mutually beneficial trades, which results in everyone being better off. Buchanan and Tullock also make other claims about the beneficial effects of vote trading. The process of vote trading reveals information about the intensity of people's preferences (we can infer that if a legislator trades influence on issue A for influence on issue B, the intensity of their preferences on B is greater), which can lead to better decisions.

On the other hand, Riker and Brams (1973) argue that the bad reputation vote trading has among the American public is deserved, because vote trading can lead to highly inefficient outcomes. This is because vote trades have external effects—when two legislators trade votes, this does not only affect them but may affect every other legislator and their constituents. When we have externalities there is no guarantee that trading will make everyone better off. Indeed, it is possible that we could have a number of deals, each of which makes the participants better off, but which yield a combined result that no one would want. Furthermore, there is a considerable empirical and theoretical literature on what Americans call pork barrel politics—government spending on inefficient (but locally identifiable) projects that are electorally beneficial to politicians in spite of their inefficiency (Mayhew 1974; Ferejohn 1974; Fenno 1978; Shepsle and Weingast 1981; Weingast, Shepsle, and Johnsen 1981; Lancaster 1986; Lancaster and Patterson 1990).

Whether logrolling and vote trading produce efficient or inefficient outcomes will depend on how centralized the bargaining is. (Following Miller [1977a], a logroll is a decisive bargain where legislators trade votes to produce an agreed outcome. Vote trading is just the trading of votes on different matters.) We would expect a single centralized logroll to produce efficiency. (An example of this would be an agreement between coalition partners in a European country that lays out all government policy.) Under majority-rule bargaining, the outcome will typically be in the uncovered set (Miller 1980; see chapter 4, this vol.). The uncovered set is a subset of the Pareto set, and thus the outcome will be efficient. Intuitively, if an alternative that is inefficient is proposed, it is possible to propose another alternative that makes everyone better off, and this will be accepted. The logic of Riker and Brams's (1973) argument depends on there not being a single centralized logroll, but rather on there being a number of successive votes on different issues. In this case it is possible for vote trading to produce a number of decisions, all of which have majority support, but which taken collectively no one would have chosen. Indeed, this scenario is quite plausible in decentralized legislatures such as the U.S. Congress. It is essentially the result of a logic similar to Sen's (1970b) as discussed in the previous chapter—decentralization is incompatible with Pareto optimality.

Another reason we may observe inefficient logrolls and pork barrel politics in countries with decentralized legislatures is a form of representative failure. Various writers on the United States (Mayhew 1974; Ferejohn 1974) have argued that the reelection prospects of U.S. Congress members do not depend on the welfare of their constituents, but on the perceived marginal effect that a Congress member has. Universalistic programs may help a member's constituents, but they are unlikely to help the member much. This is because the member cannot credibly claim much credit for bringing about a program that many other members (not to mention the president) also contributed to. What is far more valuable for the member is a locally identifiable project (such as a dam or a defense contract) that the member can credibly claim to have "won" for their district. Thus, Mayhew argues, members tend to neglect efficient national programs in favor of inefficient local projects, but tend to be rewarded for this. All these projects put together may be inefficient, but this does not stop them from being politically profitable. The cost of the projects is distributed nationally, and thus the individual member is not held accountable for it (see Shepsle and Weingast 1981; Weingast, Shepsle, and Johnsen 1981).

Let us now turn to distributional fairness. Majority-rule bargaining does not produce a core. That is to say, there is not a single outcome or set of outcomes that cannot be displaced by a challenging coalition. Although no player has an institutional advantage, this does not guarantee that we will get a fair outcome. It is possible that one set of players will form a majority coalition and gang up on the others, taking a disproportionate share of the benefits for themselves. Of course, this winning coalition is unstable—it is possible for some of the losers to offer some of the winners a better deal than they are currently getting and replace the winning coalition. Seeing that the excluded can always break up the winning coalition, those in government may be extremely careful to take the interests of those not in government into account, not wanting to provoke them into destabilizing the governing coalition. At least this is what we

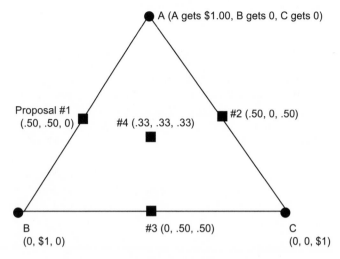

Fig. 6.3. A three-party bargaining situation

would hope would happen. Next we consider the conditions that are nec-essary to produce this outcome.

Consider the following highly simplified example. We can think of the simplest possible majority-rule legislature as a three-player divide-the-dollar game, as illustrated in figure 6.3. The single-shot version of this game has no core — if (say) players 1 and 2 make a deal to split the dol-lar, then player 3 can break this coalition by making an offer that makes player 3 and one of the other players better off. In proposals 1, 2, and 3 two players split the dollar between themselves and leave the other player with nothing. However, the outcome we typically associate with consensual democracy is proposal 4, where all three players split the dol-lar (at least roughly speaking). The question is, under what conditions is this a rational outcome to the game?

If we play the game repeatedly with a low enough discount rate, and players are risk averse (they prefer the same payoff every round to a dis-tribution of payoffs with the same expected value), then this proposal can be an equilibrium. If the result of the players playing the game competi-tively is that two random players split the dollar, then a repeated even split represents a Pareto improvement over the cycling outcome and thus can be an equilibrium by the folk theorem.[8] However, this grand coalition is still vulnerable to a smaller winning coalition. If players 1 and 2 were able to coordinate and always coalesce, then they would both be better off than by joining the grand coalition. The question is, why should a grand coalition be viable, but a permanent minimal winning coalition not? For us to get consensual outcomes, it would seem that this would have to be the case.

I can only provide a speculative answer. I suspect that evolutionary game theory may be able to provide some insight here at some point in the future, but currently most work in this field considers two-person interactions, with three-person coalition processes considered intractable (see Binmore 1994, 1998; Skyrms 1996). I also suspect that the internal contents of norms matter and that the stability of these norms is a result of forward induction. Suppose there is a commonly understood norm that everyone should split the dollar every round. Suppose also that there are two types of agents, trustworthy and cutthroat. Suppose player 2 goes to player 1 and suggests cutting out player 3. Player 1 will infer that player 2 is cutthroat and will break norms whenever it maximizes his or her short-term advantage. If the communication between the players is private (the offer cannot be proven to player 3) then player 1 will ignore the offer, because he or she can see that player 2 is untrustworthy, and the result of accepting the offer would be to return to the cycling outcome. If the communication is public, player 1 will make a deal with player 3 (who is still viewed as trustworthy) to cut out the cutthroat player 2. Anticipating this, player 2 would never make the initial offer. Another way of viewing this situation is that carrying an extra player in the coalition is a costly signal that you are trustworthy.

The conditions under which this equilibrium holds, however, are demanding. There has to be a common norm (or theory of justice, to put it in terms of Rawls 1971/1999) that is universal across the group, and subgroups cannot have sufficiently strong trust to cooperate in spite of the group norm. That is, the different groups must all distrust each other enough not to collude in a minimal winning coalition, but trust in the universal norm enough not to act opportunistically. In cases where different groups have strong ties this will probably not apply. For example, Hazan (2000) argues that Israel is only semi-consociational for this reason. The secular, traditional, and orthodox communities share consensual arrangements. However, there is a common Jewish identity that excludes Israeli Arabs, an identity that takes its political manifestation in the shape of the convention that an Arab party cannot be pivotal in a governing coalition. Thus the secular, traditional, and orthodox communities and the parties that represent them trust each other sufficiently to collude to exclude the Arab parties. That is to say, in spite of the very considerable differences between the three communities, they all resist the temptation to make a coalition with the Arab parties or even to threaten this for the sake of leverage.[9] Lijphart (1977) argues that one necessary condition for consociational democracy is a strong sense of overarching loyalty to the country that cuts across sectional boundaries. That is exactly what this model suggests is necessary.

Thus we have conditions under which we would expect majority-rule bargaining to produce efficient and distributionally equitable outcomes. Efficiency depends on there being a centralized bargain. Otherwise the logic of Riker and Brams (1973) applies, and successive deals can produce a final outcome that nobody would choose as a whole. An equitable outcome depends on far more complex factors. In particular it depends on the establishment of norms of reciprocity and the fact that the players do not trust each other well enough to form tyrannical coalitions (that is, essentially to act as if they were a single majority player). These are, of course, simply theoretical results. In chapter 8 we assess the economic efficiency and equity of countries with egalitarian political institutions—the so-called consensual democracies of Europe. To anticipate the result of that chapter, egalitarian political institutions make no difference to economic efficiency (as measured by growth, inflation, etc.) but lead to considerably greater income equality.

3. Procedural Justice and Deliberative Democracy in Electoral Systems

Deliberation in modern democracies typically takes place among elected representatives, for reasons laid out in the first section of this chapter. As Fearon (1998) argues, if we value deliberation it is necessary to explain how it is possible in societies of many millions; and if this involves representation, we need to explain how the representatives are connected to the people.[10] We will find that we will face the same trade-off between deliberation and participation that we observed earlier. Just as there is a trade-off between deliberation (which requires small group interaction) and mass participation, so there is a trade-off between modes of representation that encourage deliberation and modes that are more "participatory" in the sense of allowing localized control over the representatives. Of course, the relationship between deliberation and representation has been appreciated for a long time. For example, Edmund Burke's "Letter to the Sheriffs of Bristol" (1777/1963) considers the behavior of a representative and the deliberative nature of the legislature essentially two aspects of the same phenomenon. I will argue that large-district, closed-list proportional representation is most likely to produce reasonable deliberation between representatives. Plurality elections in some ways better fit the "direct control" or participatory conception of representation, in that they encourage more control over representatives by local activists and interests. However, the argument that plurality elections provide accountability and direct control turns out to be flawed. Direct control is only possible via direct democracy, which bypasses representation altogether and, as argued earlier, typically does not allow extensive deliberation.

A Typology of Representation

The value of political equality implies proportionality in electoral rules, as demonstrated in chapter 3. However, we can consider the nature of representation in terms of three further dimensions. The first concerns the behavior of representatives. This involves several related but logically separate distinctions: whether the representatives behave as delegates, directly implementing the wishes of their constituency, or whether they behave as trustees; whether the representatives deliberate about broad national policy or they bargain primarily for local interests; and whether representation is party centered or candidate centered. Second, there is the mode of control the voters have over their representatives. On one hand, elections may produce a division of power that leaves decision making to deliberation between the elected, while on the other, elections may produce unambiguous results giving voters direct control over the choices presented to them. Finally, there is the question of descriptive representation (Pitkin 1967). We may ask whether the legislature is an accurate microcosm of society as a whole in terms of various ascriptive characteristics such as class, gender, and ethnicity.

For the first two dimensions, we can say that one option is more compatible with a deliberative conception of representation, while the other is more compatible with the values of direct participation and direct control by the electorate. Clearly, deliberation requires that representatives are able to behave to some degree as trustees, free to engage in discussion and change their minds, whereas the value of direct control and participation are more compatible with representatives being bound to the instructions of their constituents. Advocates of deliberative democracy typically argue that one of its main virtues is its ability to elevate political discourse to the most universal and impartial terms. This is better served by broad national debate than by parochial interest advocacy. If, however, we value direct participation and control by activist citizens more than deliberation, the consequence of this may well be that representatives play to local concerns. Strong parties facilitate deliberation rather than direct control, because parties in a legislature are essentially a second level of representation. The representatives themselves choose representatives to negotiate for them. This facilitates small group deliberation, but further removes the decision from the mass public. In terms of the control of representatives, elections that do not produce a decisive result (such as a parliament where no one has a majority) necessitate deliberation and compromise, while decisive election results produce a more plebiscitarian style of politics. Descriptive representation, however, cannot be thought of in terms of the deliberative-participatory distinction. Rather, a legislature can be descriptively accurate or inaccurate with respect to various criteria. Table 6.1 summarizes our typology of representation.

Burke's (1777/1963) defense of the trustee model of representation is explicitly based on the idea of deliberation. It is the duty of the member of Parliament not to be subservient to the wishes of people possibly several hundred miles away from the debate, but to exercise independent judgment based on the arguments. Thus in order to have deliberation, we have to give up direct control over representatives. In a similar vein, Lijphart (1977) argues that consociational democracy in the small countries of Europe is possible because party leaders have sufficient independence from the subcultures they represent to make accommodations and compromises. Powell's (2000) notion of "authorized representation" is a further refinement of this idea. Homogenous communities in a plural society choose representatives who are then authorized to deliberate and negotiate on their behalf. Powell assumes homogenous communities, but this is not actually necessary to the model. We can think of the choice of representatives in the same way as we think of a choice of

TABLE 6.1. Typology of Representation

	Deliberative	Participatory— Direct Control
1. Representative behavior		
a. Mandate vs. independence	Representatives as trustees	Representatives as delegates
b. National vs. local	National representation: "deliberative body of one nation"	Particularistic representation: "congress of hostile ambassadors"
c. Party representation	Strong parties/party government	Weak parties/candidate-centered government
2. Control of representatives	Indirect/authorized representation	Direct/controlling elections
3. Descriptive representation: accurate vs. inaccurate		

attorney. We choose a representative or attorney to negotiate on our behalf, and they are authorized to do so at our pleasure.

Burke's (1777/1963) "Letter to the Sheriffs of Bristol" combines the case for national as opposed to local representation with the case for trustee representation. Members are to use their judgment independently, but not only to advance the interests of their constituency; rather they should serve the public interest. Parliament should be a "deliberative body of one nation," not a "congress of hostile ambassadors." Here there is clearly a trade-off between the values of deliberation and direct control. Deliberative democrats typically argue that deliberation should be oriented toward the general good. However, direct local control may well lead to representatives aiming primarily at ensuring that their constituents receive a fair share (or better) of the rewards of government. Indeed, there is considerable empirical evidence (see previous section) that this can lead to pork barrel spending projects that are socially inefficient but advantageous for legislators whose districts receive them.

Strong party government should promote deliberation but may dilute direct control. Party government in a legislature amounts to the representatives choosing representatives. Thus instead of maybe several hundred legislators trying to negotiate, a handful can. This allows the small-group interaction necessary for deliberation. Parties also serve as publicly visible entities that can take responsibility for decisions and have an incentive to engage in broadly defined policy-making. In a disorganized legislature, legislators can easily escape blame for failures by blaming each other, and there is an incentive to avoid broad public policy initiatives, as no single legislator can credibly claim credit for a national program. Rather, it is likely to be advantageous to legislators to try to win small projects that directly benefit their constituents. However, parties put another layer between the general public and the final decision.

Turning to the control the constituents exercise over their representatives, we can consider two models. First, there is the model where elections do not produce a definitive policy result but rather share power between parties. Proportional representation elections are obviously of this sort. Various parties receive seats, none has a majority, and these parties have to negotiate over policy. Clearly this promotes deliberation, as parties have to persuade each other since none can enact policies unilaterally. In the other model elections produce a definitive result. Elections have a winner-take-all quality. Single-member district plurality elections are the most obvious example of this. A candidate either wins the election, or not. Nationally, a single party usually wins a majority and thus control. This would appear to give the electorate, either national or local, direct control over the outcome, although we will see that this argument is problematic.

Descriptive representation is the degree that representatives resemble the people they represent according to some salient characteristics, such as class, gender, or ethnicity (Pitkin 1967). This can be justified either in terms of the need for the legislature to represent the will of the people or in more liberal terms that a person's interests can only be understood and protected by someone like them (Mill 1861/1993). We should note that descriptive representation can be justified regardless of the other characteristics of representation. For example, if representation is particularistic and oriented toward immediate interests, then a group may consider descriptive representation important, so that they receive their fair share. However, if representation is oriented toward a national public interest, a case can also be made that descriptive representation is important to make sure that a group's conception of the public interest is taken into account.

There is empirical evidence that proportional representation tends to provide more accurate descriptive representation, at least with regard to some categories (Farrell 2001). However, other factors, such as party policies toward inclusion, may be equally important. It has generally been assumed that while proportional elections provide more accurate descriptive representation, single-member district elections provide better geographical representation. However, geographical representation is simply a form of descriptive representation. It is a form that is privileged in district elections, whereas at-large proportional elections treat all "communions of interest" (to use Burke's [1792/1963] term) equally—people can vote on the basis of where they live, their gender, class, ethnicity, or whatever they think is most important. Empirically, it appears that even national list proportional representation provides more accurate geographical descriptive representation than has sometimes been assumed. Latner and McGann (2005) find that in Israel and the Netherlands (the two countries with virtually pure national list proportional representation) there is a considerable degree of geographical representation, and that the most peripheral regions are rather overrepresented.

Why Large-District, Closed-List Proportional Representation Is Most Likely to Promote Deliberation

I will argue here that PR elections are more likely than other systems to produce reasonable democratic deliberation. Thus there is no trade-off between the values of political equality and deliberation in electoral systems. As with social decision rules, there is a lack of empirical evidence due to the lack of an obvious way of measuring deliberative quality. Once again we have to rely on arguments based on the incentives that institutions create.

As with majority rule, we can begin with the argument made by Nino (1996). People are forced to adopt universalistic arguments and principles when they need to convince other people. The more people that need to be convinced, the more universalistic the argument has to be. The electoral system that demands most people to be convinced in order to form a government is proportional representation. Assuming majority rule, it is not possible to form a winning coalition without the support of the representatives of at least 50 percent of the population, whereas with all other systems a minority can form a government. If we have a supermajority required to form a government or pass legislation, proportional representation is still the system that requires convincing the most people. If 40 percent is required to block legislation, with proportional representation the representatives of 40 percent are needed, whereas with other systems the representatives of less than 40 percent can be a blocking coalition.

We would expect PR elections to produce democratic deliberation for three other reasons. First, PR elections allow for the representation of a broader range of viewpoints than plurality or elimination elections. Such elections tend to reduce the number of parties represented, create barriers to entry for new parties, and also tend to reduce the representation of interests that are not geographically concentrated. It is for this reason that Mill (1861/1993) was an early advocate of a form of PR. Indeed, under plurality elections it is possible for two parties to act as a duopoly and systematically exclude ideas or proposals from the political agenda. For example, Aldrich (1995) and Weingast (1998) argue that the second party system in the United States was able to systematically exclude the issue of slavery from political competition until the rise of the Republican Party in the 1850s. Second, proportional representation increases the incentives for parties to compete with broad national appeals. Under plurality elections parties can write off geographic regions where they can never hope to win a majority, and make particularistic appeals to their heartlands. Under PR, however, a vote is worth the same wherever it is won, so it is worthwhile to frame arguments in ways that can be convincing to everyone. Third, by increasing the number of parties represented, PR elections reduce the probability that any party will have a parliamentary majority. If no party has a majority, it is necessary for parties to negotiate coalitions. This forces parties to make concessions and take into account the interests of other parties, as opposed to being able to force through their programs on single party votes.

There are, however, many different variations on proportional representation. There are two dimensions of particular interest on which these systems vary—district magnitude and whether they use an open or closed list. These characteristics affect electoral incentives for representatives and thus may affect the way they deliberate. With a small district magnitude, a representative only has to appeal to the people in a small geographical area. If we accept the argument that the more people someone has to convince, the broader and more universalistic their arguments will be, large district magnitude should produce better deliberation. Of course, national at-large elections maximize the number of people who need to be convinced in order to win a seat. In practical terms, small district magnitude creates an incentive for representatives to look just to the interests of their constituents and to be more concerned with locally visible projects than national policy (Mayhew 1974; Lancaster and Patterson 1990). It is also possible for small district magnitude to produce weak party systems and particularistic politics under PR. Fourth Republic France (see Duverger 1962) is the most obvious example of this (see also Farrell 2001 on Ireland and de Winter 2002 on Belgium).

Open-list systems can have similar perverse effects (Chang and Golden 2003; Carey and Shugart 1995). Under some open-list systems, a very small number of personal preference votes can be vital to promote a candidate up the party list and leverage a much greater number of party votes. In these circumstances, the main competitor of a candidate will not be the other parties, but their own co-partisans. This creates a strong incentive to focus representation on the small number of people likely to give the candidate preference votes. This can lead to heavily factionalized parties, clientelism, and outright corruption, with pre-1994 Italy being an obvious example. However, it seems that open list systems such as that in the Netherlands (see chapter 3), where a small number of preference votes cannot leverage a large number of parties' votes, do not produce these perverse incentives. On the other hand, in the Netherlands, preference votes rarely result in candidates being elected out of list order. Primary elections may also force party members to compete against each other with particularistic appeals. Hazan (1997) argues that party primaries had this effect in Israel from 1996, leading to an increase in special interest legislation.

Thus we would expect PR elections with large district magnitudes and closed lists to maximize the incentives for reasonable democratic deliberation. Proportional representation produces multiparty government, which forces parties to negotiate in order to form coalitions. Large district magnitudes and closed lists increase the incentives for parties to offer broad, national programs, as opposed to candidates or factions appealing to particularistic interests.

Accountability and Direct Control

I have argued that there are two conceptions of representation, one based on deliberation, the other based on direct control. If PR elections better serve deliberation as well as political equality, it seems natural to argue that plurality elections are better at providing direct control or at least accountability (the ability to exert control by punishing governments that fail to deliver the goods). Indeed, accountability is one criterion for which even authors very well disposed toward proportional representation (Lijphart 1994; Powell 2000) admit winner-take-all has advantages. However, we will see that the argument that plurality elections provide accountability and direct control is problematic, largely due to the fact that voters have one vote while governments make many different decisions. In fact, the only way to embody the ideal of direct control is direct democracy, which I have already argued entails a strong trade-off with the value of deliberation. What low district magnitude elections (and single-member district election in particular) may be able to provide is a form of representation that is more participatory, in the sense that there is a more direct link between legislator behavior and local activists and interests.

It should be noted that the principle of local accountability and national accountability are logically mutually inconsistent. This has not stopped many opponents of proportional representation from citing both as advantages of first-past-the-post elections (see, for example, Hain 1986). National accountability means that voters have direct control over the national outcome. The Labour Party (say) puts forward a party platform, and if the voters elect the Labour Party, it carries out this platform. This, however, assumes that it is able to execute its platform. This is only the case if the Labour members of Parliament vote the party line. If Labour MPs vote according to the wishes of their constituents, it is possible for the nation to elect a Labour government but for this government to be unable to execute its program, negating popular control at the national level. However, if Labour MPs vote party line all the time, they are not accountable to their constituents, and local accountability is violated. As McLean (1991) argues, there is a logical contradiction between the will of the whole and the will of the parts.

The degree of direct popular control that plurality elections allow is severely limited by the fact that voters can only choose between a limited number of party platforms, indeed often only between two real contenders. As a result the combination of policies a voter really wants may not be on offer. Furthermore, the argument that first-past-the-post elections are more responsive to changes in public opinion than PR, and thus make parties more accountable, is true only under very restrictive conditions. First-past-the-post elections are extremely responsive over the range where a party goes from being second largest to being the largest party (typically 35 to 40 percent of the vote—see Taagepera and Shugart 1989). Whereas proportional elections are responsive over the entire range of vote shares, single-member district elections concentrate all their responsiveness into a very narrow range. Thus they are rather unresponsive if a party goes from 45 to 40 percent of the vote. This is especially problematic if (as in the case everywhere except the United States) single-member district elections fail to reduce the number of parties to two. It may indeed be possible to identify the government, but holding it accountable also means being able to replace it. If the opposition is incompetent, split, or even more obnoxious than the government, this may not be possible. These reasons may account for why Powell (2000) finds that governments in countries with single-member district elections deviate from the preferences of the median voter more than governments in countries with proportional representation.

The argument that plurality elections allow direct popular control as opposed to control by party leaders under PR is also dubious. It is certainly true that under PR, party leaders negotiate coalitions after elections to determine the future government and its program. However, under plurality elections party leaders also have considerable power. Typically the leaders of the two main parties form a duopoly that has exclusive control over the viable alternative governments that the electorate can choose between, whereas under PR systems (especially those with large district magnitude and low thresholds) there are few barriers to entry by new competitors. Under PR, party leaders have postelection power to negotiate coalitions. Under plurality elections, party leaders have preelection monopoly power to control the alternatives presented. It is far from clear in which case the party leaders have most control. Nevertheless, the argument that PR increases the power of party leaders is regularly appealed to in the electoral reform debate in the United Kingdom (see several contributors in Jenkins 1998), in spite of the fact that it is hard to see how a party leader in a democracy could be more powerful than a British prime minister is already, with exclusive control over ministerial jobs and other patronage, and the ability to pass legislation by party line votes.

If we desire direct popular control over government policy, the only way to achieve this is to dispense with representation altogether and go for direct democracy. Some deliberative democrats have been relatively favorable toward this (Nino 1996; Barber 1984). However, as argued in the previous section, direct democracy is highly unlikely to be deliberatively satisfactory for a number of reasons. Plebiscites do not allow face-to-face negotiation, the alternatives on the ballot are given and cannot be amended, and it forces the electorate to decide issues separately, which may lead to highly irrational outcomes.

It may not be possible for plurality election to provide direct popular control of government, or even more accountability than proportional elections. However, single-member district plurality or low-district-magnitude PR elections may provide outcomes more in line with the participatory model in other regards, particularly legislator behavior. Such elections may lead to legislators being closer to their constituents in the sense that they behave more as delegates and less as trustees. Furthermore, the appeals they make may be more oriented toward particularistic local interest and less toward national policy, and as a result parties may be weaker. However, these are empirical questions, and the answers are not obvious. For example, in the case of the United Kingdom, parties are strong and politics mostly national, in spite of plurality election, presumably due to the parliamentary system and the power of the prime minister, although there is some evidence that local concerns occupy an increasing amount of an MP's time (Norton 2002).

Summary

The same institutions that satisfy political equality are those most likely to provide deliberatively rational outcomes. This is obviously (indeed tautologically) true if we define deliberative rationality in terms of what people would decide under procedurally fair conditions. However, it is also the case if we define deliberative rationality in terms of changing preferences toward less egocentric and more universalistic principles. Following Nino (1996), the more people it is necessary to convince, the more necessary it is to make arguments in terms of broad principles. The social decision rule that requires the most people to be convinced in order to carry the day is majority rule, not (as claimed by some advocates of deliberative democracy) consensus. The electoral system where a candidate has to appeal to the most people is national list proportional representation.

Of course, deliberative rationality does not only depend upon the existence of political equality. It also depends on factors such as precise institutional forms and legislative norms. For example, political equality implies majority rule in the legislature. However, a majority-rule legislature may proceed by negotiating one grand bargain, or it may proceed by means of a series of decentralized logrolls. The first situation will lead to an outcome that is rational in the sense of being efficient; the second may lead to an outcome that is quite inefficient for the reasons outlined by Riker and Brams (1973). Similarly, under majority rule the threat of instability may lead all players to be careful not to threaten the vital interests of any other player, as any player can disrupt the winning coalition by offering support for a very low price. However, if the members of the current winning coalition trust each other so strongly that they are not willing to listen to outside offers, this logic breaks down and we may see a permanent majority coalition. In terms of electoral systems, there are many systems that provide for proportionality. However, some systems (large-district closed-list) are more likely to lead to national deliberation, while others are more likely to lead to particularistic politics and pork barrel.

Whereas this book has argued that there is little evidence for the perceived trade-offs between political equality and other desirable values, there is a strong trade-off between deliberation and direct participation. This trade-off is particularly troubling as many deliberative democrats esteem both values highly. If we also insist on political equality, the three values form a trilemma. Deliberation requires small group contact, so that the participants can not only hear each other's arguments but also negotiate and develop norms of reciprocity and trust. This conflicts with the value of participation, that as many people as possible should take part. In order to respect political equality, we cannot allow self-selection of participants, as those most prepared to participate will probably be an unrepresentative group perhaps with material or cognitive advantages. A similar trade-off applies to representation. If we value deliberation we will favor modes of representation and election that allow representatives freedom to deliberate and come to their own conclusions. If we are more concerned with participation, we may favor practices that allow local activists more control over representatives.

The idea of democratic deliberation, particularly in the work of Dewey (1927/1946), Habermas (1984), and Rawls (1993/1996), allows us to reformulate the idea of social reason in a way more suitable for a plural society. Previously both traditional democratic theory and social choice theory have argued that the goal of democracy is to provide a definite social choice—that is a transitive ranking of the alternatives—that could be referred to as the will of the people. This implies that all the values of society can be condensed into a single dimension—that is, into a single value. This effectively negates the plurality of values, and is not a reasonable requirement in a plural society. Rather, what is desirable is to negotiate a reasonable compromise between different values under a fair and reasonable decision rule, that is, majority rule.

The consideration of deliberation in this chapter has largely been theoretical. However, there are a group of countries that have political institutions almost completely consistent with political equality and that are considered by most commentators to have extremely deliberative and rational politics. These are the so-called consensual democracies of Western Europe—Denmark, Norway, the Netherlands, Sweden, and, to a lesser extent, Austria and Belgium (Lijphart 1984b, 1999). We consider these countries in chapter 8.

CHAPTER 7

The Logical Bases of Deliberative Democracy: The Limits of Consensus

Much (but not all) of the deliberative democracy literature takes the idea of consensus as its logical basis. Some of this literature follows Habermas, and the idea that something can be justified if it results from universal unforced agreement in an ideal deliberative situation. Others follow Rawls, justifying principles and institutions on the grounds that they would have been agreed upon unanimously in a hypothetical deliberative situation. Both these theorists, and those who follow them, rely on the idea of unforced consensus. Unfortunately, unforced consensus is logically impossible in a political context, as Rae (1975) shows. Put simply, in a political context, a decision still has to be made in the event consensus is not reached. Thus there is always an implicit threat, and consensus is not unforced (even if none of the participants makes use of the implicit threat). This problem undermines not only a great deal of the deliberative democracy literature but also the social contract tradition.

However, it is possible to build a theory of deliberative democracy on a sounder foundation, namely, majority rule. Previous chapters have shown that majority rule uniquely satisfies the value of political equality, and that it is the rule most likely to encourage reasonable deliberation. Indeed, it can be argued that the use of consensus in Rawls and Habermas is motivated by considerations of equality. However, the idea that equality is realized in consensus is clearly incorrect, as was shown in chapter 5. Nevertheless, a theory of deliberative democracy based on majority rule actually produces results quite similar to those anticipated by Rawls and Habermas. There is also, of course, a tradition of deliberative democracy based on majority rule in representative bodies as opposed to consensus. Burke (1777/1963), Hamilton, Madison, and Jay (1788/1961), and Mill (1861/1993) are classical examples. Dewey (1927/1946), Barry (1995), Nino (1996), and Knight and Johnson (1994, 1996, 1999) are modern examples of this line of thought.

Section 1 considers the problem of consensus as outlined by Rae (1975) and its relevance for social contract theory and deliberative democracy. Section 2 considers the problem of consensus in the work of

Habermas and Rawls. Section 3 defends majority rule as a basis for deliberative democracy.

1. The Problem of Consensus and Social Contract Theory

Douglas Rae's article "The Limits of Consensual Decision Making" (1975) demonstrates that no decision rule can be completely consensual if a definite decision needs to be made. This result—which I will call the problem of consensus—undercuts social contract theory by showing that social decisions cannot be based completely on consent. Formally, Rae shows that no decision rule can give everyone the right of consent and be robust. Here, *robust* means that the decision rule has to return some decision. Rae argues that this quality is inescapable in a political context, because even if no decision is taken, some outcome must result. Given that a political decision rule must be robust, it cannot give everyone the right of consent. That is to say, everyone cannot have a veto over every outcome. If there is disagreement in society, an outcome has to be imposed that at least one person objects to. Thus, any decision-making rule is to some degree coercive. Consent is always conditional on the outcome that would have been imposed if agreement had not been reached.

The intuition underlying Rae's result is simple. In politics it is not possible to not make a decision. If no agreement is reached, and no formal decision is taken, then some outcome still results. This outcome may be to do nothing for the time being. However, this is still an outcome—indeed it may be some people's preferred outcome. Alternatively, the default outcome may be to keep doing what we were doing previously, maintaining the status quo. In any case an outcome results. If agreement was not reached, then this outcome is imposed on at least one person against his will. However, even if there is agreement, this agreement is not completely free. This is because the threat of the imposed outcome hung over the discussion. If people had not agreed, a certain outcome would have to have been imposed. Of course, this threat will often weigh more heavily on some people than others. People who like the imposed outcome, or at least can tolerate it, will have a considerably stronger bargaining position than those for whom the imposed outcome is intolerable. It is for this reason that Rae argues that consensual decision making has a strong bias toward the status quo. Consensual decision making implies that everyone has a veto and the power to impose the status quo (or some other default outcome) on everyone else.

Rae's argument is aimed first and foremost against Buchanan and

Tullock's *The Calculus of Consent* (1962). Buchanan and Tullock ask which decision rule individually rational people would choose for their constitution, given the (crucial) assumption that property rights have already been settled. They argue that the optimal rule would be unanimity, because this is the only rule that guarantees economic efficiency in the sense of Pareto optimality (it is not possible to make anyone better off without making anyone worse off). We would choose unanimity, it is argued, because if a government action made people better off as a whole, it would be possible to compensate the losers, and thus gain unanimous consent. (Buchanan and Tullock accept that unanimity increases decision-making costs associated with getting universal agreement, and therefore they argue that a rule less than complete unanimity may be preferable in practice.) By Rae's argument, however, this agreement is not truly consensual. Rather, it is only consensual conditional on the initial distribution of property. What unanimity essentially does is allow those who like the initial distribution to lock in their gains and impose this distribution of property on society, even if the vast majority of the population disapproves.[1]

Similarly, Rae argues that unanimity implies a form of anarchism. This is because anyone can use their right of consent to block government action. Therefore it is impossible to use the government to protect yourself against another individual or group. Rae uses this argument against both Calhoun's (1850/1943) theory of concurrent majorities and Wolff's (1970) defense of anarchism, illustrating that logically similar arguments are made by people of apparently very different ideologies. Calhoun, of course, was insisting on the right of planters in the Southern United States to have a veto on any decision to abolish slavery, while Wolff was defending the right of the individual to oppose government actions they disapprove of. In both cases, however, the insistence on universal consent (applied only to groups in Calhoun's case) brings us back to the state of nature—individuals cannot be coerced by the government to do anything that they do not consent to. The cost of this is that individuals certainly can be coerced by each other. Unanimity is a rule very favorable to people who are powerful in the state of nature, whatever that is taken to be.

The same argument applies very naturally to classical social contract theory. People do not choose the social contract freely. Rather they only give consent conditional on what outcome would be imposed on them if they fail to agree—that is, depending on what the state of nature is like. Thus the results of social contract theory are simply a function of the state of nature described by various theorists. Hobbes (1660/1972) creates a state of nature so horrible that the sovereign has extreme bargaining power because any outcome is better than the war of all against all. In Locke (1690/1986), property rights exist in the state of nature prior to the social contract, so naturally the social contract protects these rights. In Rousseau (1762/1997), property rights do not exist in the state of nature, although morality does. As a result we get a social contract where property rights are protected but subordinate to the general will.

As a result, social contract theory loses much of its force. Social choice theory is based on the idea of consent. If everyone were to freely accept something, it is very difficult to argue against it. Unfortunately, the idea of freely given consent turns out to be illusory. Consent in classical social contract theory can only be conditional on the default outcome, the state of nature. Therefore the results depend on the state of nature, and, of course, the mythological states of nature given in classical social contract theory are not particularly compelling in any kind of literal sense. However, modern versions of social contract theory, such as the work of Rawls and Habermas, use the conditions under which deliberation takes place in a different manner. The conditions under which consent is to be reached are taken as artificial constructions, to be defended in explicitly normative terms. That is, the conditions under which the parties deliberate are chosen in order to make them deliberate fairly, rather than being chosen to represent some naturalistic situation. However, we will see that the problem of consensual decision making weighs just as heavily on these theories.

2. The Consensual Bases of Deliberative Democracy (or, Why the Ideal Speech Situation Is a Logical Impossibility)

The modern successors to social contract theory still rely on consensual agreement as the basis of legitimacy. Instead of considering agreement in a mythological or naturalistic setting, they either construct a situation so that parties are forced to argue in a moral fashion (Rawls), or they reconstruct the conditions under which an agreement reached would be morally legitimate (Habermas). However, as they still rely on the concept of consensual agreement, they are also subject to the problems raised by Rae—unconditional consensus is not possible if a decision needs to be made, as is always the case in politics.

Habermas and the Ideal Speech Situation

Habermas's philosophical project, at least since *The Theory of Communicative Action* (1984, 1987), has been to use the ideal of consensual agreement achieved through discourse to provide a justification for the concepts of truth and validity that can survive the critique of skeptical, relativistic, and postmodern philosophies.[2] Habermas accepts that metaphysical justifications are no longer viable—it is not possible to argue convincingly that there is a transcendent truth that resides beyond human reason. However, if we engage in discourse in good faith, we must engage in what Habermas describes as communicative action. That is, we enter into communication with the intention of finding agreement with another person. We make statements that can be valid or not (they can be correct or incorrect; morally valid or invalid; aesthetically authentic or inauthentic), and we try to convince others of their validity. Doing this assumes that such agreement is possible, otherwise our speech would be futile and our action self-contradictory. Therefore we must believe that agreement (and thus validity) can be obtained, at least under ideal conditions. These ideal conditions comprise what Habermas (1984, 42) calls the "ideal speech situation," in which unforced argumentation is conducted openly, without strategic manipulation and without time constraints. Thus the possibility of consensual agreement in ideal conditions provides the basis for the belief in truth and validity.

Habermas's work since *The Theory of Communicative Action* has sought to apply this principle in more concrete settings. *Moral Consciousness and Communicative Action* (1990a), particularly the essay within it entitled "Discourse Ethics: Notes on a Program of Philosophical Justification," applies the principles of communicative action to moral philosophy. Once again, it is the possibility of consensus through discourse that creates the philosophical basis for the validity of moral claims. Following Strawson (1974) he argues that moral claims can be seen as relative from the vantage point of a disinterested observer but not from the point of view of a participant. If we enter into an argument about what is right, we accept that our statements can be valid or not. This validity is provided by the discourse principle: "Only those norms can claim to be valid that meet (or could meet) with the approval of all affected in their capacity as participants in a practical discourse" (Habermas 1990a, 66). It should be noted that Habermas's (1990a, 211) goal here is quite modest. He does not claim to be making any substantive contribution to morality, only providing a refutation of moral skepticism. (See Heath 2003 for an excellent reconstruction of Habermas's argument without some of the harder-to-defend assumptions, notably the assumption that engaging in discourse commits a participant to reaching agreement on the moral claims underlying norms.)

Between Facts and Norms (1996b) applies the discourse principle to the legitimacy of law and democratic decision making. Once again, it is the possibility of agreement under ideal conditions that provides the basis for validity claims. Law differs from morality in that it is codified and enforceable by state coercion. Thus law facilitates social cooperation by ensuring that people know what their legal duties are, that others will in general comply with their duties, and that people's duties and rights are coordinated in an organized manner (114). The problem is to show how positively existing law can be justified in a moral sense. Habermas continues to hold that norms (legal and otherwise) can only be validated by agreement in a discourse including all involved. However, in *Between Facts and Norms* this discourse can take the form of decentralized social discourse that generates "influence" and "communicative power," which in turn is mediated by procedures in a representative parliament that produces binding decisions. Thus the people ideally adopt morally valid norms that they impose freely upon themselves. This, incidentally, gives equal and co-original status to the political right to self-govern and the liberal rights to individual self-determination: self-governance is only possible if individuals are free to enter into discourse; while the only legitimate way to decide the limits of individual self-determination is through discourse. Again, it should be noted that Habermas is only providing conditions under which laws generated by parliamentary procedures can be morally legitimate; he explicitly denies providing "anything original at the level of particular details" (444).

In *Between Facts and Norms*, Habermas (1996b, 179) does allow for the legitimate use of majority rule and bargaining, but this remains subordinated to consensual agreement and communicative action. Majority rule produces legitimate norms, but only in a provisional sense. It represents a "caesura" in discourse—we have not reached the agreement necessary for full validity, but the majority-rule result represents a fallible interim result of discussion that is presumed to continue. Furthermore, the majority-rule decision is only morally valid if the discussion that led to it was rationally motivated (informed and oriented toward reaching agreement, rather than toward strategic advantage). Habermas also accepts the role of bargaining (that is, strategic negotiation as opposed to argument seeking agreement) in politics. Indeed, he accepts (282) that most of politics consists of bargaining. However, bargaining is subordinated to communicative discourse in two ways (167). First, the terms under which bargaining takes place can only be morally validated using the discourse principle; second, only particular interests can be involved, because generalizable interests require moral discourse. These concessions to practical decision making are not particularly problematic from a philosophical point of view—consensus through rationally motivated discourse is intended as a counterfactual ideal, after all, not a description of reality. However, we will see that the ideal of consensus is problematic for more intrinsic reasons.

The problem is that Rae (1975) shows unconditional consensus is logically impossible when a decision needs to be made. If this is so, then the ideal speech situation is a logical—not just a practical—impossibility in these cases. As a result, it is not possible to conceive—even as an ideal—a completely free situation in which people reach agreement by means of consensus. This undercuts the principle on which Habermas bases the legitimation of moral and legal norms. It should be noted that the problem here is that the ideal speech situation is *logically* impossible. If it were merely impossible as a practical matter, it could still serve as a counterfactual ideal. Indeed Habermas himself emphasizes that the ideal speech situation is intended as a counterfactual. As we have seen, in *Between Facts and Norms* he argues that majority rule is legitimate in political institutions precisely because it represents a provisional and temporary stopping point on the road to the ideal of consensus. However, if the ideal of unforced consensus is illusory and impossible, this kind of argument is no longer viable. It is no longer possible to argue that unforced agreement is the source of legitimacy, because unforced agreement can never exist even under ideal conditions.

Thus the ideal speech situation is logically impossible for precisely the type of practical questions that we encounter in politics. The ideal speech situation may still be possible for theoretical questions. If we do not have consensus on some point of (say) physics or chemistry, then we can simply say that this question is not yet resolved. Indeed the same is true of moral questions, as long as these remain on a theoretical level— we can say that there remain unresolved questions as to which moral principles are valid. We hope that as more research is done and better arguments are made, we will move toward the agreement that currently eludes us. However, we cannot do this in the case of practical questions of the type "What are we to do?" In these cases, not making a decision is effectively a decision to do nothing (at least for the time being) or some other default outcome. Furthermore, in these kinds of practical situation, we cannot choose the question—rather the question presents itself. If we cannot agree whether a man is guilty or not, we cannot substitute a more abstract question, such as whether acts of type x are in general culpable. (This is not to say that considering the more abstract question may not help in our deliberations.) Rather we have to decide whether to change a policy, whether to enact a constitution, whether to go to war, or whether to punish a defendant. For these kinds of decisions—which are precisely the kind of decisions we are concerned with in politics—an ideal speech situation is logically impossible.

We should note that the problem here is not simply the lack of time. Rather it is that a decision has to be made, which makes unconditional consensus impossible. Habermas acknowledges the problem of time and accepts that in practical settings majority rule may have to be used instead of consensus when a decision needs to be made within a limited time. However, time is not really the issue here, as illustrated by the following thought experiments. Suppose that we were able to get unlimited time for argumentation by means of a time machine. That is to say, a decision has to be made at time x, but we can go back in time as far as we like in order to give us enough time to deliberate. (Assume also that we have indefinite life spans and patience.) This would not solve the problem of unconditional consensus. We would still have to make a decision at time x, and thus the threat of the imposed outcome would still hang over us. Suppose, alternatively, that we had a technology that allowed us to talk and think at an infinite speed. We would then have effectively unlimited time to deliberate. However, this would not help us either. We would still have to make a decision at time x, with the implicit threat of the imposed outcome. The problem does not result from a lack of discursive resources (time, goodwill, etc.) but from the threat implicit in the fact that a definite decision of some kind has to be made.

It is interesting that Habermas (1987, 310–11) accepts an argument very similar to the one made here when considering organizational behavior. Consider the following passage.

> Members of organizations act communicatively only with reservation. They know they can have recourse to formal regulations, not only in exceptional but in routine cases; there is no necessity for achieving consensus by communicative means. Under conditions of modern law, the formalization of interpersonal relations means the legitimate demarcation of scopes for decision making that can, if necessary, be utilized in a strategic manner. Innerorganizational relations constituted via membership do not replace communicative action, but they do disempower its validity basis so as to provide the legitimate possibility of redefining at will spheres of action oriented to mutual understanding into action situations stripped of lifeworld contexts and no longer directed to achieving consensus.

People in organizations can behave communicatively—that is, in a manner oriented toward reaching consensus. However, they always have the fallback option of being able to resort to bureaucratic rules and procedures. This strips the communicative action of its "validity basis," because the participants are acting communicatively only "with reservation," knowing that they do not have to reach a consensus by communicative means. This situation, however, applies to all practical political matters, and not just to members of bureaucracies. There is always an outcome that will be imposed if agreement is not reached, so consensus can only be conditional.

Thus the logical impossibility of the ideal speech situation in the case of practical political questions undermines the applicability of Habermas's approach to politics. However, I will argue that a considerable amount of Habermas's project is still viable, if we replace consensus with the principle of majority rule. However, before turning to this, let us consider the implications of the problems of consensus for the work of Rawls.

Rawls and the Problem of Consensus

Rawls, like Habermas, uses consensus reached through discourse as a means to provide a justification for political and moral norms without having to resort to metaphysical foundations. In *A Theory of Justice* (1971/1999), the concept of justice derived is moral, covering all aspects of life. In the series of articles and lectures that culminate in *Political Liberalism* (1993/1996), however, Rawls makes the conception of justice more strictly political and relevant only to the consensus reached in certain modern, liberal societies. However, although *A Theory of Justice* has a broader scope, I will argue that it is considerably more rigorous than *Political Liberalism* at least in terms of how it deals with the problem of consensus. In *A Theory of Justice*, the problem of consensus is recognized and "solved" by making everyone identical in the hypothetical original position in which the terms of society are negotiated. This, of course, opens the author up to other criticisms, such as that the results claimed are just an artifact of the author's precise construction of the original position and the solution concept he imposes on it. *Political Liberalism* attempts to deal with such criticism but, I will argue, fails to deal with the problem of consensus.

In *A Theory of Justice* (1971/1999) the problem is to specify just terms for social cooperation between people. To do this he considers the agreement that people would come to if placed in a situation where they are deprived of information that is morally irrelevant to choosing just terms, such as information about their personal interests and how various terms would affect them. Thus Rawls's participants are forced to deliberate in an "original position" where they decide the terms of social cooperation behind a "veil of ignorance"—they know enough about society to be able to conceptualize the issues that are relevant, but not enough to be able to tailor the terms in their favor. According to Rawls, in this position people would use the maximin principle (choose the terms that gives you the highest guaranteed outcome, given that the worst event for you happens) as their solution concept. Rawls argues that this would lead to the adoption of "justice as fairness," which is comprised of Rawls's two principles of justice, with the first taking absolute priority.[3] With these principles of justice established, the veil of ignorance is lifted slightly in successive stages, and people receive more information about the specific character of society. People are then able to consider what constitution would best serve the principles, and after another relaxation of the veil, consider legislation and its application. If the resulting principles of justice, constitution, legislation, and application can then be accepted by everyone who was socialized in this society with full knowledge, then we have stability and the society is "well-ordered."

It is apparent that Rawls (1971/1999, 120–21) considers the problem of consensus, as the following passages illustrate.

> To begin with, it is clear that since the differences among the parties are unknown to them, and everyone is equally rational and similarly situated, each is convinced by the same arguments. Therefore, we can view the agreement in the original position from the standpoint of one person selected at random. If anyone after due reflection prefers a conception of justice to another, then they all do, and a unanimous agreement can be reached.

> Thus there follows the very important consequence that the parties have no basis for bargaining in the usual sense. No one knows his situation in society nor his natural assets, and therefore no one is in a position to tailor principles to his advantage.

> The veil of ignorance makes possible a unanimous choice of a particular conception of justice. Without these limitations on knowledge the bargaining problem of the original position would be hopelessly complicated. Even if theoretically a solution were to exist, we would not, at present anyway, be able to determine it.

The problem of consensus is resolved by making argument monological. In the original position everyone is assumed to have the same information and to be equally rational. Therefore everyone is convinced by the same arguments, and we can consider a single person chosen at random. We achieve unanimity by the complete absence of differing interests or perspectives. Thus there is no real bargaining (or discourse), but simply the reflection of a single hypothetical individual. Rae (1975), as we have seen, shows that this complete lack of differing interests is the only way to achieve unforced consensus.

This consensus, however, is bought at a considerable cost—the cost of making the argument monological. This exposes Rawls to the argument that the results he claims are not the result of agreement reached through discourse but simply artifacts of the solution concept[4] and the original situation imposed by the theorist. As a consequence the results cannot claim the legitimacy that comes from consensus. For example, Rawls's argument for the difference principle (allow inequality only if it benefits the least advantaged) over utilitarianism with a basic social minimum relies on the information constraints of the original position preventing the participants from knowing what the basic minimum would be (see Rawls 1971/1999, 278–85). Habermas (1995) argues that the construction of the original position requires the theorist to decide what information is morally relevant and what information will lead participants to partial judgments. This logically requires a theorist to make impartial judgments on what information leads to partial judgments. (Habermas is critiquing *Political Liberalism* here, but the argument applies even more to *A Theory of Justice*.) Of course, it could be argued that a particular set of information constraints is justified in terms of ensuring impartial decisions. However, this merely shifts the argument up one level of abstraction. To argue that the decision is consensual, we have to argue that there is consensus about what conditions are appropriate. Furthermore, this consensus would have to be among concrete people, not the constructions of a theorist, as we are arguing precisely about what the appropriate constructed situation should be.

It should be noted that Rawls prior to *A Theory of Justice* did not rely on such a monological construction. In the article "Justice as Fairness" (1958) he justifies principles of justice very similar to those in his later work on the grounds that they would be adopted by a group of individuals deciding on how complaints about the terms of social cooperation should be handled. These individuals are not assumed to be ignorant about their situations. The only thing forcing them to argue reasonably is the knowledge that principles they adopt may work against them in the future. Of course, it is clear why Rawls moves from this position to the identical (and thus monological) deliberators of *A Theory of Justice*. As the passages quoted show, Rawls realized (correctly) that without identical agents it was impossible to draw any definite conclusions about what autonomous agents would agree on.

Thus *A Theory of Justice* clearly recognizes the problem of consensual decision making but avoids it by making the "consensus" be among identical, hypothetical agents. This, of course, gives up much of the claim to validity that would result from freely reached agreement among actual people. *Political Liberalism,* on the other hand, considers the possible grounds of consensus among actual people but does not consider the problem of consensus rigorously. There are actually two positions taken in *Political Liberalism,* one in the original hardback edition and a second in the introduction to the paperback edition and Lecture IX ("Reply to Habermas"). The "Reply to Habermas," originally published in the *Journal of Philosophy* in 1995 in response to Habermas's review of *Political Liberalism,* amends Rawls's position considerably; the paperback introduction seems to take into account Rawls's response to Habermas's objections. The original text of *Political Liberalism* argues that in a plural society, it is not reasonable to expect that any single moral doctrine will be universally accepted. Therefore, all society can be expected to agree on is a political conception of justice, which leaves people to hold any moral doctrine compatible with political justice. However, justice as fairness is still conceived as the appropriate political conception of justice (together with a slightly modified version of the two principles outlined in *A Theory of Justice*), and the original position is taken as the appropriate representation people should use to reason politically. The "Reply to Habermas" and the paperback introduction, however, accept that there are many reasonable political conceptions of justice, and that justice as fairness is simply Rawls's favored solution. Similarly, it is accepted that the original position is merely one possible representation, and that it needs to be defended in public discourse. This brings Rawls far closer to Habermas's position that validity comes from agreement reached between actual people. It also exposes him to the problem of consensus, in the same way that Habermas is exposed.

Political Liberalism considers what kind of political conception of justice might be approved by an "overlapping consensus" in a free, plural society. The conception of justice proposed is a version of justice as fairness that is very similar to that in *A Theory of Justice,* including the two principles (slightly modified). In *Political Liberalism,* however, Rawls accepts that in a modern, plural society, we should not expect agreement on which comprehensive moral doctrine is correct. Nevertheless, Rawls argues that there may still be a consensus on a political conception of justice. Various reasonable comprehensive doctrines (*reasonable* is defined in terms of seeking fair terms of social cooperation) may agree on the basic issues of political justice, although they may disagree on issues as to what the good life is, and indeed why the consensus on political justice is justified. Thus there are different comprehensive doctrines (that may include religions, comprehensive philosophies, and political ideologies), but there is agreement on the key issues required for these doctrines to coexist. However, it must be noted that the overlapping consensus Rawls envisions is not a modus vivendi or compromise between various existing comprehensive doctrines. Rather, it has to be justified as a "freestanding" conception independent of comprehensive doctrines, and Rawls terms this process that abstracts from specific comprehensive doctrines "public reason." The device of representation Rawls advocates for this is the original position, as used in *A Theory of Justice*.

However, it is not clear whether the political conception of justice is really justified by the reasoning from the original position, or whether it is justified by the actual achievement of an overlapping consensus of actual people. This presents a dilemma. If justification is through reasoning from the original position, then the argument is subject to the same objections made against *A Theory of Justice*. The reasoning is monological and conducted under conditions constructed by a political philosopher. Thus it cannot claim the legitimacy that would come from an agreement freely reached by actual people. In this case, the achievement of an overlapping consensus is not necessary for the validity of the "freestanding" conception of political justice, but only important to its empirical acceptance and stability. On the other hand, if justification is through the actual achievement of consensus, then there is no guarantee that actual people will agree on the political conception of justice that John Rawls presents—they could just as well agree on something else. This is the basis of Habermas's (1995) objection that Rawls does not distinguish sufficiently between the acceptance and the validity of the political conception of justice. Habermas, of course, advocates leaving the actual specification of justice to actual participants, with the philosopher merely providing the terms and procedures that can make any agreement legitimate.

Rawls's (1995/1996) "Reply to Habermas" and the introduction to the paperback edition of *Political Liberalism* take the second course. He accepts that a political conception of justice is justified by the agreement of actual people, which brings Rawls's position far closer to Habermas's. Rawls (382) argues that justice as fairness as a political conception of justice and the original position as a device of representation are to be judged by debate in the public sphere, as the following passage illustrates.

> From what point of view are the two devices of representation to be discussed? And from what point of view does the debate between them take place? Always, we must be attentive to where we are and whence we speak. To all these questions the answer is the same: all discussions are from the point of view of citizens in the culture of civil society, which Habermas calls the public sphere. There, we as citizens discuss how justice as fairness is to be formulated, and whether this or that aspect of it seems acceptable—for example, whether the details of the set-up of the original position are properly laid out and

whether the principles selected are to be endorsed. In the same way, the claims of the ideal of discourse and of its procedural conception of democratic institutions are considered.

Thus these concepts are justified by actual agreement obtained in discourse. Furthermore, it is emphasized that the philosopher does not have a privileged role in this discussion (1993/1996, 382–84), and that it is denied that the original position makes reasoning monological, because the original position is itself subject to debate by citizens (1993/1996, 383ff.). Of course, a consequence of this is that justice as fairness and the original position lose their privileged position—people could just as easily agree on other conceptions of justice or devices of representation. In the introduction to the paperback edition of *Political Liberalism,* Rawls (1993/1996, xlviii–xlix) merely states that justice as fairness is the conception of justice that he believes is most reasonable, but he does not deny that there are other conceptions that are also reasonable. Indeed any conception that accepts the fallibility of human reason and the principle of reciprocity is taken as a candidate.

Thus Rawls's final position is that the political conception of justice is justified through agreement reached through discourse in the public sphere. This is a position very similar to Habermas's and brings with it the same problems. Most notable for us is the problem of consensus. As Rae (1975) shows, completely unforced agreement is a logical impossibility in a political matter, because there is always the threat of what will happen if agreement is not reached. Therefore we cannot base legitimacy even on the counterfactual ideal of unforced consensus. To the extent that Rawls appeals to agreement reached in the public sphere, this applies as much to his argument as it does to Habermas's. *A Theory of Justice* recognized the problem of consensus and avoided it by relying not on a genuine consensus but on the monological reasoning of a single, constructed individual. *Political Liberalism* relies (at least after the exchange with Habermas) on consensus between actual people and thus is subject to the problem of consensus.

3. A Nonconsensual Justification for Deliberative Democracy

It has been argued in the previous two sections that the problem of consensus undermines both social contract theory and theories of deliberative democracy based on consent, including the projects of Rawls and Habermas. If there are people with differing interests, it is logically impossible for consent to be unforced, because some outcome has to be enforced in the absence of consensus. The only way to get around this is to limit deliberation to identically constructed agents and thus not have divergent interests, as Rawls does in *A Theory of Justice*. This, however, gives up most of the moral force of the idea of consent. I will argue that it is possible to construct a theory of deliberative democracy on a nonconsensual basis. This involves going back to the basic value of political equality. If we start with political equality, we can show that this implies majority rule and not consensus as a decision rule. Indeed, a great deal of the existing deliberative democracy literature assumes majority rule rather than consensus (Dewey 1927/1946; Knight and Johnson 1994, 1996, 1999; Barry 1995; Nino 1996).

Actually, it is the value of equality that underlies the justification of consensus. As Dworkin (1975, 53) argues, equality is the basic value that motivates the construction of the original position in *A Theory of Justice*. The original position is a device of representation (to use a term from Rawls 1993/1996) that ensures that the interests of all people are treated equally. Similarly, Habermas's ideal speech situation is premised on the idea that everyone affected by a norm has an equal right to consent to it or not. The problem is that both Rawls and Habermas assume that equality implies consensus, and that consensus does not involve coercion. Chapter 5 has shown that consensus is anything but egalitarian, while Rae (1975) has shown that unforced consensus is a logical impossibility. Instead I have argued that the decision rule correctly derived from equality is majority rule.

Of course, it is possible to argue along constructivist lines (Rawls 1971/1999; Scanlon 1982; Beitz 1989) that equality should be applied to agents in hypothetical choice situations, as opposed to actual participants. I have already rejected this argument in chapter 2. The most telling argument against this approach is the argument made by Habermas (1995) against Rawls. If we create a hypothetical situation of choice under equality as a representational device, then different people may come to different opinions as to what the hypothetical participants would choose. We are then faced with the question of how to arbitrate between them. There has to be some procedure for coming to an outcome, and this procedure needs to respect the values represented in the hypothetical choice situation, or the final choice is arbitrary. Thus the conditions for an acceptable choice situation have to apply to actual participants, not just hypothetical deliberators.

Whereas Habermas criticizes Rawls's approach for being monological, Habermas's definition of the ideal speech situation is open to the charge that it is dialogical, when it should be polylogical. The standard case for Habermas is a conversation between two people seeking agreement. For Habermas, adding participants does not seem to change the nature of the interaction. However, a polylogical decision situation is qualitatively different from a dialogical one. If we have two people, the only way they can resolve their differences (without one enforcing their will by coercion) is by mutual agreement. Indeed, in a two-person situation consensus and majority rule are equivalent—the only possible majority is for both people to agree. However, if we have a third person, we have other possibilities. If two people are unable to agree, they may attempt to persuade the third person that their proposed action plan is reasonable. As such the third person can act as an audience or judge. The situation is further complicated by the fact that the third person may also have interests that need to be negotiated with the other two players. It is at this point that social choice theory becomes relevant. Rae (1975) has shown that when a decision is required, unforced consensus is a logical impossibility. The only decision rule that is fair in the sense of treating everyone equally is majority rule. Therefore the best we can hope for is a fair and reasonable decision process—that is, decision by majority rule with sufficient time for deliberation.

We can compare the ideal of a fair and reasonable decision process to the ideal speech situation defined by Habermas. Habermas requires that the ideal speech situation be without coercion, strategy, and time limits, so the outcome is determined only by the "forceless force of the better argument." However, as Rae (1975) shows, all decision rules where a decision must be made are to some degree coercive. A fair and reasonable decision process based on majority rule does not claim to be exempt from coercion. Rather, it is equally coercive to all participants— the coercion is distributed evenly. For this decision-making process to be reasonable as well as fair, some other conditions are required. It is necessary that the participants have sufficient time to deliberate, and that any question can always be raised again. As we have seen, unlimited time does not solve the problem of consensus. However, sufficient deliberation to recognize one's interests and engage in negotiation is necessary for a decision to be reasonable. Furthermore it is necessary that the participants be granted such basic rights as are necessary to realize what their interests are and to argue for them.

It may be asked how much this formulation varies from Habermas's in practice. After all, Habermas allows the legitimacy of norms validated by majority rule, on the grounds that majority rule serves as a "caesura" on the road to consensus. In our derivation majority rule provides the basis for a fair and reasonable decision process. In Habermas's formulation, majority rule serves as a stand-in for agreement reached in an ideal speech situation for decisions that have to be made in a timely way. Although the justification is different, the practical prescription is the same. However, there are two significant differences. First, the fair and reasonable decision process recognizes the plurality of reason—it does not imply that there is a single true solution to a political question, which we could find if only we had enough time and goodwill. Second, it forces us to view deliberation and negotiation—communicative action and strategic action—as intrinsically linked, not separate modes of action, as Habermas argues.

Let us first consider the plurality of reason. The ideal speech situation implies that if we had enough time and could argue openly enough, we would come to an agreement, and this would be *the* true, right, or authentic outcome. The fair and reasonable decision process makes no such promise. Majority rule does not produce a single, best outcome. Rather it produces cycling. This is not to say that some outcomes are not far more defensible than others, or that majority rule produces arbitrary results. Indeed, as was argued in chapter 4, majority rule is an extremely effective way of eliminating unreasonable outcomes. However, it does not produce a single outcome that can claim to be uniquely valid. This is appropriate when dealing with questions of social cooperation. As Rawls (1971/1999, 1) argues, social cooperation typically makes everyone better off than a situation of no cooperation, but some terms of cooperation benefit some people more than others. Thus the argument over the terms of social cooperation is partially distributive. As argued in the previous chapter, such arguments do not admit a single, correct answer.

This, incidentally, provides a justification for Rawls's (1993/1996) use of the word *reasonable* rather than *true* to describe fair terms of social cooperation in a plural society. Habermas (1995, 119–26) criticizes Rawls's use of *reasonable,* because he thinks that Rawls is actually raising truth claims. However, I would argue that the use of the word *reasonable* is appropriate, although for reasons quite different from Rawls's. Rawls defines the reasonable as being that which is oriented toward fair terms of social cooperation, as opposed to the rational, which is oriented toward the fulfillment of some goal. This definition of *reasonable* does not imply that there is a single, reasonable outcome—more than one set of terms can be fair. Describing an outcome as reasonable does not make the claim that it is the one, true outcome. In the case of outcomes that are partially distributive, we would not want to make such a claim, so Rawls's use of the word *reasonable* is more appropriate than describing these terms as *true.*

The fair and reasonable decision process forces us to treat the rational and reasonable—or strategic and communicative action—as inseparable. Rawls (1993/1996, 48–54) does argue just this, but Habermas (1984, 286) argues that strategic and communicative action should be treated as quite separate modes of action. This, of course, has led to criticism, notably from Johnson (1991) who argues that the two concepts cannot be coherently separated even in Habermas's work. If people engage in argument, then they are attempting to influence others. Therefore the action is strategic. Indeed the concept of action oriented solely toward the reaching of agreement is problematic for the reasons given by Elster (1983). It makes little sense for the reaching of agreement to be the final goal—reaching agreement can only be valuable as a side effect. If two people aim primarily to reach agreement, then the agreement will be trivial—the one makes a proposal and the other agrees primarily in order to get an agreement.[5] Agreement can only be valuable if the parties have something to argue about and thus have (strategic) interests. Or, as Rawls puts it, the reasonable assumes the rational. We can only reach a reasonable agreement if we have interests to come to an agreement or compromise about.

A fair and reasonable decision process involves the final decision being made by majority rule. In majority-rule bargaining it is not possible to completely distinguish strategic and communicative action. In order to further one's strategic goals, one has to seek allies. This means seeking agreement with others and thus acting communicatively. However, seeking agreement with others has the inevitable side effect of improving one's strategic situation. Furthermore, it should be noted that in a multilateral, majority-rule bargaining situation, a participant being too accommodating does not necessarily produce a fairer outcome. A participant giving ground too easily may encourage other participants to behave in a predatory manner, and harm the interests not only of the accommodating participant but of other participants as well. Therefore we need to avoid simplistic judgments about communicative action oriented to agreement necessarily being morally superior to strategic action. Finally, given that we are not going to have a final "correct" solution to most political matters, compromise is inevitable. Compromise here is not a second-best we resort to when agreement fails; rather it is an essential part of being reasonable. When dealing with distributive matters, all reasonable outcomes are to some degree compromises.

Other Majority-Rule-Based Theories of Deliberative Democracy

The argument that has been developed in the last two chapters bears many similarities to other theories of deliberative democracy that are based on majority rule, such as the work of Dewey (1927/1946), Knight and Johnson (1994, 1996, 1999), Barry (1995), and Nino (1996). The arguments are generally compatible with one another, differing more in emphasis than in practical implications. There are two main differences. First, Barry and Nino both accept the value of consensus as an ideal representing unforced, uncoerced agreement. However, they reject unanimity (and indeed supermajoritarian rules) as an empirical decision rule for practical reasons. This chapter, however, has argued that the idea that consensus is not coercive is logically flawed, and that majority rule is the most impartial rule because the (inescapable) coercion is equally distributed.

Second, and more significant, our argument starts from a procedural conception of political equality, derives institutions from this, and then argues that these are optimal for facilitating reasonable discourse. Thus the value of political equality has primacy over deliberation, although it appears that there is unlikely to be an empirical trade-off. The procedural arguments from political equality are valid regardless of the behavioral question about what institutions best promote deliberation. Furthermore, following Dewey, Rawls, and Habermas, the procedural conditions of political equality constitute in part what is meant by social reason. This is not to say that politically egalitarian institutions always produce reasonable outcomes (the previous chapter outlines the conditions in which they do not) but merely that there is no external standard for defining reason in a social context. Thus deliberation under egalitarian conditions is the most reliable means for finding a solution we may presume to be reasonable.

This difference in emphasis can be illustrated by considering a thought experiment. Imagine we had a supremely wise and good facilitator-king. This monarch's objective is to make social reasonable decisions based on inclusive deliberation. (Let us ignore the [im]possibility of finding a guardian of sufficient wisdom and goodwill.) The monarch could hold extensive consultations before making decisions, or realizing his own fallibility with regard to knowledge of the interests of others, could even hold straw polls or referenda. If the goal is to promote reasonable deliberation, then such a monarch could provide as high a quality of deliberation as any truly democratic system. (Note that the monarch requires participation, and that this participation affects outcomes, so Mill's [1861/1993] argument that a benevolent despot promotes servility does not apply.) However, this situation could not be described as a fair and reasonable decision process, in the sense outlined earlier. The monarch may provide incentives for deliberation, make good use of the information he receives, and even make reasonable substantive decisions; however, the situation is not democratic, in that the monarch has the final say. The point is that democracy has value as an intrinsically fair procedure for distributing power, not just as a mechanism for facilitating reasonable deliberation.

In a much quoted passage, Dewey (1927/1946, 206–7) argues that the main value of majority rule is that it forces deliberation that allows the public interest to be defined. However, Dewey (146–47) also argues that the details of the political institutions under which this happens are only of secondary importance. The primary problem is that of how a diffuse public can recognize itself and define its interests. Once this problem was solved, appropriate democratic forms would emerge. This contrasts with our emphasis on the extreme importance of the details of institutions in both determining outcomes and determining how people deliberate.

Knight and Johnson's recent work on Deweyan pragmatism puts far more emphasis on institutions. They argue that pragmatism implies a commitment to radically democratic institutions (1996), and that rational choice theory is a useful tool in determining which institutions may be satisfactory in this respect (1999). In this light, our theoretical justifications of proportional representation and majority rule can be seen as a contribution to this agenda.

Barry's (1995) approach is very similar to that taken here in that the theory of deliberative democracy is embedded in a more general theory of justice as impartiality. As was argued in chapter 2, if we consider equality in liberal (that is, individual) terms, impartiality and equality are equivalent. Barry, however, does not proceed directly from impartiality to political institutions. Rather he defines impartial justice in contractualist terms, using the criterion proposed by Scanlon (1982).[6] As with Rawls (1971/1999), justice is defined as what would be agreed by reasonable people in a hypothetical choice situation. Although this does not reduce all individuals to identical agents as Rawls (1971/1999) does, this construction inherits all the problems of contractualism that have been discussed in this chapter. In particular, it is monological in that it relies on the opinion of the particular philosopher conducting the thought experiment as to what can be reasonably rejected.

Barry (1989) recognizes that the Scanlonian procedure admits a great deal of uncertainty, and he proposes supplementing the consideration of hypothetical deliberators ("the a priori method") with the consideration of actual deliberation under conditions that approximate impartiality ("the empirical method"). Barry is also well aware of the problems of consensual rules—indeed he has been critical of supermajoritarianism at least since *Political Argument* (1965). He argues (1995, 104–5) that the best empirical approximation of the Scanlonian situation where anyone can veto a proposal on reasonable grounds is not a situation where any-one can veto a proposal on any grounds, reasonable or not; rather the best approximation is majority rule. It is interesting that the countries that Barry considers best examples of the "circumstance of impartiality" (the small, "consensual" democracies of Europe) are precisely the coun-tries that I argue best satisfy the procedural requirements of political equality. Barry's (1989, 347–48) argument that these countries satisfy the conditions of impartiality seems to be mainly sociological—there exist multiple, organized interests with access to government, political candi-dacy is not determined by access to money, there is a culture of accom-modation and debate. The arguments in this book provide strict institu-tional criteria for judging which countries best satisfy the conditions of impartiality. They also provide a far more direct route for getting to Barry's conclusions—instead of arguing that impartial institutions are the best approximation of a hypothetical (and logically flawed) choice situation, we can directly apply the value of impartiality to the political institutions themselves.

Nino (1996) likewise argues that a parliamentary system with major-ity rule and proportional representation is the most reliable set of institu-tions to promote deliberative democracy, although he views representa-tion as at best a necessary evil and is sympathetic toward direct democracy (132). Indeed many of the arguments in our previous chapter arguing that politically egalitarian institutions can be expected to promote deliberation were taken directly from Nino's *The Constitution of Deliberative Democ-racy*. Nino, however, does not argue that these institutions are justified in terms of being intrinsically fair. Rather, they are justified as promoting de-liberation, which he argues is the most reliable way of arriving at moral truth, a position he refers to as epistemic constructivism. Nino (117–18) argues that unanimity is the situation best capturing impartial decision making, because it involves unforced consent. However, when unanimity is not possible for pragmatic reasons, majority rule is the rule most likely to lead to the reasonable conduct of deliberation. (Nino refutes the argu-ment that the next best thing to unanimity is something close to unanim-ity—such a situation may be extremely partial, as in a situation where the majority imposes a large cost on a minority of one.)

Summary

This chapter has considered the logical basis of theories of deliberative democracy built on the idea of consensus, as well as classical social con-tract theory. They are all problematic for the same reason, which I call the problem of consensus. Rae (1975) shows that no decision rule can give everyone the right of consent if a definite decision needs to be made. Thus unforced consensus is impossible—if everyone does not agree, then some agreement needs to be imposed. Furthermore, even if agreement is reached, it was not unforced—the threat of the imposed outcome was hanging over the procedure. Thus Habermas's ideal speech situation is a logical—not just empirical—impossibility and cannot even serve as a counterfactual ideal. Similarly, any social contract agreement reached in a state of nature cannot be completely consensual. Rawls recognizes the problem of consensus in *A Theory of Justice* but overcomes only by making the reasoning monological—it is not based on actual consensus, but on hypothetical consensus choreographed by the philosopher. To the extent that Rawls's *Political Liberalism* ceases to be based on monological reasoning, it is vulnerable to the problem of consensus.

The problem of consensus, however, does not undermine the idea of deliberative democracy or the deliberative justification of democracy. On a practical level, democratic deliberation takes place within the context of majority rule. Indeed much of the deliberative democracy literature is based on majority rule rather than consensus (Dewey 1927/1946; Knight and Johnson 1994, 1996, 1999; Barry 1995; Nino 1996). However, majority rule should not be regarded as a practical stand-in for the utopian ideal of consensus. Consensus seems to offer the possibility of free, uncoerced choice, but this is illusory. All social decision rules involve some degree of coercion. The best we can do is to distribute coercive power equally. Thus we need to replace Habermas's ideal speech situation with the idea of a fair and reasonable decision process. As has been shown previously, the only social decision rule that treats all people equally is majority rule. Thus the theory of deliberative democracy is compatible with the theory of procedural democracy developed in the rest of this book.

PART 4

STABILITY, ECONOMICS, AND OTHER VALUES

CHAPTER 8

Political Equality in Practice:
Stability and Economic Outcomes
in the Consensual Democracies

Part 1 of this book demonstrated that political equality implies proportionality in the electoral system and majority rule in the legislature. Parts 2 and 3 have considered the relationship between political equality and the values of minority protection and deliberation. However, these are not the only values we are concerned about when choosing political systems. For example, the value of stability is sometimes used as an argument against proportional representation in some countries and also as an argument for systems of checks and balances as opposed to simple majority rule. There is considerable literature on the effects of political institutions on economic performance. The liberal emphasis on procedural equality in this book could be criticized on the grounds that it ignores substantive (in particular, economic) inequality. The only way to address these concerns is to see whether there is an empirical trade-off between political equality and these other values.

There is a group of countries that have institutions very similar to those I have argued are implied by political equality. The so-called consensual democracies of Western Europe (Denmark, the Netherlands, Norway, Sweden, and, to a lesser extent, Austria and Belgium) are characterized by a combination of proportional representation and majority rule with very few constitutional checks. We can therefore use these countries to test the empirical performance of the institutions covered in this book. However, most of the existing literature on these countries does not view these countries as examples of majority rule. Rather it emphasizes the difference between the consensual mode of politics found in small European countries and majority rule as practiced in the United Kingdom, United States, and France, as exemplified by the title of Jürg Steiner's (1973) *Amicable Agreement versus Majority Rule* and by Lijphart's (1984b, 1999) distinction between "consensual democracy" and "majoritarian democracy." By contrast, I will argue that the consensual outcomes in the small European democracies do not occur because of constitutionally mandated consensual rules but are rather the natural result of the type of majority-rule negotiation outlined in this book. I will also propose an alternative typology of political institutions to Lijphart's, based on whether the seat allocation rules respect political equality on one hand, and whether the social decision rules do so on the other.

Section 1 considers the existing literature on consensual democracy. Section 2 demonstrates that the so-called consensual democracies are indeed characterized by a combination of proportional representation and majority rule, and establishes a typology for classifying constitutions. Section 3 considers the performance of consensual democracies in terms of stability, economic outcomes, and also minority protection and deliberation. This allows us to determine whether there are trade-offs between these values and political equality.

1. Theories of Consensual Democracy

Lijphart's concept of consensual democracy grew out of the idea of consociational democracy. Lijphart (1968, 1977) sought to produce a characterization of democracy as it was practiced in the small countries of Europe. The current understanding of democracy was that it consisted of competition for power between (ideally two) parties, resulting in alternation of power. This not only fit the pattern observed in the Anglo-Saxon democracies (Australia, Canada, New Zealand, the United Kingdom, and the United States) but also fit the recent experience of Fifth Republic France and Germany quite well, in that politics in these countries was essentially bipolar. Fourth Republic France and Italy were considered unstable and frankly dysfunctional forms of democracy. However, the small European democracies (as Lijphart [1977] considered Austria, Belgium, the Netherlands, and Switzerland) were clearly stable but were not characterized by alternation of power. Rather all the major parties negotiated policy, even if all parties were not represented in government all the time. Lijphart laid out four features that typified politics in these countries: grand coalitions; norms of mutual veto; proportionality in elections, but also in allocation of resources and positions; and federalism or segmented authority. Given that the countries Lijphart studied were all culturally pluralistic, he suggested that the consociational form of democracy might be more suitable for many emerging democracies than the Westminster style of democracy.

Lijphart's later work (1984b, 1999) further generalizes these ideas. In addition to the Low Countries and the Alpine republics, the consensual democracies come to include the Nordic countries. Consensus democracy remains a single concept, contrasted with majoritarian democracy. For example, in Lijphart (1999), New Zealand is given as an exemplar of the "majoritarian" Westminster model, typified by plurality elections (until 1997) and lack of power-sharing institutions, while Belgium and Switzerland are given as examples of consensual democracy, with proportional elections and power sharing. However, the empirical part of Lijphart's 1984 and 1999 books reveals distinct aspects of consensual democracy. Factor analysis on the constitutional features and electoral outcomes of thirty-six different democracies shows two dimensions. The first of these Lijphart calls the *executive-parties dimension;* it is loaded on mostly by the proportionality of the electoral system, the effective number of parties, the frequency of one-party government, the average cabinet length, and the interest group system. The second dimension, called by Lijphart the *federal-unitary dimension,* is loaded on by bicameralism, federalism, judicial review, constitutional rigidity, and central bank independence. Lijphart (1999) finds that most of the outcomes that lead him to consider consensual democracy "a kinder, gentler democracy" (higher turnout, more satisfaction with democracy, lower inequality, more environmental protection, more rights for women) are linked to the first dimension rather than the second. However, Lijphart does not theorize using the distinction between the two dimensions but rather argues in terms of the consensual/majoritarian dichotomy.

Unfortunately this dichotomy between consensual and majoritarian democracy conflates two important distinctions. The first is between the rule for electing legislators and the rule that the legislators use to make collective decisions. Majority rule correctly refers to a decision rule for deciding between two alternatives, as in a legislature. However, the term *majority rule* is frequently (and incorrectly) used to refer to elections by single-member district plurality (as in the United Kingdom and United States) and plurality runoff (as in France). There is no reason why majority rule in the legislature cannot be combined with proportional representation elections, as indeed is the case in most of the "consensual democracies." Furthermore, majority rule does not imply government by a single majority party. Where no single party has a majority, majority rule is necessarily government by coalition.

Second, Lijphart's distinction between "majoritarian" and "consensual" democracy conflates consensual outcomes with consensual institutions. At some points, consensual democracy is identified in terms of the outcomes it produces—essentially, power sharing, compromise, and broad coalitions—as opposed to the winner-take-all outcomes allegedly produced by majority rule. At other times, however, consensual democracy is identified with constitutional features that demand, if not a complete consensus (unanimity), at least more than a simple majority to make a decision. Such institutions include strong bicameralism, federalism, and judicial review. Whether such constitutional features are necessary to produce consensual outcomes is surely an empirical question, not something to be embedded in the definition of consensual government. Indeed I argued in chapter 6 that many of these features may actually obstruct arriving at consensual outcomes. It may be that the worst way to achieve consensus is to insist that no decision can be made until a consensus exists.

Birchfield and Crepaz (1998) and Crepaz (2001) provide a theoretical justification for the two dimensions of consensual democracy generated by Lijphart. They identify the first (executive-parties) dimension with what they call "collective veto points." A high score on collective veto points results when different agents share power and responsibility within a single body, especially when there are face-to-face contact and negotiation. They identify the second dimension (federal-unitary) with "competitive veto points." Constitutional features such as strong bicameralism (where the two chambers have equal powers but are elected differently) and federalism create "competitive veto points" by allowing agents controlling different bodies to prevent policies being enacted. Competitive veto points tend to lead to policy deadlock and immobilism, whereas as collective veto points enable common policies to be agreed upon and implemented. Thus collective veto points lead to lower income inequality, as they facilitate government responsiveness to public opinion, whereas competitive veto points lead to higher income inequality, as it is easier to block redistributive policies. In this way Birchfield and Crepaz claim to overcome the contradiction between the theory of consensual democracy and veto points theory. Veto points theory argues that more consensual government entails more veto players, more policy immobilism, and thus higher inequality, whereas Lijphart shows that consensual democracy produces lower inequality. The solution is simply that the two different dimensions of consensual democracies work in quite different ways.

Birchfield and Crepaz (1998) is a response in part to the veto point literature. Their approach is consistent with the results of Huber, Ragin, and Stephens (1993) who find that constitutional checks and balances lead to smaller, less redistributive welfare states. However, their results contrast with those of Tsebelis (1995, 2002). Tsebelis conflates the two dimensions that we have discussed, arguing that more veto points (whether they be of the collective or competitive variety) lead to greater policy stability. When calculating the number of veto players Tsebelis uses the principle of absorption—veto points that are superfluous, in that the same party already has access to another veto point, are disregarded. Thus the number of veto points amounts to the number of parties that have access to a veto point. This approach yields some interesting insights, such as the fact that countries normally classified as quite different like the United States and pre-1994 Italy actually experience similar policy deadlock. However, the claim that coalition partners in multiparty governments are veto players is problematic and has met with severe criticism (see Strom 2000; Birchfield and Crepaz 1998).

Lijphart (1977) argues that consociational democracy is effective precisely when society is plural and characterized by cross-cutting political and social cleavages. These are precisely the conditions that social choice theorists argue should lead to instability and "chaotic" voting outcomes, in that any winning coalition can be displaced by mobilizing on different dimensions or cleavages, producing arbitrary outcomes. Miller (1983) shows, however, that the theories of pluralism and social choice can be reconciled, given that in practice voting cycles are likely to be confined to a limited area, and that cycling may actually be beneficial to democratic stability, as it ensures that there are no permanent losers. As argued in chapters 5 and 6, this insight is central to our understanding of the working of democracy.

The theory of democracy developed in this book leads to an understanding of "consensual democracy" very different from that put forward in both the "consensual democracy" literature (with the exception of Birchfield and Crepaz 1998) and the "veto points" literature. In our theory, consensual democracy does not produce consensual outcomes because there are institutions that demand consensus, but as a natural outcome of majority-rule bargaining. Because there is proportional representation, no single party has a majority, and thus it is necessary to make coalitions. There are always multiple possible winning coalitions, so it is always possible to break the current winning coalition by offering some of its members a better deal. This protects minorities and makes intransigence a very risky strategy. If a party digs its heels in, it is always possible to make a winning coalition around it, rendering the party irrelevant. The only way a party can protect its interests is to compromise with other parties. Thus self-interested behavior leads to reasonable negotiation.

2. Consensual Democracy = PR + MR: A Typology of Constitutions

We can categorize constitutions along two dimensions according to how closely the institutions fit the requirements of political equality. In chapters 3 and 4 I showed that political equality implies proportionality in the seat allocation rule, and majority rule in the parliamentary decision rule.

Thus the first dimension is simply the degree to which the electoral system is proportional. The second dimension is the degree to which the policy-making is supermajoritarian (requiring more than a simple majority, as results of institutions such as division of power, presidentialism, checks and balances, or qualified majority voting). This classification is based completely on constitutional features and does not confuse institutions with outcomes. Most of the countries regarded as consensual (Denmark, Norway, the Netherlands, Sweden, and to a lesser degree Austria and Belgium) have proportional elections and simple majority-rule parliaments. However, there are a few cases where elections are proportional, but the decision-making process is quite supermajoritarian, such as Germany, Italy, and Switzerland.

These two dimensions correspond to Lijphart's (1984b, 1999) executive-party and federal-unitary dimensions. They correspond even more closely to Birchfield and Crepaz's concepts of collective and competitive veto points but are simpler in that they avoid the introduction of new "veto points" concepts. Essentially the idea of "collective veto points" refers to nothing more than power sharing and proportionality within a legislature. Indeed Birchfield and Crepaz measure this with an additive scale of proportionality and the number of parties. In a legislature where no party has a majority (or enough seats to block legislation if there is qualified majority voting), no individual party is a veto player, and the only veto players are majority coalitions (or blocking coalitions under a qualified majority rule). Therefore it is more straightforward to replace the concept of collective veto points here with proportionality. And competitive veto points can be subsumed under the concept of supermajoritarianism. Since Condorcet (1787/1986) it has been recognized that the effect of dividing power between different bodies is to require an effective supermajority. Although "collective veto point" institutions (bicameralism, federalism) are the most common institutions leading to legislative supermajoritarianism, they are not the only ones. For example, qualified majority voting (such as the 60 percent rule required to invoke cloture and end a filibuster in the U.S. Senate) and presidentialism can have a similar effect.

The approach here is quite at odds with the Tsebelis (1995, 2002) veto points approach. Tsebelis's claim that coalition partners in multiparty governments are veto players is logically and empirically incorrect. Tsebelis (1995, 293) defines a veto player as "an individual or collective actor whose agreement is required for a policy decision." Under simple majority rule, the only such veto player is a majority coalition. If no party has a majority, then no party is a veto player. The claim that coalition partners are veto players in a practical sense, because they have the power to leave the government and provoke a crisis, is also flawed. First, a party leaving the government does not necessarily provoke a crisis. In some countries it may not even lead to a change of administration if the government can find new allies and survive a vote of confidence. Indeed in some countries, such as Italy from 1949 through 1994, government partners came and went with depressing frequency. Second, and more important, major policy decisions in most of the consensual democracies are made in negotiations after elections but before a new government is formed. Parties negotiate elaborate policy programs before taking office. Contra Tsebelis (2002, 87) parties are not in government "to agree on a government program." Rather they are in the government because they have *already* agreed and signed off on the government's program. Of course, no contract is ever totally comprehensive, but parties do bind themselves to a very definite program of legislation. If (as is most commonly the case) forming a government requires a simple majority vote of investiture, no party is a veto player at this stage, as it cannot unilaterally prevent a government from being formed.

Table 8.1 scores the constitutional features of the OECD countries

TABLE 8.1.   Electoral System Proportionality and Constitutional Supermajoritarianism

	Electoral System Proportionality	Supermajoritarianism						
		Federalism	Bicameralism	Presidentialism	Judicial Review	Referenda	Filibuster	Total
Australia	0	1	2	0	2	0	0	5
Austria	2	1	0	0	2	0	0	3
Belgium	3	0	1	0	1	0	0	2
Canada	0	2	0	0	2	0	0	4
Denmark	3	0	0	0	1	0	0	1
Finland	3	0	0	1	0	0	0	1
France	0	0	0	1	2	0	0	3
Germany	2	2	2	0	2	0	0	6
Iceland	3	0	0	0	1	0	0	1
Ireland	2	0	0	0	1	0	0	1
Italy	3	0	1	0	2	0	2	5
Japan	1	0	1	0	1	0	0	2
Netherlands	3	0	1	0	0	0	0	1
Norway	3	0	0	0	1	0	0	1
Sweden	2	0	0	0	1	0	0	1
Switzerland	3	2	2	1	0	2	0	7
United Kingdom	0	0	0	0	0	0	0	0
United States	0	2	2	2	2	0	2	10

that have been democracies continuously since World War II.[1] Electoral system proportionality is simply scored 0 for single-member district elections, 1 for mixed systems and single nontransferable vote, 2 for proportional representation with a high threshold (4 percent or more), and 3 for proportional representation with a low threshold (<4 percent). A high effective threshold may be the result of a legal threshold of representation, as in Germany, or low district magnitude, as in Ireland. Supermajoritarianism was scored as an additive index of constitutional and legislative features that allow a minority to block government action. These features are: federalism (0—unitary, 1—weak federalism, 2—strong federalism); bicameralism (0—unicameralism or weak bicameralism, 1—moderate bicameralism, 2—strong bicameralism); presidentialism (0—parliamentarianism, 1—semipresidentialism, 2—presidentialism); judicial review (0—none, 1—weak, 2—strong); referenda (0—unimportant, 1—moderately important, 2—highly significant); filibuster (0—impossible, 1—unimportant, 2—significant). The scores on federalism, presidentialism, judicial review, and referenda are taken from Huber, Ragin, and Stephens (1993). Strong bicameralism involves two chambers elected by different means, each having at least a veto; while weak bicameralism involves two identically elected chambers having a veto.

Table 8.2 compares how our measure and other measures of consensual democracy correlate together. Unsurprisingly, the various measures of the electoral system (electoral system proportionality, Lijphart's executive-parties dimension, and Birchfield and Crepaz's collective veto points) are all strongly correlated with one another, as are the measures of supermajoritarianism (supermajoritarianism, Lijphart's federal-unitary dimension, Birchfield and Crepaz's competitive veto points, and Huber, Ragin, and Stephens's constitutional index). The electoral system proportionality index and Lijphart's executive-parties dimension correlate with each other more strongly than with the collective veto points index. This is probably due to the fact that the collective veto points index relies heavily on the effective number of parties, which is only indirectly related to electoral institutions. It is notable that Tsebelis's (2002, 182) two measures of the number of veto points (a qualitative assessment of the number of veto players, and an average of the number of veto players for 1981 through 1991) correlate with both sets of measures. However, they correlate with the measures of the electoral system more strongly than with the measures of supermajoritarianism and federalism.

Figure 8.1 plots the various countries in terms of their scores on electoral system proportionality and supermajoritarianism. This allows us to divide them into four categories. Most of the countries considered consensual democracies (Austria, Belgium pre-1994, Denmark, Finland,

TABLE 8.2. Correlation between Measures of Consensual Democracy

	Proportionality	Lijphart dim 1	Crepaz Collective Veto Points	Supermajoritarianism	Lijphart dim 2	Birchfield and Crepaz Competitive Veto Points	Huber et al. Constitutional Checks	Tsebelis Qualitative Veto Points	Tsebelis Numerical Veto Points
Proportionality	1.000								
Lijphart dim 1	0.830	1.000							
Birchfield and Crepaz collective veto points	0.476	0.563	1.000						
Supermajoritarianism	0.222	0.222	−0.345	1.000					
Lijphart dim 2	0.358	0.177	−0.220	0.809	1.000				
Birchfield and Crepaz competitive veto points	0.222	0.148	−0.266	0.794	0.881	1.000			
Huber et al. constitutional checks	−0.127	−0.004	−0.506	0.795	0.662	0.830	1.000		
Tsebelis qualitative veto points	0.693	0.827	0.499	0.445	0.448	0.318	0.147	1.000	
Tsebelis numerical veto points	0.533	0.795	0.520	0.377	0.109	0.181	0.136	0.790	1.000

Note: Lijphart dim 1 = executive-parties dimension; Lijphart dim 2 = federal-unitary dimension.

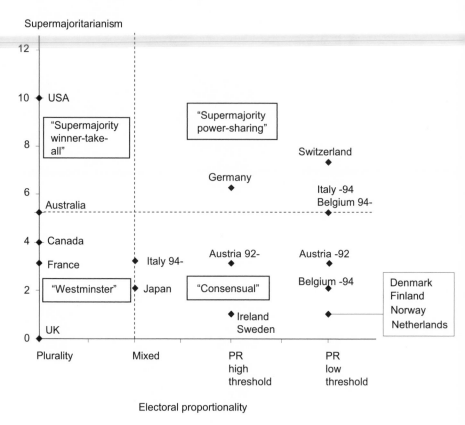

Fig. 8.1. Constitutional types in the OECD. -92 and -94 indicate pre-1992 and pre-1994; 92- and 94- indicate post-1992 and post-1994.

the Netherlands, Norway, Sweden, as well as Ireland) are in the bottom right quadrant, combining proportional representation elections with majority-rule parliaments with very few constitutional checks. There are a few cases that combine proportional representation with extensive supermajoritarianism, which I label as "supermajority power-sharing." These include Germany and Switzerland, with Italy and post-1994 Belgium as borderline cases. (According to Di Palma [1977], many features of the Italian legislature not considered here such as consensual agenda making, secret voting, and the unacceptability of the Communists made it extremely easy to block action, so pre-1994 Italy probably should be classified in the supermajoritarian group.) The Westminster model combines winner-take-all elections with a relatively unchecked majority-rule parliament. The United Kingdom, France, and to some degree Australia and Canada fit in this category. Japan and post-1994 Italy can also be seen as marginal cases, in that they have few checks and mixed electoral systems. Finally, there is the U.S. pattern of winner-take-all election with multiple checks and balances ("supermajority winner-take-all"). The only other countries that are candidates for this category are Australia and perhaps Canada, due to their high degree of federalism.

It should be noted that the way several countries are classified changed during the 1990s. For the 1992 election Austria adopted a 4 percent threshold where previously there was none. In 1994 Japan moved from single nontransferable vote to a mixed system. In the same year Belgium adopted a new constitution with a far higher degree of formal federalism, particularly concerning matters affecting the ethnolinguistic communities. Thus Belgium goes from being firmly within the consensual group to being on the border between this category and the "supermajority power-sharing" countries. In 1994 the Italian political system was also reformed. Most attention has focused on the changes on the electoral system, which went from open-list proportional representation to a mixed system. However, it may be that the other changes that took place at this time were equally significant. Secret voting in the legislature was abolished, as was the ability to filibuster, and the agenda was set by the majority coalition rather than consensually. Equally important, the exclusion of the (ex) Communists came to an end, so it was no longer necessary to assemble a supermajority of the non-Communist parties to govern. Thus Italy ceases to be supermajoritarian at the same time it ceases to have pure proportional representation. I would speculate that the ability of Italy to make hard budgetary decisions to meet European Monetary Union convergence criteria may be at least as much the result of these changes as it was the result of electoral system change.

3. Empirical Outcomes in Consensual Democracy

We have established that the consensual democracies typically have proportional representation electoral rules and simple majority-rule parliamentary decision-making rules. We now turn to the empirical effects of these rules on stability, on economic performance and equality, and on minority protection and the quality of democratic deliberation. To summarize the results, in terms of basic rights protection and economic performance, there is little evidence that the type of political regime makes any difference. However, consensual democracies are economically more egalitarian and provide more social rights and services. In terms of stability, consensual democracy appears, if anything, more stable than other forms.

Stability

Stability is clearly a value that can be held up as something against which the claims of political equality have to be balanced. Indeed both proportional representation and majority rule have been criticized as leading to instability. Of course, political science's preoccupation with stability has itself come in for criticism, as has the assumption that stability—any kind of stability—is a good thing. Przeworski et al. (2000, 187–88), for example, suggest that the structural functionalist approaches popular in the 1950s combined with cold war ideology often led to normal facets of democratic competition (alternation of governments, strikes, peaceful demonstrations) being categorized alongside coups and political assassinations. For this reason it is extremely important to distinguish between different kinds of stability. There are three kinds of stability that are relevant in this context. First there is cabinet stability, which is the frequency with which governments last or break up. Second there is policy stability, or how rapidly government policy changes over time. Finally there is regime stability, or whether the basic political institutions are able to maintain themselves.

Cabinet Stability.   Opponents of proportional representation (in the United Kingdom in particular) frequently cite cabinet instability as a problem of proportional elections. The case usually cited is Italy, where (prior to 1994) cabinets rarely lasted a whole year. Of course, proponents of proportional representation would point to other countries with PR elections that were far more stable. When we systematically examine the relationship between electoral systems, multiparty government, and cabinet duration, there is little evidence of a strong relationship. Lijphart (1984a) finds that the average cabinet duration of multiparty governments is somewhat shorter than that of single-party governments. However, this difference is mostly accounted for by a small number of outliers, notably Italy and Israel. Italy is particularly noteworthy here, as Italy had institutions other than PR that encourage instability—open-list elections to the legislature and secret voting in it, both of which undermined party discipline. Israel in the 1980s had very short cabinet duration as a result of a string of virtually tied elections. It could be argued that such elections would lead to short government duration in any system (consider the United Kingdom in the 1970s). Strom (1990) finds that minority governments (where the governing party does not have a majority but has to rely on the tacit support of nongoverning parties, an arrangement common in some countries with PR) are not particularly unstable. Thus there is little evidence that proportional representation leads in general to cabinet instability.

Policy Stability.   Next we turn to policy stability. Even here it is necessary to distinguish between two kinds of policy stability. The first is the absence of short-term oscillation in policy (as when consecutive governments switch sides on important issues or radically change spending priorities back and forth).This first kind of stability is needed for effective government. However, the second kind of stability is not necessarily so desirable. This is long-run stability in policy, or put more negatively, policy inflexibility. Policies are locked in over the medium term so that they are stable even as the demands on government change. In a rapidly changing global economy it is easy to make a case that this kind of policy sclerosis is a liability.

As for the first kind of policy stability, there is little empirical evidence on how systems of government affect this. Tsebelis and Chang (2001) provide an interesting measure of policy stability, using the Euclidean distance between vectors of government spending. However, they do not relate the variation to constitutional features such as proportionality, supermajoritarianism, or veto players. They do show that instability is greatest when there is an alternation of government, and when the distance between the ideological placement of the parties in government changes greatly. Given that proportional representation is associated with fewer complete alternations of government than winner-take-all systems, we would expect proportional systems to exhibit less short-term policy oscillation. However, this is an argument based on indirect evidence. Further research is to determine directly the effect of different election systems.

Concentrating on the second kind of policy stability (long-run stability versus flexibility) allows us to discriminate between theories that argue that consensus democracy is characterized by veto players, on one hand, and theories that characterize consensual democracy as driven by mutual accommodation and flexible adjustment, on the other. Tsebelis (2002) argues that consensual democracies have many veto players and thus a high degree of policy stability if not deadlock. Tsebelis (2002) tests this proposition, although his measures are extremely problematic.[2] Birchfield and Crepaz (1998) on the other hand argue that electoral proportionality and power sharing (what they call "collective veto points") are enabling and allow governments to implement redistributive policies. There is also a considerable political economy literature (for example, Cameron 1978;

Katzenstein 1985) that argues that the countries that we call consensual are small, open economies that tend to be extremely flexible in terms of policy and indeed have to be, given their exposure to world markets.

In this chapter policy stability is measured using the simple proxy of total government spending as a percentage of gross domestic product, taken from OECD Historical Statistics. Whereas this does not capture subtle changes in the direction of policy, it does provide a crude measure of flexibility. In particular the ability to cut government spending is a strong test of flexibility, as the literature on government retrenchment (for example, Pierson 1994) argues that government spending is far more difficult to cut than to increase, because the beneficiaries of programs form concentrated groups. If such groups have access to veto points, they will be able to prevent retrenchment. The standard deviation of government expenditure/GDP provides a first measure of flexibility. However, it is possible that a high standard deviation is simply the result of a constant upward trend, essentially locked in by an inflexible political system. Therefore we also consider the standard deviation of the annual change in expenditure/GDP. The countries that score highest will be those that can increase and decrease spending, whereas countries that have a constant trend will score zero.

Table 8.3 considers the mean and standard deviation of government expenditure/GDP and the standard deviation of the annual changes, averaged across countries with different constitutional types. Contra Tsebelis, the consensual democracies actually display the most variation. The consensual democracies (those with proportional elections and simple

TABLE 8.3.   Variation in Total Government Expenditure for Different Constitution Types

	Winner-Take-All		Proportional		
Supermajority	"Supermajority winner-take-all"		"Supermajority power-sharing"		
	Mean	34.59	Mean	37.93	(42.22
	Standard deviation	4.24	Standard deviation	4.87	(5.24
	Standard deviation		Standard deviation		
	annual change	1.23	annual change	1.33	(1.48
Majority-rule	"Westminster"		"Consensus"		
	Mean	35.79	Mean	44.04	
	Standard deviation	4.70	Standard deviation	7.01	
	Standard deviation		Standard deviation		
	annual change	1.11	annual change	1.92	

Note: Figures in parentheses exclude Switzerland (see text).

majority rule) have high government spending (an average of 44 percent of GDP) but also a high standard deviation in annual changes. The Westminster systems and the "supermajority winner-take-all countries" have on average lower expenditures, but also lower variability. The "supermajority power-sharing" countries (proportional elections and checks and balances) have average expenditure slightly lower than the consensual countries, but also considerably less variability. Note that figures in parentheses for these countries exclude Switzerland. This is because OECD figures for the size of the Swiss government are considered suspect by many observers (Lane and Maitland 2001; Armingeon 2001) because they do not include state mandated contributions to theoretically private insurance programs. If Armingeon's estimate of the size of the Swiss state (45 percent of GDP) is correct, then the mean expenditure of the "supermajority power sharing" countries would be almost identical to that of the consensual countries.

Figure 8.2 charts the evolution of public expenditure in Germany, the Netherlands, and the United States. The Netherlands increased public spending extremely quickly in the 1970s. However, in the 1980s it halted the rise and retrenched somewhat. In the late 1990s there were drastic cuts in the state's share of the economy. This experience is typical of many of the consensual democracies. It is possible to expand expenditure rapidly to deal with external shocks, but once a decision has been made that retrenchment is necessary, the government faces no veto players that can stop it. Even in Sweden, long famous for its government expenditure in excess of 60 percent of GDP, had reduced this to 52.4 percent by 2000. In Germany, however, there has been a steady trend toward greater spending, so that by the late 1990s it actually overtook the Netherlands. In the United States there has also been a trend toward greater expenditure, although this growth is far slower than Germany's. It has long been accepted that the consensual democracies have higher government expenditure than other countries. However, it also seems to be the case that they are better at retrenching. It should be no surprise that a lack of supermajoritarian institutions makes blocking retrenchment harder. However, it is less clear why proportional election should facilitate retrenchment, given that broad coalitions have to be constructed. In a provocative paper, Kitschelt (1996) suggests that retrenchment is hard in systems with bipolar party systems because the opposition party will always opportunistically attack any government that takes hard economic decisions. In a consensual system, however, these hard choices would be negotiated among all the parties.

Table 8.4 gives the results of regressing electoral system proportionality and the supermajoritarianism index on the standard deviation of

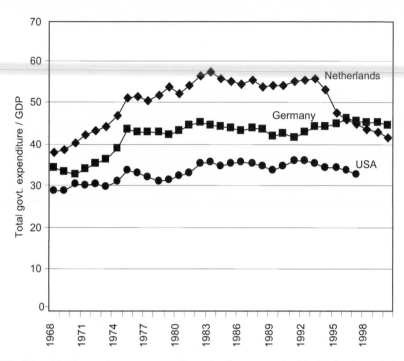

Fig. 8.2. Total government expenditure in Germany, the Netherlands, and the United States

TABLE 8.4. Regression of Constitutional Type on Deviation in Total Government Expenditure

Dependent Variable Adjusted $R^2 = 0.287$	Deviation in Expenditure/GDP ($N = 18$)			
	Effect			
	Coefficient	Std. error	t	P(1 tail)
Constant	5.766	1.008	5.717	0.000
Electoral system porportionality	0.546	0.345	1.582	0.0675
Supermajoritarianism	−0.320	0.167	−1.916	0.0375

Dependent Variable Adjusted $R^2 = 0.394$	Deviation in Change in Expenditure/GDP ($N = 18$)			
	Effect			
	Coefficient	Std. error	t	P(1 tail)
Constant	1.536	0.225	6.833	0.000
Electoral system proportionality	0.155	0.077	2.018	0.0361
Supermajoritarianism	−0.083	0.037	−2.234	0.0205

government expenditure/GDP and the annual change in government expenditure/GDP. As expected, election system proportionality increases the standard deviations, while supermajoritarianism decreases them. All the coefficients are significant to the 5 percent level (1-tailed test) except proportionality on the standard deviation of government expenditure, and even this is close. This is in spite of a low sample size ($N = 18$). Table 8.5 regresses Tsebelis's two measures of the number of veto points on the same dependent variable. The coefficients have the opposite sign to that predicted by Tsebelis's theory, with a higher number of veto points producing more deviation in expenditure. However, the results are not statistically significant. This is to be expected, as Tsebelis's concept of veto points conflates two variables (proportionality and supermajoritarianism) that work in opposite directions.

In summary, it is clear that short-term policy instability is undesirable, but we cannot come to any firm conclusions as to how consensual democracy performs relative to other forms. We would suspect, however, that consensual democracies are more stable in the short run because they have fewer complete alternations of governments. It is not clear that long-run stability is desirable. If a country is a small, open economy in the world market (as most of the consensual democracies are), policy flexibility is likely to be very important. Our evidence suggests that the consensual democracies are actually far more flexible than other forms of democracy over the long run, at least as measured by overall levels of government spending. Not only was it possible for these countries to develop large welfare states, but it has been possible for these countries to

TABLE 8.5. Regression of Tsebelis Veto Points on Deviation in Total Government Expenditure

Dependent Variable Adjusted $R^2 = 0.027$	Deviation in Expenditure/GDP ($N = 12$)			
	Effect			
	Coefficient	**Std. error**	***t***	***P*(1 tail)**
Constant	3.816	2.409	1.584	0.072
Tsebelis veto points	1.067	0.933	1.143	0.140

Dependent Variable Adjusted $R^2 = 0.000$	Deviation in Change in Expenditure/GDP ($N = 12$)			
	Effect			
	Coefficient	**Std. error**	***t***	***P*(1 tail)**
Constant	1.364	0.600	2.275	0.023
Tsebelis veto points	0.135	0.232	0.582	0.2865

retrench their welfare states far more than other countries. This disconfirms the hypothesis that consensual democracies are stable because they have a large number of veto players. Rather, they appear to be the democracies most capable of flexible adjustment.

Regime Stability.   Within the advanced industrial democracies, there is little evidence that the type of democracy has any effect on regime stability. In high-income countries, democracy—whatever its type—appears extremely stable. As Przeworski and Limongi (1997) famously pointed out, there is no case of democracy failing in a country with a per capita GDP of more than $6,000 per year. Przeworski et al. (2000) show that national income is by far the strongest predictor of whether democracy will survive. Thus, in advanced industrial democracies there does not appear to be any trade-off between political equality and regime stability.

In the case of lower-income countries, there is no evidence that the consensual form of democracy leads to higher regime instability. Indeed as Colomer (2001) argues, parliamentary proportional representation systems (a distinction that roughly corresponds to our characterization of consensual democracy) have had far fewer breakdowns than parliamentary-majoritarian or presidential systems. The reason we cannot come to a strong conclusion about consensual systems being more stable than other forms is that the consensual model has rarely been applied in low-income countries (the only cases that Colomer gives of proportional-parliamentary systems outside of Europe are South Africa after 1994 and Lebanon from 1943 through 1976). However, the consensual model did prove stable in Western Europe in the interwar period when income was much lower and regime breakdown common in many countries. It also appears stable in several middle-income postcommunist countries. Indeed the only cases of breakdown in parliamentary-proportional systems (excluding foreign invasion) are Estonia (1934), Latvia (1934), Lithuania (1926), Italy (1922), Austria (1933), and Lebanon (1976) (Colomer 2001).

There is considerable evidence that presidential systems are less stable than parliamentary ones. For example, Przeworski et al. (2000) find that presidential systems are three times as likely to suffer a breakdown in a given year as parliamentary systems, and that this difference cannot be explained by differences in income or by the fact that many presidential systems are in Latin America. Furthermore, presidential systems are found to be particularly unstable when the governing party controls between a third and a half of the lower house. Przeworski et al. argue that this is the situation in which deadlock between the executive and the legislature is likely—in our terms, when the supermajoritarian nature of presidentialism produces inflexibility. Shugart and Carey (1992) argue

that presidentialism does not necessarily produce instability, but their results are actually quite consistent with those of Przeworski et al. (2000).
They find that the greater the powers of the president (legislative and executive), the greater the chance of a breakdown. This is particularly the
case when the president has strong legislative powers, which can lead to
deadlock between the president and the legislature.

Of course, there are theoretical reasons to expect consensual democracy to exhibit higher levels of regime stability than other forms. Lijphart
(1977) argues that consociational democracy is a direct result of the need
to pacify a deeply divided society and commends it to developing nations
for precisely this reason. Miller (1983) and Przeworski (1991) suggest that
regime stability depends upon all actors expecting a better payoff from
playing by the political rules than by taking up arms. This in turn depends
on the probability of each player being able to win future elections and
on the difference in payoff between winning and losing. Consensual
democracy is likely to increase the chance of stability on both counts.
Even a minority has a chance of being in the government coalition under
proportional elections, whereas under a winner-take-all system it has no
chance. Second, a consensual power-sharing system typically reduces the
difference in payoff between winning and losing. Even if a group expects
to lose an election, it still may not take up arms if it expects to continue
to have some influence over the government. Although there are few
cases of consensual parliamentary-proportional systems outside Europe,
there are other systems that can be described as power sharing. For example, India, the longest established non-OECD democracy, typically has
multiparty governments in spite of having single-member district elections. Thus government coalitions have to be negotiated as in the consensual model. The same is true in several recent democracies in Africa (such
as Mali). It may be that the crucial factor in regime stability is multipartism and power sharing, not specific institutions. This, however, is a hypothesis for future research.

Economic Performance and Economic Equality

There is little evidence that either dimension of consensual democracy is
related strongly to overall economic performance. Lijphart (1999) finds
no significant relationship between the executive-parties scale and economic growth or inflation. He does find that the federal-unitary dimension is correlated with low inflation, but this is unsurprising as the federal-unitary dimension includes central bank independence as one of its
components. Rogowski and Kayser (2002) claim that the price level is
significantly higher in countries with proportional representation, and

that this shows that producers have more power than consumers in these countries. However, what they actually show is that the real exchange rate is more overvalued in countries with proportional representation. This results in exports from these countries being more competitively priced vis-à-vis the rest of the world, which benefits internationally competitive producers as opposed to producers for the domestic market. Given that countries with proportional representation in Europe tend to be small, open economies, it is hardly surprising that export industries get their way on exchange rate policy.

Economic corruption is very low in the consensual democracies. Denmark, Norway, the Netherlands, Sweden, and Switzerland are all among the ten least corrupt countries in the world according to Transparency International (2005). Considering all the world's democracies, Rose-Ackerman and Kunicova (2005) do find a positive relationship between proportional representation and corruption, but this is completely driven by the interaction between proportional elections and presidentialism. The coefficients for parliamentarianism with proportional representation are not significantly different from zero and actually tend slightly toward lower corruption. In terms of pork barrel spending (spending on inefficient, but locally popular projects), this is extremely hard to measure objectively, especially across countries. However, Milesi-Ferretti et al. (2002) suggest that we should expect countries with proportional representation to spend a higher proportion of their revenue on transfers (which are universal), while countries with "majoritarian" elections should spend a higher proportion on "public goods" (which can be geographically targeted). They produce econometric evidence that seems to confirm this.

When we consider income equality, consensual democracies do vary from other constitutional types. Lijphart (1999) shows that income inequality tends to be lower in the consensual democracies, while social spending and redistribution are higher. Birchfield and Crepaz (1998) show that "collective veto points" (essentially proportionality and multipartism) lead to lower inequality, while "competitive veto points" (checks and balances) increase inequality. Theoretically it is very easy to explain why supermajoritarian checks and balances increase inequality. Such institutions allow minority groups that lose from redistribution to veto it. However, explaining why proportional elections produce lower inequality than winner-take-all elections is more complex.

Crepaz (2001) suggests that the reason proportional elections facilitate redistribution is that to build redistributive institutions requires time and planning. Proportional elections enable long-term planning, whereas winner-take-all elections make this difficult. Essentially we can think of winner-take-all elections as being a stochastic veto point. Given that the electoral system magnifies changes in support, the party in government is likely to lose power in the near future for reasons beyond its control such as economic cycles. Furthermore, the party in power cannot afford to make temporarily unpopular decisions that may prove advantageous in the long run. With proportional elections, however, the parties are able to negotiate a long-term settlement. The idea that winner-take-all elections are a form of veto gate, with uncertainty and alternation of power preventing long-term policy development, is consistent with our findings on policy stability. Countries with single-member district elections have low variation in the level of government expenditure, even when they have very few constitutional checks.

There have been numerous other models proposed recently to account for the difference in redistribution between countries with proportional and winner-take-all elections (for example, Austen-Smith 2000; Iversen and Soskice 2002; Persson and Tabellini 1999). Many of them build on the insight that the median voter is not poor, and that the poor, as a minority group, do better under a proportional system. Further research is necessary to determine which of the many plausible mechanisms is actually responsible for the fact that countries with proportional representation tend to have lower income inequality.

However, it should not surprise us that we find low income inequality in countries with proportional representation electoral systems and simple majority-rule decision-making rules. In these countries political resources are distributed in a highly egalitarian manner. If economic assets are distributed less equally, it is not surprising that those who have votes but few assets leverage their votes for economic redistribution. What is interesting is that redistribution does not appear to proceed to the point where it damages economic growth, as consensual democracies appear to perform just as well as other forms. (In fact, there is little economic evidence that income inequality and growth are correlated—see Furman and Stiglitz 1998.) Thus democracy can be seen as a form of distributional justice, as Esping-Andersen suggests in *Politics Against Markets* (1981). Dahl (1988, 191) makes a similar point.

> The democratic process not only presupposes a broad array of fundamental rights: It is itself a form of distributive justice, since it directly influences the distribution of power and authority over the government of the state and, because of the importance of the decisions made by the government of the state, over other substantive goods as well.

Thus there is not convincing evidence that there is a trade-off between political equality and either economic performance or economic equality. Consensual democracies appear to perform economically at least as well as other forms in terms of growth and inflation. In terms of economic equality, consensual democracy appears considerably more egalitarian and redistributive. The argument advanced by the traditionalist left in the United Kingdom and by Roemer (1999a,b) that winner-take-all elections may allow more redistribution is empirically false: Winner-take-all elections actually lead to less redistribution than proportional elections. Again, it should not be surprising that institutions enshrining political equality should be most favorable to the disadvantaged: If an electoral system or decision-making rule is fiddled in somebody's favor (that is, is not anonymous and neutral), it is highly unlikely that it will be fiddled in favor of a disadvantaged group. If a group is powerful enough to get the constitution fiddled in its favor, it is almost by definition not a disadvantaged group.

Minority Protection, Rights, and Democratic Deliberation

In terms of protection of basic rights, there seems little evidence that there is any difference between consensual democracies and other forms in the advanced industrial democracies. This is because advanced industrial democracies of all constitutional types in general respect the basic rights necessary for democratic governance. For example, if we consider the score on political and social freedom compiled by Freedom House (2004) we find very little variation between OECD countries, all of them receiving near perfect marks. When we consider Amnesty International's (2004) annual report, we do see that some countries appear to be cited more (the consensual democracies are often conspicuous by their absence). However, Amnesty International does not provide a comparable, quantitative measure and specifically states that the absence of a country in the report does not mean that the organization has no concerns. Thus there is no evidence that any constitutional form is necessary for the respect of basic rights. Certainly there is no evidence for the American constitutionalist assumption that a system of checks and balances is better able to protect rights than a parliamentary system with no such checks (see Dahl 1988, 2001).

Of course, human rights violations often take place when a regime collapses or is overthrown. If one constitutional form is less stable than another, it is more likely to lead to a breakdown situation where rights violations occur. As noted earlier, it appears that presidential systems are considerably more likely to break down than parliamentary ones.

Consensual democracies appear to provide more broadly defined "social" rights. Indeed there are various characteristics that appear to make these "kinder, gentler democracies" in Lijphart's (1999) words. As discussed later, consensual democracies tend to have lower income inequality and greater provision of public services. Lijphart (1999) also finds that they appear to be more egalitarian in respect to gender, with more female legislative representation and more expansive family policies. They also appear to be less punitive, with lower incarceration rates and less inclination to use the death penalty. Finally, they appear more environment friendly, at least when environmentalism is measured by outcomes such as emission levels and energy efficiency (see also Scruggs 1999, 2001).

In terms of the conduct of democracy, countries with proportional representation have notably higher rates of voting (Lijphart 1997, 1999) and legislatures that are descriptively more representative in terms of variables such as gender (see Farrell 2001). The consensual democracies also appear to be different in other ways that are harder to measure. Because there is multiparty competition, observers of these countries often emphasize collaboration and negotiation among elites, rather than adversarial competition (Steiner 1973; Lijphart 1977). Strom (1990) argues that in some consensual democracies the power differential between parties that are in government and those that are not is slight, because parliamentary committees are powerful and chairs are distributed proportionally. Greater reliance appears to be placed on outside expert testimony, leading to a highly consultative form of democracy relying on institutions like the Social Economic Council in the Netherlands and the Royal Commissions in Scandinavia (Katzenstein 1985; Rochon 1999; Gladdish 1991; Cox 1993 on the Netherlands; Arter 1999 on Scandinavia). Of course, the reliance on outside expertise should not be surprising when no party has the political muscle to guarantee its preferred outcomes single-handed. Thus politics in consensual democracies appears extremely deliberative—a negotiated process aimed at finding better alternatives. Consensual democracy is, well, more consensual.

Conclusion

We have seen that the consensual democracies typically have proportional representation at the electoral stage, and simple majority rule (with very few checks and balances) at the lawmaking stage, precisely the institutions demanded by political equality. In terms of the empirical performance of consensual democracy, there is no evidence that there is a trade-off between political equality and stability. There is no evidence that countries with proportional representation and simple majority rule have significantly more turnover of governments. Neither is there any evidence of more short-term policy instability, although policy does seem to be more flexible in the long run. This, however, would appear at first sight to be an advantage in a changing world economy. In terms of regime stability, type of constitution makes little difference in developed countries, as democracy in whatever form appears stable. However, there is evidence that consensual forms may be more stable in developing countries.

Neither does there appear to be a trade-off between political equality and economic performance or equality. There is little evidence of a relationship between the form of democracy and economic performance. However, countries with PR and simple majority rule do have less income inequality and more public services. This provides a rebuttal to the argument that there is a trade-off between the value of procedural equality, on which this book is based, and substantive equality (particularly in terms of economics). Of course, such a trade-off may exist in theory, but in practice it is precisely where political procedures are most egalitarian that income equality and redistribution by government is highest. This should not surprise us—political institutions are highly unlikely to be biased in favor of the economically disadvantaged. Political equality is the most that the economically disadvantaged can practically hope for (and considerably more than they get in many cases). Furthermore the empirical literature shows that it is precisely where there is political equality that governments do most to reduce economic inequality.

We find that the consensual democracies perform at least as well as other forms of democracy in terms of rights protection and the quality of democratic deliberation. Therefore it is difficult to make a case that there is a trade-off between the value of political equality and these other values. Where there may be a trade-off is between political equality and participation (see chapter 6). Consensual democracy emphasizes intensive negotiation, which implies discussion among small groups and a representative rather than a direct form of democracy. This hypothesis, however, requires systematic study.

The central characteristic of consensual democracy is that it has power sharing rather than domination by a single majority. The consensual democracy literature has tended to contrast this power sharing with majority rule. However, majority rule does not typically produce domination by a single majority when combined with proportional representation, because no single party typically wins a majority. Rather it tends to produce coalition and compromise. In most consensual democracies, consensus is not the result of "consensual" (i.e., supermajoritarian) institutions that demand consensus as a condition for making a decision. Rather, consensual decision making results from the fact that no party can get its way without convincing allies, and that furthermore any coalition can be undercut by an alternative coalition. Consensual outcomes, it seems, result from the instability inherent in majority rule.

CHAPTER 9

Conclusions: Political Equality and the Beauty of Cycling

I have argued that it is necessary to bring together the three literatures—social choice theory, normative political philosophy, and the empirical study of democratic institutions—that study democracy. When we do political philosophy, it is necessary to take heed of the analytic results derived by social choice theory. These lay out the logical consequences of the values we advocate—for example, the fact that political equality implies majority rule and proportional representation. Social choice theory also set limits on what is logically possible; it is pointless to argue that something should be the case when it logically cannot be. When we use social choice theory, on the other hand, we start from axioms. For our results to have any normative force or relevance, it is necessary to justify these axioms normatively, which involves us in political philosophy. Finally, in order to be relevant to practical politics, it is necessary to combine the insights of both literatures with the empirical literature on political institutions. This allows us to argue about what is desirable, what is possible, and how it might be achieved.

Unfortunately, the three literatures have been largely disconnected from one another, if not overtly hostile. I have argued that a great deal of the difficulty in translating across these literatures comes from the interpretation (and misinterpretation) of the phenomenon of cycling (the fact that whatever is chosen by majority rule, it is possible to find another alternative that a majority prefers). Generally, social choice theory has treated majority-rule cycling as a problem to be overcome, or even as a problem that is fatal for the theory of democracy. As a result, political philosophers with a normative commitment to democracy argued that social choice theory was wrong, while empirical researchers (not observing cycles) often ignored it altogether. Miller's (1983) "Social Choice and Pluralism," however, argues that cyclical social preferences are likely to be pervasive but are actually an important part of the normal working of democracy. Building on this insight, it is possible to bring the three literatures back together. This forces us to reevaluate the assumptions of all three literatures, and it changes how we think about democracy. In particular, it allows us to simultaneously satisfy the demands of political equality—which implies majority rule—and other democratic values such as minority protection and reasonable deliberation.

Combining the three approaches, we get the following results.

1. *Political equality implies majority rule and proportional representation. All other institutions privilege some citizens over others.* Following Dahl (1956) we can understand democracy as a system of government that satisfies popular sovereignty and political equality. Popular sovereignty simply means that the political process has the final say over all issues. Political equality means that all citizens are treated equally. Dahl argues that this axiomatically implies majority rule, but that this is of little relevance to modern democracies, because these are representative, not direct. Contrary to this, I have argued that political equality does imply a very specific set of institutions. Representative democracy consists of two stages: In the first representatives are chosen by elections, while in the second these representatives make decisions using a voting rule. Political equality implies specific institutions for both stages.

(a) At the electoral stage, political equality axiomatically implies proportionality. That is to say, any electoral system that does not satisfy proportionality violates political equality. National list proportional representation is the most obvious system that satisfies proportionality (ignoring rounding error). However, many other systems are also possible (mixed-member systems, small district proportional representation with national compensation seats, etc.).

(b) At the decision-making stage, political equality implies majority rule. That is to say, majority rule is the only binary decision-making rule that satisfies political equality. It should be noted that to satisfy political equality it is not sufficient that majority rule be used as part of the process; rather the process has to satisfy majority rule. Procedures that are effectively supermajoritarian—which includes most institutional features we refer as checks and balances (bicameralism, presidentialism, federalism, division of power)—violate political equality just as much as explicitly supermajoritarian rules.

2. *Majority rule is the decision rule offering most protection to minorities. The standard defense of liberal constitutionalism on the grounds that it offers more protection to minorities in general is not logically tenable—it is not possible to protect every minority more than every other minority.* Chapter 5 argues that majority rule provides the greatest possible

protection to the worst-off minority. This is because majority rule is the decision rule that makes it easiest to form an alliance to overturn an unfavorable outcome. Any supermajoritarian decision rule has the effect of locking in the status quo to some extent. If the status quo turns out to be oppressive (and we do not know what conditions will be like in the future), it will be harder to change. Empirically, in terms of basic liberal rights, there is no evidence that there is any difference between countries with simple majority rule and countries with checks and balances, at least among advanced industrial democracies. Countries with simple majority rule, however, do provide more protection for social rights.

3. *Majority rule and proportional representation are the institutions that most promote democratic deliberation. The idea of unforced consensus (which underlies much of the deliberative democracy literature, as well as social contract theory) is logically flawed.* We would expect majority rule to be the decision rule best suited to produce rational deliberation because majority rule maximizes the number of people that need to be persuaded to pass a decision. (With supermajority rule a minority may prevail if it is defending the status quo.) By forcing people to seek allies and making it impossible for narrow alliances to prevail, majority rule creates an incentive to argue reasonably. This conclusion is in line with a considerable amount of existing work on deliberative democracy based on majority rule (Dewey 1927/1946; Knight and Johnson 1994, 1996, 1999; Barry 1995; Nino 1996). Similarly it can be argued that proportional representation (especially national list proportional representation) creates an incentive to frame arguments broadly. However, there is to date no comparative empirical study on the degree to which different systems produce rational deliberation, due presumably to the fact that no one has found a convincing way to measure it.

Rae (1975) shows that unforced consensus when there is initial disagreement and an outcome has to come about is logically impossible. If an outcome has to happen (which is always the case in politics, as a nondecision is a decision to do nothing, at least for the time being), then some outcome has to be imposed in the event no agreement is reached. This implicit threat hangs over the deliberation, and thus even if agreement is reached, it is not free but conditional on the threat of the imposed outcome. This undermines the logic of both classic social contract theory and modern discourse theory. In particular, it shows that Habermas's ideal speech situation, which logically underlies much of the deliberative democracy literature, is a logical impossibility and therefore cannot even serve as a counterfactual ideal.

4. *There is no evidence of a trade-off between political equality and the values of political stability, economic efficiency, and economic equality.*

(a) *Stability.*   Whether we consider regime stability, policy stability, or cabinet stability, there is no evidence that countries with proportional representation and simple majority rule are more unstable than other countries. (Countries with PR do have slightly shorter cabinet duration on average, but this is most accounted for by a small number of cases such as Italy and Israel, where special conditions apply.) Indeed in terms of regime stability, countries with PR and parliamentarianism may actually be more stable.

(b) *Economic Equality and Performance.*   This book takes no position on whether economic equality (or its opposite) is intrinsically desirable or not. However, if the political system is egalitarian, we would expect this to lead to greater economic equality. If a valuable asset (political power) is distributed equally in an otherwise unequal society, we would expect this asset to be traded to some extent for greater equality in other spheres. Empirically this appears to be the case. Countries with egalitarian political systems (proportional representation and majority rule) have higher levels of economic equality than other countries. Therefore the argument that reducing economic inequality can justify political inequality has little empirical basis. In terms of economic performance, the degree of political equality seems to make no difference at all.

5. *There will be a trade-off between the values of deliberation and direct participation.* Deliberation requires small group interaction, where people can persuade, be persuaded, and negotiate. The value of direct participation requires that as many people as possible take part in the process as completely as possible. There is an obvious conflict between these two values, which is intensified if we insist on political equality (which requires that everyone counts equally). This will manifest itself in:

(a) *The Decision Rule.*   A representative system can be highly deliberative and satisfy political equality but still limit direct participation. Most people can only vote or participate indirectly by lobbying their representative or arguing in civil society. A plebiscitarian system can be egalitarian and participatory (everyone votes on all the main issues), but it does not allow for reasonable deliberation, as decisions are taken by mass publics that cannot meet to deliberate. A "participatory" system where anyone who wants may participate directly may be deliberative and participatory but will violate political equality, as some are more able to participate than others. Thus it is impossible to maximize all three values simultaneously.

(b) *Representation.*   There will be a similar trade-off in the choice of electoral system. If we wish to promote deliberation, we will choose an electoral system that allows representatives sufficient freedom from their immediate constituents, so they can listen to arguments and be persuaded. However, if we value participation more, we will want representatives to be more directly controlled by their (active) constituents. Similarly, if we value deliberation, we will want representatives to have to persuade as broad an audience as possible and will prefer national list systems; whereas if we value direct participation we may prefer systems with small district magnitudes so that local activists can have an impact on the behavior of representatives.

6. *The consensual democracies of western Europe typically have the institutions required for political equality (proportional representation and majority rule), not a system of minority vetoes, as previously theorized.* The consensual democracies of Western Europe (Denmark, the Netherlands, Norway, Sweden, and to a lesser extent Austria and Belgium) combine proportional representation with majority-rule parliaments that have very few checks and balance. Thus they are characterized by almost precisely the institutions that are required to satisfy political equality. (The only country generally characterized as consensual that is strongly supermajoritarian is Switzerland.) The politics of consensus and accommodation in these countries does not result from minority vetoes but from agreement reached with the framework of majority-rule bargaining. Far from the stasis or gridlock we would expect from political systems with many veto points, these countries have been extremely adaptable in terms of policy, which is important as they are all small, open economies.

7. *Cycling is essential to the understanding of democracy. It should not be seen as a problem to be overcome but rather as the thing that makes democracy as we know it possible.* The presence of cyclical social preferences does not imply that we will observe instability, much less chaos. Cycling merely means that there are multiple overlapping winning coalitions. Whichever coalition is currently winning, it is possible for the losers to buy off enough of the winners to undermine the current winning coalition. This typically does not produce chaos, because the winners realize

they have to accommodate the losers sufficiently that they do not seek to undermine the winning coalition. Following Miller (1983), I argue that this leads to normatively desirable results. Cycling allows us to combine majority rule (and thus political equality) with minority protection. The minority is protected because there is no permanent winning bloc, but rather a number of potential winning coalitions, any one of which can be split. If the minority feels that its essential interests are being attacked, they can "sell" their support on issues they care less about to anyone who will agree to protect their vital interests. In a similar manner, cycling promotes deliberation. No one can get their own way without allies, and thus everyone has to make reasonable accommodations.

It is the final conclusion—that cycling is a normal part of the democratic process—that allows us to reconcile the three literatures. In particular, this allows us to get beyond the "confrontation" between social choice theory and the normative theory of democracy. It is, of course, Riker's *Liberalism Against Populism* (1982) that most explicitly framed the relationship between the two literatures as a confrontation, arguing that the findings of social choice theory—and cycling in particular—render traditional democratic theory empty. There have been many attempts to refute Riker's conclusions (Coleman and Ferejohn 1986; D. Miller 1992; Mackie 2003; Dryzek and List 2003). These try to minimize or overcome the effects of cycling, but they accept Riker's key premise that the only alternative to minimal liberalism (the idea that voting has no intrinsic value except occasionally removing governments) is populism (the idea that democracy produces a single best outcome or "General Will"). While Riker's interpretation of the social choice results is certainly questionable, the phenomenon of cycling surely does undermine the idea that democracy can produce a single best outcome, and hence populism fails. However, if we discard populism and the idea of a single best outcome— that is, if we accept cycling as a normal part of democracy—then there are still many ways to justify democracy other than minimal liberalism.

It is not necessary to resort to untenable arguments—about social choice theory being wrong or about the existence of an anthropomorphic "General Will" for the whole of society—in order to justify majority-rule democracy. Cycling does not undermine a procedural justification of majority rule on the ground of its inherent fairness. Majority rule can be seen as a fair game for producing social decisions. Majority rule does not in general produce a single determinate outcome that we can call the "Will of the People," but neither are its results arbitrary or random. Furthermore, majority-rule bargaining typically produces reasonable outcomes—the most unreasonable outcomes have no chance of winning over a majority. We can also justify democracy on pragmatic or deliberative grounds (democracy is justified because it facilitates rational social inquiry or reasonable deliberation). Thus without the unnecessary metaphysical weight of the "Will of the People," it is possible to provide arguments practically identical to those sought by populist democrats — the institution of majority rule is justified, voting procedures must be fair, and democratically agreed outcomes have moral force.

The phenomenon of cycling gives us other normatively desirable results. One of the central problems for democratic theory has been the problem of the tyranny of the majority. Cycling allows us to overcome this problem without empowering a minority that may itself become tyrannical. Providing that there is not a single, permanent, cohesive majority, majority rule relies on a coalition of minorities. Any such coalition can be split. If a minority feels its vital interests are threatened, it can offer its support on all other issues at a very low price in order to obtain concessions on the one issue it views as essential. We do not get a tyrannical majority, because there are multiple, overlapping potential winning coalitions — the current majority knows that it can be divided and replaced. It was argued in chapter 5 that this is essentially the argument that James Madison made for a large republic. Furthermore, cycling is the only way to reconcile political equality and protection from majority tyranny: Any artificial check on the majority logically implies a form of minority rule, violating political equality and producing the possibility of minority tyranny. Far from cycling being a problem for democracy, we should be worried when cycling is not present. This is because the absence of cycling implies a single majority, which poses the problem of majority tyranny.

It was argued in chapter 8 that cycling is vital to the operation of Western European consensual democracy. In these countries minorities are protected precisely by the possibility of alternative winning coalitions under majority rule. Contrary to much of the existing literature, these countries do not have institutions that force consensus by giving various groups vetoes; in fact they have very few institutional veto points. Rather they have precisely the institutions required to satisfy political equality — proportional representation elections and majority-rule parliaments with very few checks and balances. Consensual outcomes and norms in these countries are a result of majority-rule bargaining in a situation where cyclical majorities are inevitable. Reasonable accommodations are reached within the framework of majority-rule bargaining, not because of institutions that frustrate majority rule or demand consensus at the cost of producing gridlock. It is notable that when changes in the international economy have necessitated changes in policy, the consensual democracies have typically made very significant policy adjustments very rapidly. Thus we can theorize consensual democracy in social choice theoretic terms.

It has been argued that majority rule is in practice a rule that defines the conditions under which people negotiate their differences. This has implications for the standards we use for judging the procedures used for making social decisions. Social choice theory has typically started with the concept of a social choice functional. This is a mapping that takes the preferences of individuals and returns a preference ordering for society. However, we do not use democratic procedures in such a mechanical manner. Rather, elections choose representatives, who then engage in negotiation and deliberation. When we judge the quality of election rules we are interested in whether they are procedurally fair and whether they create appropriate incentives for representatives when they engage in deliberation. When we consider the quality of the decision rule, we are concerned once again with procedural fairness and whether it leads to a deliberative process that produces reasonable outcomes. Thus we are interested in the deliberative games that representatives play. Of course, there is a massive literature on how we should expect rational agents to bargain. The problem is that there is typically a multiplicity of equilibria, a problem recognized at least since Schelling (1960).

In particular, the requirement of transitivity, assumed as normatively vital in much of the social choice literature, is inappropriate for a decision-making rule in a plural society. Requiring that a procedure produce a transitive ranking of all alternatives is actually equivalent to the demand in the normative literature that a procedure produce a single "Will of the People." It demands that we take all the values of every individual in society and condense them into one supervalue that can order every alternative. Given that different individuals have different preference orders, we need some way to weight these differences to come up with a single order. The problem is that how to weight the values of different people is itself a value. Different people will rank different procedures differently, which simply reproduces the original problem at a higher level. In a plural society where people have different values, a reasonable outcome will have to be a compromise between different values, not a transitive supervalue. Arrow's theorem does not show that there is no appropriate social decision rule; rather it shows that it is impossible to achieve a single, transitive ranking of values in a plural society. As a result, it is necessary to make compromises. This requires a deliberative or bargaining procedure, which implies that there will in general be a plurality of reasonable outcomes.

Thinking about democratic procedures as rules that govern deliberation forces us to rethink the way we use social choice theory; however, the results of social choice theory also force us to reconsider the normative literature on deliberative democracy. The deliberative democracy literature also holds out the hope of a single, correct solution to a social decision, based on the idea of an unforced consensus. However, as Rae (1975) demonstrates, an unforced consensus in a political matter is logically impossible. Given that a decision needs to be made, there is always the threat of the outcome to be imposed if consensus should fail, and all outcomes agreed to are conditional on this. Given that there is an element of coercion in any collective decision where there is initial disagreement, the best we can do is distribute the coercion equally. Thus majority rule is the only procedurally fair decision rule for deliberating over social decisions. Of course, majority rule does not produce a single, determinate outcome, and the outcomes will result in part from bargaining. As a result, the terms agreed upon will to some degree be a compromise, one reasonable solution among many. Even at an abstract philosophical level, it is necessary to acknowledge the plurality of social reason.

While fair and reasonable procedures will not produce a single, determinate answer but rather a reasonable compromise, it is possible to be more specific about the procedures themselves. Most of the empirical literature on political institutions has been extremely agnostic concerning what are good institutions, preferring instead to argue instrumentally about the effect of institutions. The theoretical literature, on the other hand, has rarely got down to the level of institutional details. However, combining the two approaches, it can be shown the basic value of fair democratic procedure—political equality—implies very specific institutions: proportional representation at the electoral stage and at the decision-making stage simple majority rule.

Notes

CHAPTER 2

1. It is notable that Arrow (1951/1963, 20–21) considered a game-theoretic approach to social choice. He did not pursue this, however, instead taking the social welfare function approach to its logical conclusion. The example Arrow gave was of noncooperative games, rather than the cooperative coalition-type games suggested earlier. "Thus, the model of rational choice as built up from pair-wise comparisons does not seem to suit well the case of rational behavior in the described game situation. It seems that the essential point is, and this being of general bearing, that, if conceptually we imagine a choice being made between two alternatives, we cannot exclude any probability distribution over those two choices as a possible alternative. The precise shape of a formulation of rationality which takes the last point into account or the consequences of such a reformulation on the theory of choice in general or the theory of social choice in particular cannot be foreseen; but it is at least a possibility, to which attention should be drawn, that the paradox to be discussed below might be resolved by such a broader concept of rationality."

2. Rawls (1995/1996) accepts that the original position construction has no privileged status and is simply a device that has to be justified in actual discourse with real people. However, Rawls does not talk about the rules for such discourse.

3. "If we exclude the possibility of interpersonal comparisons of utility, then the only methods of passing from individual tastes to social preferences which will be satisfactory and which will be defined for a wide range of sets of individual orderings are either imposed or dictatorial."

4. The Borda procedure has every voter rank order all the n alternatives, and then gives $n - 1$ points to each voter's first choice, $n - 2$ to each voter's second choice, etc. The scores for each alternative are then summed, and the alternative with the highest score is the winner.

5. Mathematically speaking, we do have a metric for the space of alternatives.

CHAPTER 3

1. For example, it would be possible to implement pure PR by distributing some seats by a lottery where each alternative's chance of getting the seat is proportional to the difference between its vote share and the seat share it has received.

2. Subject to other institutional features. For example, Germany has a mixed-member system of this type. The results are approximately proportional, except that there is a 5 percent electoral threshold and that parties who win more district seats than their overall vote share would dictate are allowed to keep the "excess" seats.

3. With single transferable vote, a candidate requires a certain quota to be elected, typically the Droop quota = (number of voters / (number of seats + 1)) + 1. Once a candidate is elected, their excess votes are distributed to the candidates ranked second on the excess ballots. If there are still seats to be distributed, the candidate with the lowest vote is eliminated and their votes are redistributed to the candidates ranked second on the ballots. This procedure is repeated until all seats are filled.

4. If there are n candidates, the Borda procedure gives $n − 1$ points to each voter's first choice, $n − 2$ to their second, etc. The scores are then totaled.

5. Strictly speaking, Rae (1967) uses three dimensions of classification: district magnitude, electoral formula, and whether the vote is categorical or ordinal (whether the voter gets a single vote or whether they get to rank-order the candidates). However, systems with ordinal vote typically use distinctive mechanisms, such as single transferable vote, so we can treat ordinal voting as a different kind of formula.

6. Strictly speaking, the Netherlands is divided into smaller electoral subunits. However, seats are allocated on a nationwide basis. See Gladdish (1991).

7. Strictly speaking, majority rule implies the winning candidate receives more than 50 percent of the vote against any other candidate. Plurality runoff violates this. It is possible that a candidate could beat either of his opponents in a head-to-head race but would lose in plurality runoff by being eliminated in the first round.

8. A variation of this is cumulative vote, which allows voters to award more than one vote to one candidate.

9. The debate between the two methods can be traced back to the dispute between Jefferson (who advocated a divisor method) and Hamilton (who advocated a quota method) over how to allocate House of Representative seats to the various states (see Balinski and Young 1982/2001; Nurmi 1999; Saari 2001).

10. Voters in the Netherlands have one vote, which they can cast for the head of a list (usually a party leader) or for any person on the list. Prior to 1998 the votes for the list head were distributed in list order, so list position overwhelmed personal vote, and very few candidates were elected on the basis of their personal following. Since 1998 personal votes can overturn list order, but only if a candidate receives votes equivalent to half a quota, a very high requirement.

11. I use the term *plurality* instead of *majoritarian* because there is no guarantee that a candidate elected from a district receives a majority of the votes in that district, nor is there any guarantee that a party that receives a majority of seats won a majority of the vote.

12. Party system fractionalization is defined as $\sum V_i^2$ or $\sum S_i^2$, where V_i is the vote share of party i and S_i is its seat share. The effective number of parties is defined as $1/\sum V_i^2$ or $1/\sum S_i^2$.

CHAPTER 4

1. To recap, anonymity means that the rule treats all voters equally—if we exchange the preferences of any pair of voters, it does not affect the outcome. Neutrality means all alternatives are treated equally—if one alternative gets a certain set of voters and wins, then if these voters all switch their support to another alternative, it must then win. Decisiveness simply means that the rule must produce a result, which may be a draw. Positive responsiveness means that if we have a draw, and one voter switches his support to alternative 1, then alternative 1 must win.

2. This amounts to saying that if someone prefers alternative a to b, then there is another alternative, very close (possibly infinitesimally close), that the person also prefers to b.

3. Strictly speaking, Schofield gives a characterization of the "heart" or locally uncovered set, which is a superset of the uncovered set.

4. Note that this definition of logrolling implies separable preferences over the issues in question. Logrolling involves people voting for measures they do not like. We could not talk about people liking or not liking specific measures unless their preferences are separable—that is, they like or dislike the measure regardless of how other measures are resolved.

5. That is to say, *some* representatives vote for things that they do not want in order to get things that they do, but there is no cycle or intransitivity because other representatives have a very particular kind of nonseparable preference that effectively cancels the cycle. Suppose that we change Representative C's preferences. Representative C still wants his measure adopted, and prefers that measures A and B are both not adopted. However, he despises the situation where measure A is adopted and not B, to the extent of preferring that both measures be adopted to only one being adopted. (Perhaps C has a strong sense of equity, and thinks that adopting A but not B is unfair.) With this change, Representative C will no longer support a motion to go from funding measures A and B to just funding A. Therefore the cycle in figure 4.4 disappears, essentially because we have assumed an agent who despises the intermediate step in the cycle. This situation, incidentally, is morally troubling. Representative C does not get his measure, but he has to pay for A and B, precisely because A and B can exploit his sense of equity. In the previous version of the example, Representative C can defend himself against a coalition of A and B by trying to cut a deal with one of them; however, the new preferences we have given C make this line of defense impossible.

6. Riker (1982, 242–43) anticipates this objection, arguing that this randomness gives elected officials an even stronger incentive not to offend voters. However, this response is extremely unconvincing. Coleman and Ferejohn (1986) are surely right that if voters' rejection is strictly random, officials can do nothing about it and will treat it as an act of God.

7. Przeworski (1999) does not rely on elections removing bad governments but rather argues that if elections were completely random, the exercise would still be worthwhile. Given that there is a probability for the incumbent to be removed

in the future, it is worthwhile for the opposition to continue to play the constitutional game, as opposed to taking up arms. It is also in the interest of the incumbent not to be too oppressive, as he may lose power in the future. Przeworski also argues that elections are useful as a measure of the relative strength (in the case of civil war) of the government and the opposition. I do not dispute Przeworski's claim that even minimalist democracy may have some value; the argument in this chapter is that a more expansive theory of democracy is viable.

8. Other justifications could be given for fairly distributing political resources, such as the symbolic value of fair representation. This argument is not pursued here, as it simply reinforces the case for majority rule as pure procedure.

9. Thus power indices, such as the Penrose, Shapley-Shubik, and Banzhaf indices, which are based upon the percentage of possible coalitions in which a player is crucial, are monotonic to the voting weight of the players. That is, as players get more voting weight, their power increases, all other things being equal. See Penrose (1946); Shapley and Shubik (1954); Banzhaf (1965).

10. Schwartz (1995) shows that a group of voters can become worse off by getting more representation. However, this argument relies on sincere voting. If their representatives vote strategically, they can at least reproduce the outcome they got when they were less represented.

11. Although majority rule is generally not transitive (it allows cycles), there is typically a great deal of transitivity within the web of preference relations. The covering relation can be restated as follows: a covers b implies that the social preference between a, b, and any other alternative is transitive. It is this transitivity information that allows us to reject certain alternatives as never being reasonable choices.

CHAPTER 5

1. This would rest on empirical evidence. As we will see, empirical evidence that supermajoritarian rules provide better rights protection does not exist.

2. See Madison's remarks to the Constitutional Convention on June 19, 1787 (Madison 1840/1966) and "Vices of the Political System of the United States" (Madison 1999).

3. On June 6 at the Federal Convention, Madison argued that extending the scope of the republic was the *only* way to protect minorities: "In a Republican Govt. the majority if united have always an opportunity. The only remedy is to enlarge the sphere, and thereby divide the community into so great a number of interests and parties, that in the 1st place a majority will not be likely at the same moment to have a common interest separate from that of the whole or of the minority; and in the 2nd place that in case they should have such an interest, they should not be apt to unite in the pursuit of it" (Madison 1840/1966, 77).

4. Madison most famously opposed equal representation of the states in the Senate. However, he also championed the supremacy of the national government over the states (including a national veto on all state legislation), supported a simple majority override of judicial review, and opposed the prohibition of legislators taking executive posts.

5. See also Federalist 22 (authored by Hamilton).

6. It is notable that Buchanan and Tullock (1962, 47) do not state how these rights come about but merely state that "it will be useful to 'jump over' the minimal collectivization of activity that is involved in the initial definition of human and property rights and the enforcement of sanctions against violations of these rights."

7. Rae quotes Sen (1970a): "An economy can be optimal in this sense even when some people are rolling in luxury and others are near starvation as long as the starvers cannot be made better off without cutting into the pleasures of the rich. If preventing the burning of Rome would have made Emperor Nero feel worse off, then letting him burn Rome would have been Pareto-optimal. In short, a society or economy can be Pareto-optimal and still be perfectly disgusting."

8. The term *core* is used differently here than in Laing and Slotznick (1987). We define the core as the set of points that cannot be defeated under the q-rule. This is equivalent to the set of points that cannot be overturned if that point is established as the status quo. Laing and Slotznick define the core as the set of points that are undefeated under the q-rule and dominate the current status quo. The definition of *core* used here is equivalent to Laing and Slotznick's *heartland*.

9. Thanks to Donald Saari for pointing me to this source.

10. Rae (1975) gives the example of people building chimneys that pollute their neighbors in a jurisdiction that does not yet have effective regulation of pollution.

11. Rawls (1993/1996, 332–33) accepts that rights cannot be maximized and replaces "the most extensive possible scheme of equal basic liberties" in *A Theory of Justice* with "a fully adequate scheme."

12. Sen's illustration involves two people, one a prude, the other a libertine. The library has one copy of D. H. Lawrence's *Lady Chatterly's Lover.* The libertine wishes to read this, while the prude does not. If they are both free to decide whether to read the book, this will be the outcome. However, the libertine would get more pleasure from the prude reading it (and suffering embarrassment), while the prude would rather read it himself than see the libertine enjoy the book. Therefore both would prefer for the prude to read the book, even though the prude does not want to read the book and the libertine does.

13. The most commonly cited case of the U.S. Supreme Court extending basic rights is, of course, *Brown v. Board of Education* (1954), which outlawed segregation in public schools. This, however, did not protect a minority for a national legislative majority. Rather, it overturned the actions of state and local governments. Indeed, by 1954 there was already a clear national majority in favor of desegregation, and (ironically) the reason this could not be enforced by legislation was actually the supermajoritarian nature of the U.S. Congress, notably the filibuster in the Senate and the Southern domination of the committee system. Furthermore, the *Brown* decision only had practical impact because the most majoritarian branch of the U.S. government, the executive, chose to implement it by force.

CHAPTER 6

1. However, the deliberative polls organized by Fishkin do involve briefing by expert witnesses.

2. Essentially the argument is that people have a mutual interest in cooperation, but some forms of cooperation may suit some people better than others. When I talk, I try to convince you that society will coordinate on the outcome that suits me, and you will discount my communication somewhat. However, you will not discount it entirely, as it does provide some information about the outcome society is most likely to coordinate on.

3. Strictly speaking, Dryzek (1990) uses the term *discursive democracy* rather than *deliberative democracy.*

4. Johnson argues that communicative action involves persuasion. Persuasion, however, is necessarily perlocutionary and strategic, trying to change the opinion of another.

5. In *Political Liberalism* (1993/1996, 39–40) Rawls argues that political justice in a plural society requires an overlapping consensus on how reasonable claims can be reconciled. This consensus may originate historically from a compromise between different communities, but it eventually needs to become a consensus that can be justified on its own terms. See chapter 7 for a fuller account.

6. Knight and Johnson (1994) are a notable exception.

7. Barber uses the term *strong democracy* rather than *deliberative democracy,* but there is a strong emphasis both on collective will formation by discussion and on mass participation.

8. The folk theorem is that virtually any outcome that gives every player at least the minimum payoff they can guaranteed themselves can be an equilibrium in a repeated game with a low enough discount rate. It is so called because it was widely recognized before anyone published it.

9. The one partial exception of this was the Rabin government from 1993, which had Arab parties as part of the support coalition of a minority government.

10. Fearon (1998) actually prefers the term *discussion* to *deliberation,* as he feels that *deliberation* is too normatively loaded.

CHAPTER 7

1. Rae argues against Buchanan and Tullock on other grounds. See chapter 5.

2. See, in particular, *The Philosophical Discourse of Modernity* (1990b) for Habermas's reaction to the work of Derrida, Foucault, Bataille, and others.

3. The principles are: (1) everyone receives the greatest possible liberties compatible with the same liberties being universal; (2) all social goods are distributed by means of offices open to all, with inequality only being tolerated when it advantages the least advantaged.

4. See Harsanyi (1975), Hare (1973/1975), and Sen (1975) for critiques of the maximin principle as a solution concept. See Hart (1975) for a critique of the

elaborate "four-stage process" by which Rawls gets from principles of justice to their implementation.

5. Habermas does not, of course, argue that people engaged in communicative action lack their own action plans. However, they pursue them only on condition that their plans can be harmonized with others. Thus their action is oriented toward agreement first and goal attainment second (1984, 285–86).

6. Scanlon's criterion is: "An act is wrong if its performance under the circumstances would be disallowed by any system of rules for the general regulation of behaviour which no one could reasonably reject as a basis for informed, unforced general agreement."

CHAPTER 8

1. France's 1958 coup d'état is ignored for this purpose.

2. Tsebelis (2002) uses two measures of stability. The first measure, based on Doering (1995), is the number of significant laws on working time and working conditions in the period 1981 through 1991. Apart from the concern about the generalizability of conclusions from one policy area, it is far from clear that the amount of actual change in "the law" is at all related to the number of laws passed. Tsebelis deals with this problem in part by correcting for Sweden (where every amendment is counted as a law) and by only considering "significant" laws to correct for legislative inflation. However, the judgment of which laws are significant are made by legal scholars, not by economists or political scientists. Indeed an economist might well suggest that labor policy is often impacted far more by social security rules and business regulation than by labor law per se. There is no attempt to validate the measure of legal change by correlating it with outcomes in the real economy such as changes in working hours, female participation, or part-time work. In addition to validating Doering's measure, changes in these variables may actually be better measures of change in labor market conditions.

Tsebelis's other measure of policy change is the Euclidean distance between the vectors of government spending in ten categories between consecutive years, based on work with Eric Chang (Tsebelis and Chang 2001). As a measure of policy change, this has considerable potential as it measures changes in the allocation of hard resources, as opposed to legislative gestures. However, Tsebelis uses the expenditure in each category as a percentage of total government spending. Thus, if a government doubles spending in every category, this counts as no change. Interestingly, Tsebelis does not use the distance measure to test the effect of the number of veto points, but only variables such as government alternation and the ideological cohesion of the governing coalition.

References

Aldrich, John. 1977. "The Dilemma of a Paretian Liberal: Some Consequences of Sen's Theorem." *Public Choice* 30:1–22.

———. 1995. *Why Parties? The Origin and Transformation of Political Parties in America.* Chicago: University of Chicago Press.

Amnesty International. 2004. *Amnesty International Report 2004.* London: Amnesty International.

Anscombe, Gertrude. 1976. "On Frustration of the Majority by Fulfillment of the Majority's Will." *Analysis* 36:161–68.

Armingeon, K. 2001. "Institutionalizing the Swiss Welfare State." *West European Politics* 24, no. 2: 145–68.

Arrow, Kenneth. 1951/1963. *Social Choice and Individual Values.* New York: John Wiley and Sons.

Arter, David. 1999. *Scandinavian Politics Today.* Manchester: Manchester University Press.

Austen-Smith, David. 1990a. "Credible Debate Equilibria." *Social Choice and Welfare* 7:75–93.

———. 1990b. "Information Transmission in Debate." *American Journal of Political Science* 34, no. 1: 124–52.

———. 1992. "Strategic Models of Talk in Political Decision Making." *International Political Science Review* 16, no. 1: 45–58.

———. 2000. "Redistributing Income under Proportional Representation." *Journal of Political Economy* 108, no. 6: 1235–69.

Austen-Smith, David, and Jeffrey Banks. 2000. *Positive Political Theory I: Collective Preference.* Ann Arbor: University of Michigan Press.

———. 2005. *Positive Political Theory II: Strategy and Structure.* Ann Arbor: University of Michigan Press.

Balinski, Michael, and H. Peyton Young. 1982/2001. *Fair Representation: Meeting the Ideal of One Man, One Vote.* Washington, DC: Brookings Institute.

Banzhaf, John, III. 1965. "Weighted Voting Doesn't Work: A Mathematical Analysis." *Rutgers Law Review* 19:317–43.

Barber, Benjamin. 1984. *Strong Democracy: Participatory Politics for a New Age.* Berkeley: University of California Press.

Barry, Brian. 1965/1990. *Political Argument.* New York: Harvester Wheatsheaf.

———. 1979. "Is Democracy Special?" In *Philosophy, Politics, and Society,* ed. P. Laslett and J. Fishkin. 5th ser. New Haven: Yale University Press.

———. 1989. *Theories of Justice.* Berkeley: University of California Press.

———. 1995. *Justice as Impartiality.* Oxford: Clarendon.

Beetham, David. 1992. "The Plant Report and the Theory of Political Representation." *Political Quarterly* 63, no. 4: 460–67.

Beitz, Charles. 1989. *Political Equality: An Essay in Democratic Theory.* Princeton: Princeton University Press.

Benoît, Jean-Pierre, and Lewis Kornhauser. 1994. "Social Choice in a Representative Democracy." *American Political Science Review* 88, no. 1: 185–92.

Bernholz, Peter. 1973. "Logrolling, the Arrow Paradox, and Cyclical Majorities." *Public Choice* 15:87–96.

———. 1975. "Logrolling and the Paradox of Voting: Are They Really Logically Equivalent? A Comment." *American Political Science Review* 69, no. 3: 961–62.

Bianco, William, Ivan Jeliazkov, and Itai Sened. 2004. "The Uncovered Set and the Limits of Legislative Action." *Political Analysis* 12, no. 3: 256–77.

Binmore, Ken. 1994. *Game Theory and the Social Contract.* Vol. 1, *Playing Fair.* Cambridge: MIT Press.

———. 1998. *Game Theory and the Social Contract.* Vol. 2, *Just Playing.* Cambridge: MIT Press.

Birchfield, Vicki, and Markus Crepaz. 1998. "Veto Points on Income Inequality in Industrialized Democracies." *European Journal of Political Research* 34:175–200.

Black, Duncan. 1948. "On the Rationale of Group Decision Making." *Journal of Political Economy* 56:23–34.

———. 1958/1971. *The Theory of Committees and Elections.* Cambridge: Cambridge University Press.

Black, Duncan, and R. A. Newing. 1951/1998. "Committee Decisions with Complementary Valuation." In *The Theory of Committees and Elections,* by Duncan Black, and *Committee Decisions with Complementary Valuation,* by Duncan Black and R. A. Newing. Rev. 2d eds. Ed. Iain McLean, Alistair McMillan, and Burt Monroe. Boston: Kluwer Academic Press.

Borda, Jean-Charles de. 1770/1995. "On Ballot Votes." In *Classics of Social Choice,* ed. Iain McLean and Arnold Urken. Ann Arbor: University of Michigan Press.

Bowler, Shaun, and Bernard Grofman. 2000. *Elections in Australia, Ireland, and Malta under the Single Transferable Vote: Reflections on an Embedded Institution.* Ann Arbor: University of Michigan Press.

Brown, D. J. 1975 "Aggregation of Preferences." *Quarterly Journal of Economics* 89:456–69.

Brunel-Petron, Anne. 1998. "Contribution à l'analyse des droits en théorie du choix social." Thèse pour le doctorat de L'Université de Caen, spécialité sciences économiques. Mimeo, L'Université de Caen.

Buchanan, James, and Gordon Tullock. 1962. *The Calculus of Consent: Logical Foundations of Constitutional Democracy.* Ann Arbor: University of Michigan Press.

Burke, Edmund. 1777/1963. "Letter to the Sheriffs of Bristol." In *Edmund Burke: Selected Writings and Speeches,* ed. Peter Stanlis. New York: Anchor Books.

————. 1792/1963. "Letter to Sir Hercules Langrishe." In *Edmund Burke: Selected Writings and Speeches,* ed. Peter Stanlis. New York: Anchor Books.

Calhoun, John. 1842/1982. "On the Veto Power." In *The Portable Conservative Reader,* ed. Russell Kirk. New York: Penguin Books.

————. 1850/1943. *A Disquisition on Government.* New York: P. Smith.

Cameron, David. 1978. "The Expansion of the Public Economy: A Comparative Analysis." *American Political Science Review* 72, no. 4: 1243–61.

Carey, John, and Matthew Shugart. 1995. "Incentives to Cultivate a Personal Vote: A Rank Ordering of Electoral Formulas." *Electoral Studies* 14, no. 4: 417–39.

Chamberlin, John, and Paul Courant. 1983. "Representative Deliberations and Representative Decisions: Proportional Representation and the Borda Rule." *American Political Science Review* 77, no. 3: 718–33.

Chang, Eric, and Miriam Golden. 2003. "Electoral Systems, District Magnitude and Corruption." Paper prepared for presentation at the 2003 annual meeting of the American Political Science Association, August 28–31, Philadelphia.

Cohen, Joshua. 1986. "An Epistemic Conception of Democracy." *Ethics* 97, no. 1: 26–38.

————. 1996. "Procedure and Substance in Deliberative Democracy." In *Democracy and Difference: Contesting the Boundaries of the Political,* ed. Seyla Benhabib. Princeton: Princeton University Press.

————. 1998. "Democracy and Liberty." In *Deliberative Democracy,* ed. Jon Elster. Cambridge: Cambridge University Press.

Coleman, Jules, and John Ferejohn. 1986. "Democracy and Social Choice." *Ethics* 97, no. 1: 6–25.

Colomer, Josep. 2001. *Political Institutions: Democracy and Social Choice.* Oxford: Oxford University Press.

Condorcet, M. J. A. N. de Caritat, Marquis de. 1785/1995. "An Essay on the Application of Analysis to the Probability of Decisions Rendered by a Plurality of Votes." In *Classics of Social Choice,* ed. Iain McLean and Arnold Urken. Ann Arbor: University of Michigan Press.

————. 1787/1986. "Lettres d'un Bourgeois de New Heaven à un Citoyen de Virginie, Sur L'Inutilité de Partager Le Pouvoir Legislatif en Plusieurs Corps." In *Cordorcet Sur Les Elections,* ed. Olivier de Bernon. Paris: Fayard.

————. 1788/1995. "On the Constitution and the Functions of Provincial Assemblies." In *Classics of Social Choice,* ed. Iain McLean and Arnold Urken. Ann Arbor: University of Michigan Press.

Cox, Gary. 1997. *Making Votes Count: Strategic Coordination in the World's Electoral Systems.* Cambridge: Cambridge University Press.

Cox, Robert. 1993. *The Development of the Dutch Welfare State.* Pittsburgh: University of Pittsburgh Press.

Crepaz, Markus. 2001. "Veto Players, Globalization, and the Redistributive Capacity of the State: A Panel Study of 15 OECD Countries." *Journal of Public Policy* 21, no. 1: 1–22.

Dahl, Robert. 1956. *A Preface to Democratic Theory.* Chicago: University of Chicago Press.

———. 1988. *Democracy and Its Critics.* New Haven: Yale University Press.

———. 2001. *How Democratic Is the American Constitution?* New Haven: Yale University Press.

De Winter, Lieven. 2002. "Belgian MPs: Between Omnipotent Parties and Disenchanted Citizen-Clients." In *Parliaments and Citizens in Western Europe,* ed. Philip Norton. London: Frank Cass.

Deemen, A. M. A. van. 1993. "Paradoxes of Voting in List Systems of Proportional Representation." *Electoral Studies* 12:234–41.

Dewey, John. 1927/1946. *The Public and Its Problems: An Essay in Political Inquiry.* Chicago: Gateway Books.

Di Palma, G. 1977. *Surviving without Governing: The Italian Parties in Parliament.* Berkeley: University of California Press.

Dodgson, Charles. 1876/1995. "A Method of Taking Votes on More than Two Issues." In *Classics of Social Choice,* ed. Iain McLean and Arnold Urken. Ann Arbor: University of Michigan Press.

———. 1884/1995. "The Principles of Parliamentary Representation." In *Classics of Social Choice,* ed. Iain McLean and Arnold Urken. Ann Arbor: University of Michigan Press.

Doering, H. 1995. *Parliaments and Majority Rule in Western Europe.* New York: St. Martin's Press.

Downs, Anthony. 1957. *An Economic Theory of Democracy.* New York: Harper and Row.

Dryzek, John. 1990. *Discursive Democracy: Politics, Policy, and Political Science.* Cambridge: Cambridge University Press.

———. 2000. *Deliberative Democracy and Beyond: Liberals, Critics, Contestations.* Oxford: Oxford University Press.

Dryzek, John, and Christian List. 2003. "Social Choice Theory and Deliberative Democracy: A Reconciliation." *British Journal of Political Science* 33:1–28.

Dummett, Michael. 1984. *Voting Procedures.* Oxford: Clarendon.

———. 1997. *Principles of Electoral Reform.* Oxford: Oxford University Press.

Duverger, Maurice. 1954/1963. *Political Parties: Their Organization and Activity in the Modern State.* New York: Wiley.

———. 1962. *Les Institutions Françaises.* Paris: Presses Universitaires de France.

Dworkin, Ronald. 1975. "The Original Position." In *Reading Rawls: Critical Studies on Rawls' 'A Theory of Justice,'* ed. Norman Daniels. Stanford: Stanford University Press.

———. 1978. *Taking Rights Seriously.* Cambridge: Harvard University Press.

Elster, Jon. 1983. *Sour Grapes: Studies in the Subversion of Rationality.* Cambridge: Cambridge University Press.

Enelow, John, and Melvin Hinich. 1984. *The Spatial Theory of Voting: An Introduction.* Cambridge: Cambridge University Press.

Epstein, David. 1998. "Uncovering Some Subtleties of the Uncovered Set: Social Choice Theory and Distributive Politics." *Social Choice and Welfare* 15:81–93.

Esping-Andersen, Gøsta. 1981. *Politics Against Markets: The Social Democratic Road to Power.* Princeton: Princeton University Press.

Farquharson, Robin. 1969. *Theory of Voting.* New Haven: Yale University Press.

Farrell, David. 2001. *Electoral Systems: A Comparative Introduction.* Basingstoke, UK: Palgrave.

Fearon, James. 1998. "Deliberation as Discussion." In *Deliberative Democracy,* ed. Jon Elster. Cambridge: Cambridge University Press.

Feld, Scott, and Bernard Grofman. 1986. "On the Possibility of Faithfully Representative Committees." *American Political Science Review* 80, no. 3: 863–79.

———. 1987. "Necessary and Sufficient Conditions for a Majority Winner in N-Dimensional Spatial Voting Games: An Intuitive Geometric Approach." *American Journal of Political Science* 31, no. 4: 709–28.

Feld, Scott, Bernard Grofman, Richard Hartly, Marc Kilgour, Nicholas Miller, with the assistance of Nicholas Noviello. 1987. "The Uncovered Set in Spatial Voting Games." *Theory and Decision* 23:129–55.

Feld, Scott, Bernard Grofman, and Nicholas Miller. 1988. "Centripetal Forces in Spatial Voting: On the Size of the Yolk." *Public Choice* 59:37–50.

———. 1989. "Limit on Agenda Control in Spatial Voting Games." *Mathematical and Computer Modeling* 12, no. 4/5: 405–16.

Femia, Joseph. 1996. "Complexity and Deliberative Democracy." *Inquiry* 39: 359–97.

Fenno, Robert. 1978. *Homestyle: House Members in Their Districts.* Boston: Little, Brown.

Ferejohn, John. 1974. *Pork Barrel Politics.* Palo Alto: Stanford University Press.

Ferejohn, John, Richard McKelvey, and Edward Packel. 1984. "Limiting Distributions for Continuous State Markov Voting Models." *Social Choice and Welfare* 1:45–68.

Fishkin, James. 1995. *The Voice of the People: Public Opinion and Democracy.* New Haven: Yale University Press.

Freedom House. 2004. *Freedom in the World 2003: The Annual Survey of Political Rights and Civil Liberties.* Lanham, MD: Rowman and Littlefield.

Furman, Jason, and Joseph Stiglitz. 1998. "Economic Consequences of Income Inequality." In Federal Reserve Board of Kansas, *Income Inequality and Policy Options, A Symposium Sponsored by the Federal Reserve Bank of Kansas City,* Jackson Hole, WY, August 27–29.

Gibbard, Alan. 1969. "Intransitive Social Indifference and the Arrow Dilemma." Mimeo.

———. 1973. "Manipulation of Voting Schemes: A General Result." *Econometrica* 41:587–602.

Gladdish, Ken. 1991. *Governing from the Center: Politics and Policy-Making in the Netherlands.* Dekalb: Northern Illinois University Press.

Glendon, Mary Ann. 1991. *Rights Talk: The Impoverishment of Political Discourse.* New York: Free Press.

Guinier, Lani. 1994. *The Tyranny of the Majority: Fundamental Fairness in Representative Democracy.* New York: Free Press.

Gutmann, Amy. 1980. *Liberal Equality.* Cambridge: Cambridge University Press.

Gutmann, Amy, and Dennis Thompson. 1996. *Democracy and Disagreement.* Cambridge: Belknap Press of Harvard University Press.

Habermas, Jürgen. 1984. *The Theory of Communicative Action*. Vol. 1, *Reason and the Rationalization of Society*. Boston: Beacon.

―――. 1987. *The Theory of Communicative Action*. Vol. 2, *Lifeworld and System: A Critique of Functionalist Reason*. Boston: Beacon.

―――. 1990a. *Moral Consciousness and Communicative Action*. Cambridge: MIT Press.

―――. 1990b. *The Philosophical Discourse of Modernity*. Cambridge: MIT Press.

―――. 1995. "Reconciliation through the Public Use of Reason: Remarks on John Rawls's Political Liberalism." *Journal of Philosophy* 92, no. 3: 109–31.

―――. 1996a. "Three Normative Models of Democracy." In *Democracy and Difference: Contesting the Boundaries of the Political,* ed. Seyla Benhabib. Princeton: Princeton University Press.

―――. 1996b. *Between Facts and Norms: Contributions to a Discourse Theory of Law and Democracy*. Cambridge: MIT Press.

Hain, Peter. 1986. *Proportional Misrepresentation: The Case Against PR in Britain*. Hampshire, UK: Wildwood House.

Hamilton, Alexander, James Madison, and John Jay. 1788/1961. *The Federalist Papers*. New York: Mentor.

Hare, R. M. 1973/1975. "Rawls' Theory of Justice." *Philosophical Quarterly* 23:144, 241. Reprinted in *Reading Rawls: Critical Studies on Rawls' 'A Theory of Justice,'* ed. Norman Daniels. Stanford: Stanford University Press.

Harsanyi, John. 1975. "Can the Maximin Principle Serve as a Basis for Morality? A Critique of John Rawls' Theory." *American Political Science Review* 69: 594–606.

Hart, H. L. A. 1975. "Rawls on Liberty and Its Priority." In *Reading Rawls,* ed. Norman Daniels. Palo Alto: Stanford University Press.

Hartley, Richard, and D. Marc Kilgour. 1987. "The Geometry of the Uncovered Set in the Three-Voter Spatial Model." *Mathematical Social Sciences* 14:175–83.

Hazan, Reuven. 1997. "The 1996 Intra-Party Elections in Israel: Adopting Party Primaries." *Electoral Studies* 16, no. 1: 95–103.

―――. 2000. "Religion and Politics in Israel: The Rise and Fall of the Consociational Model." In *Parties, Elections, and Cleavages: Israel in Comparative and Theoretical Perspective,* ed. Reuven Hazan and Moshe Maor. Portland, OR: Frank Cass.

Heath, Joseph. 2003. *Communicative Action and Rational Choice*. Cambridge: MIT Press.

Hees, Martin van. 1998. "On the Analysis of Negative Freedom." *Theory and Decision* 45:175–97.

―――. 2003. "Acting Autonomously versus Not Acting Heteronomously." *Theory and Decision* 54:337–55.

Hobbes, Thomas. 1660/1972. *Leviathan*. Harmondsworth, UK: Penguin Books.

Hout, Eliora van der, Harrie de Swart, and Annemarie ter Veer. 2002. "Axioms Characterizing the Plurality Ranking Rule." Paper presented at the annual meeting of the Public Choice Society, San Diego, March 22–24.

Hout, Eliora van der, and Anthony McGann. 2004. "Equal Protection Implies

Proportional Representation." Institute of Mathematical Behavioral Sciences Working Paper. University of California, Irvine.

Huber, Evelyn, Charles Ragin, and John Stephens. 1993. "Social Democracy, Christian Democracy, Constitutional Structure, and the Welfare State." *American Journal of Sociology* 99, no. 3: 711–49.

Iversen, Torben, and David Soskice. 2002. "Electoral Systems and the Politics of Coalitions: Why Some Democracies Redistribute More than Others." Paper prepared for the 2002 annual meeting of the American Political Science Association, Boston, August 29, September 2.

Jenkins, Roy. 1998. *Report of the Independent Commission on the Voting System.* London: Stationery Office Cm 4090-1.

Johnson, James. 1991. "Habermas on Strategic and Communicative Action." *Political Theory* 19, no. 2: 181–201.

Katz, Richard. 1997. *Democracy and Elections.* Oxford: Oxford University Press.

Katzenstein, P. 1985. *Small States in World Markets: Industrial Policy in Europe.* Ithaca: Cornell University Press.

Kernell, Sam. 2003. "The True Principles of Republican Government: Reassessing James Madison's Political Science." In *James Madison: The Theory and Practice of Republican Government,* ed. Sam Kernell. Palo Alto, CA: Stanford University Press.

Kitschelt, Herbert. 1996. "Defense of the Status Quo as Equilibrium Strategy? New Dilemmas for European Social Democracy." Paper presented to the 1996 annual meeting of the American Political Science Association, San Francisco, August 29–September 1.

Knight, Jack, and James Johnson. 1994. "Aggregation and Deliberation: On the Possibility of Democratic Legitimacy." *Political Theory* 22, no. 2: 277–96.

Knight, Jack, and James Johnson. 1996. "Political Consequences of Pragmatism." *Political Theory* 24, no. 1: 68–96.

———. 1999. "Inquiry into Democracy: What Might a Pragmatist Make of Rational Choice Theories?" *American Journal of Political Science* 43, no. 2: 566–89.

Kramer, Gerald. 1977. "A Dynamical Model of Political Equilibrium." *Journal of Economic Theory* 16:310–44.

Krehbiel, Keith. 1998. *Pivotal Politics: A Theory of U.S. Lawmaking.* Chicago: University of Chicago Press.

Lacy, Dean, and Emerson Niou. 2000. "A Problem with Referendums." *Journal of Theoretical Politics* 12, no. 1: 5–32.

Laing, James, and Benjamin Slotznick. 1987. "Viable Alternative to the Status Quo." *Journal of Conflict Resolution* 31:63–85.

Lancaster, Thomas. 1986. "Electoral Structures and Pork Barrel Politics." *International Political Science Review* 7, no. 1: 67–81.

Lancaster, Thomas, and W. David Patterson. 1990. "Comparative Pork Barrel Politics: Perceptions from the West German Bundestag." *Comparative Political Studies* 22, no. 4: 458–77.

Lane, Jan-Erik, and Reinert Maitland. 2001. "The Growth of the Public Sector in Switzerland." *West European Politics* 24, no. 2: 169–90.

Latner, Michael, and Anthony McGann. 2005. "Geographical Representation under Proportional Representation: The Cases of Israel and the Nether-lands." *Electoral Studies* 24:709–34.

Lijphart, Arend. 1968. *The Politics of Accommodation; Pluralism and Democracy in the Netherlands.* Berkeley: University of California Press.

———. 1977. *Democracy in Plural Societies.* New Haven: Yale University Press.

———. 1984a. "Measures of Cabinet Durability: A Conceptual and Empirical Evaluation." *Comparative Political Studies* 17:265–79.

———. 1984b. *Democracies: Patterns of Majoritarian and Consensus Government in Twenty-one Countries.* New Haven: Yale University Press.

———. 1994. *Electoral Systems and Party Systems: A Study of Twenty-seven Democracies, 1945–1990.* Oxford: Oxford University Press.

———. 1997. "Unequal Participation: Democracy's Unresolved Dilemma." *American Political Science Review* 91, no. 1: 1–14.

———. 1999. *Patterns of Democracy: Government Forms and Performance in Thirty-six Countries.* New Haven: Yale University Press.

Lindblom, Charles. 1965. *The Intelligence of Democracy: Decision Making through Mutual Adjustment.* New York: Free Press.

Locke, John. 1690/1986. *The Second Treatise of Civil Government.* Amherst, NY: Prometheus.

Mackie, Gerry. 1998. "All Men Are Liars: Is Democracy Meaningless?" In *Deliberative Democracy,* ed. Jon Elster. Cambridge: Cambridge University Press.

———. 2003. *Democracy Defended.* Cambridge: Cambridge University Press.

Madison, James. 1840/1966. *Notes of Debates in the Federal Convention of 1787 Reported by James Madison.* Athens: Ohio University Press.

———. 1999. *Writings.* New York: Library of America.

May, Kenneth. 1952. "A Set of Independent Necessary and Sufficient Conditions for Simple Majority Decision." *Econometrica* 20:680–84.

Mayhew, David. 1974. *Congress: The Electoral Connection.* New Haven: Yale University Press.

McGann, Anthony. 2004. "The Tyranny of the Supermajority: How Majority Rule Protects Minorities." *Journal of Theoretical Politics* 16, no. 1: 53–77.

McKelvey, Richard. 1976. "Intransitivities in Multidimensional Voting Models and Some Implications for Agenda Control." *Journal of Economic Theory* 16:472–82.

———. 1979. "General Conditions for Global Intransitivities in Formal Voting Models." *Econometrica* 47, no. 5: 1085–1112.

———. 1986. "Covering, Dominance, and the Institution-Free Properties of Social Choice." *American Journal of Political Science* 30, no. 2: 283–314.

McLean, Iain. 1991. "Forms of Representation and Voting Systems." In *Political Theory Today,* ed. David Held. Palo Alto: Stanford University Press.

McLean, Iain, and Arnold Urken, eds. 1995. *Classics of Social Choice.* Ann Arbor: University of Michigan Press.

Milesi-Ferretti, Gian Maria, Roberto Perotti, and Massimo Rostagno. 2002. "Electoral Systems and Public Spending." *Quarterly Journal of Economics* 117, no. 2: 609–57.

Mill, David van. 1996. "The Possibility of Rational Outcomes from Democratic Discourse and Procedures." *Journal of Politics* 58, no. 3: 734–52.

Mill, John Stuart. 1861/1993. *Considerations on Representative Government.* In John Stuart Mill, *Utilitarianism, On Liberty, Considerations on Representative Government.* Everyman Edition. London: J. M. Dent.

Miller, David. 1992. "Deliberative Democracy and Social Choice." *Political Studies* 40 (supplement): 54–67.

Miller, Nicholas. 1975. "Logrolling and the Arrow Paradox: A Note." *Public Choice* 21:107–10.

———. 1977a. "Logrolling, Vote Trading, and the Paradox of Voting." *Public Choice* 30:51–76.

———. 1977b. "Social Preference and Game Theory: A Comment on 'The Dilemma of a Paretian Liberal.'" *Public Choice* 30:23–27.

———. 1980. "A New Solution Set for Tournaments and Majority Voting: Further Graph-Theoretical Approaches to the Theory of Voting." *American Journal of Political Science* 24, no. 1: 68–96.

———. 1983. "Social Choice and Pluralism." *American Political Science Review* 77, no. 3: 734–47.

———. 1995. *Committees, Agendas, and Voting.* Chur, Switzerland: Harwood Academic Publishers.

———. 1996. "Majority Rule and Minority Interests." In *Political Order: Nomos XXXVIII,* ed. Ian Shapiro and Russell Hardin. New York: New York University Press.

Miller, Nicholas, Bernard Grofman, and Scott Feld. 1989. "The Geometry of Majority Rule." *Journal of Theoretical Politics* 1:379–406.

Moe, Terry. 1989. "The Politics of Bureaucratic Structure." In *Can the Government Govern?* ed. John Chubb and Paul Peterson. Washington, DC: Brookings Institution.

Moe, Terry, and William Howell. 1999. "The Presidential Power of Unilateral Action." *Journal of Law, Economics, and Organization* 15:132–79.

Monroe, Burt. 1995. "Fully Proportional Representation." *American Political Science Review* 89, no. 4: 925–40.

Moulin, Hervé. 1988. *Axioms of Cooperative Decision Making.* Cambridge: Cambridge University Press.

Mueller, Dennis. 2003. *Public Choice III.* Cambridge: Cambridge University Press.

Nakamura, Kenjiro. 1979. "The Vetoers in a Simple Game with Ordinal Preferences." *International Journal of Game Theory* 8:55–61.

Nino, Carlos Santiago. 1996. *The Constitution of Deliberative Democracy.* New Haven: Yale University Press.

Norton, Philip. 2002. "Parliaments and Citizens in Western Europe." In *Parliaments and Citizens in Western Europe,* ed. Philip Norton. London: Frank Cass.

Nozick, Robert. 1974. *Anarchy, State, and Utopia.* New York: Basic Books.

Nurmi, Hannu. 1987. *Comparing Voting Systems.* Dordrecht: D. Reidel.

———. 1999. *Voting Paradoxes and How to Deal with Them.* Berlin: Springer.

Oppenheimer, Joe. 1975. "Some Political Implications of 'Vote Trading and the Voting Paradox: A Proof of Logical Equivalence': A Comment." *American Political Science Review* 69, no. 3: 963–66.

Park, R. E. 1967. "The Possibility of a Social Welfare Function: Comment." *American Economic Review* 57, no. 5: 1300–1304.

Pateman, Carole. 1970. *Participation and Democratic Theory.* Cambridge: Cambridge University Press.

Pattanaik, Prasanta, and Kotaro Suzumura. 1994. "Rights, Welfarism, and Social Choice." *American Economic Review* 84, no. 2: 435–39.

Penrose, Lionel. 1946. "The Elementary Statistics of Majority Voting." *Journal of the Royal Statistical Society* 109:53–57.

Persson, Torsten, and Guido Tabellini. 1999. "The Size and Scope of Government: Comparative Politics with Rational Politicians." *European Economic Review* 43:699–735.

Pierson, Paul. 1994. *Dismantling the Welfare State: Reagan, Thatcher, and the Politics of Retrenchment.* Cambridge: Cambridge University Press.

Pitkin, Hanna Fenichel. 1967. *The Concept of Representation.* Berkeley: University of California Press.

Plott, Charles. 1967. "A Notion of Equilibrium under Majority Rule." *American Economic Review* 57:787–806.

Poole, Keith, and Howard Rosenthal. 1997. *Congress: A Political-Economic History of Roll Call Voting.* Oxford: Oxford University Press.

Powell, G. Bingham, Jr. 2000. *Elections as Instruments of Democracy: Majoritarian and Proportional Visions.* New Haven: Yale University Press.

Przeworski, Adam. 1991. *Democracy and the Market: Political and Economic Reforms in Eastern Europe and Latin America.* Cambridge: Cambridge University Press.

———. 1998. "Deliberation and Ideological Domination." In *Deliberative Democracy,* ed. Jon Elster. Cambridge: Cambridge University Press.

———. 1999. "Minimalist Conception of Democracy: A Defense." In *Democracy's Value,* ed. Ian Shapiro and Casiano Hacker-Cordón. Cambridge: Cambridge University Press.

Przeworski, Adam, Michael Alvarez, Jose Antonio Cheibub, and Fernando Limongi. 2000. *Democracy and Development: Political Institutions and Well-Being in the World, 1950–90.* Cambridge: Cambridge University Press.

Przeworski, Adam, and Fernando Limongi. 1997. "Modernization: Theories and Facts." *World Politics* 49, no. 2: 155–83.

Rae, Douglas. 1967. *The Political Consequences of Electoral Laws.* New Haven: Yale University Press.

———. 1969. "Decision-Rules and Individual Values in Constitutional Choice." *American Political Science Review* 63, no. 1: 40–56.

———. 1975. "The Limits of Consensual Decision Making." *American Political Science Review* 69, no. 4: 1270–94.

Rawls, John. 1958. "Justice as Fairness." *Philosophical Review* 67, no. 2: 164–94.

Rawls, John. 1971/1999. *A Theory of Justice.* Rev. ed. Cambridge: Belknap Press of Harvard University Press.

————. 1993/1996. *Political Liberalism.* New York: Columbia University Press.

————. 1995/1996. "Reply to Habermas." In John Rawls, *Political Liberalism.* New York: Columbia University Press. First appeared in *Journal of Philosophy* 92, no. 3: 132–80.

Regenwetter, Michel, Bernard Grofman, Anthony Marley, and Ilia Tsetlin. Forthcoming. *Foundations of Behavioral Social Choice Research.* Cambridge: Cambridge University Press.

Riker, William. 1982. *Liberalism Against Populism: A Confrontation between the Theory of Democracy and the Theory of Social Choice.* San Francisco: Freeman.

Riker, William, and Steven Brams. 1973. "The Paradox of Vote Trading." *American Political Science Review* 67, no. 4: 1235–47.

Rochon, Thomas. 1999. *The Netherlands: Negotiating Sovereignty in an Interdependent World.* Boulder, CO: Westview.

Roemer, John. 1999a. "Does Democracy Engender Justice?" In *Democracy's Value,* ed. Ian Shapiro and Casiano Hacker-Cordón. Cambridge: Cambridge University Press.

————. 1999b. "The Democratic Political Economy of Progressive Income Taxation." *Econometrica* 67:1–19.

Rogowski, Ronald. 1981. "Representation in Political Theory and in Law." *Ethics* 91, no. 3: 395–430.

Rogowski, Ronald, and Mark Kayser. 2002. "Majoritarian Electoral Systems and Consumer Power: Price-Level Evidence from the OECD Countries." *American Journal of Political Science* 46, no. 3: 526–39.

Rose-Ackerman, Susan, and Jana Kunicova. 2005. "Electoral Rules and Constraints on Corruption." *British Journal of Political Science* 35, no. 4: 573–606.

Rousseau, Jean-Jacques. 1762/1997. *The Social Contract and Later Political Writings.* Cambridge: Cambridge University Press.

Saari, Donald. 1997. "The Generic Existence of a Core for Q-Rules." *Economic Theory* 9:219–60.

————. 2001. *Decisions and Elections: Explaining the Unexpected.* Cambridge: Cambridge University Press.

————. 2003. "Capturing the 'Will of the People.'" *Ethics* 113, no. 2: 333–49.

Saari, Donald, and Katri Sieberg. 2001. "The Sum of the Parts Can Violate the Whole." *American Political Science Review* 95, no. 2: 415–34.

Satterthwaite, M. 1975. "Strategy-proofness and Arrow's Conditions: Existence and Correspondence Theorems for Voting Procedures and Social Welfare Functions." *Journal of Economic Theory* 10:187–217.

Scanlon, T. M. 1982. "Contractualism and Utilitarianism." In *Utilitarianism and Beyond,* ed. Amartya Sen and Bernard Williams. Cambridge: Cambridge University Press.

Scharpf, Fritz. 1988. "The Joint-Decision Trap: Lessons from German Federalism and European Integration." *Public Administration* 66:239–78.

Schelling, Thomas. 1960. *The Strategy of Conflict.* Cambridge: Harvard University Press.

Schofield, Norman. 1978. "Instability of Simple Dynamic Games." *Review of Economic Studies* 45, no. 3: 557–94.

———. 1999. "The C[1] Topology on the Space of Smooth Preference Profiles." *Social Choice and Welfare* 16, no. 3: 445–70.

Schumpeter, Joseph. 1942. *Capitalism, Socialism, and Democracy*. New York: Harper.

Schwartz, Thomas. 1995. "The Paradox of Representation." *Journal of Politics* 57: 309–23.

Scruggs, Lyle. 1999. "Institutions and Environmental Performance in Seventeen Western Democracies." *British Journal of Political Science* 29, no. 1: 1–31.

———. 2001. "Is There Really a Link between Neo-Corporatism and Environmental Performance? Updated Evidence and New Data for the 1980s and 1990s." *British Journal of Political Science* 31, no. 4: 686–92.

Sen, Amartya. 1970a. *Collective Choice and Social Welfare*. San Francisco: Holden-Day.

———. 1970b. "The Impossibility of a Paretian Liberal." *Journal of Political Economy* 78:152–57.

———. 1975. "Rawls versus Bentham: An Axiomatic Examination of the Pure Distribution Problem." In *Reading Rawls,* ed. Norman Daniels. Palo Alto: Stanford University Press.

———. 1976. "Liberty, Unanimity, and Rights." *Economica* 43:217–45.

———. 1979. "Personal Utilities and Public Judgments: or What's Wrong with Welfare Economics." *Economic Journal* 89:537–58.

Shapley, Lloyd, and Martin Shubik. 1954. "A Method for Evaluating the Distribution of Power in a Committee System." *American Political Science Review* 48:787–92.

Shepsle, Kenneth, and Barry Weingast. 1981. "Political Preferences for the Pork Barrel." *American Journal of Political Science* 25:96–111.

Shugart, Matthew, and John Carey. 1992. *Presidents and Assemblies: Constitutional Design and Electoral Dynamics.* Cambridge: Cambridge University Press.

Shugart, Matthew Soberg, and Martin Wattenberg. 2001. "Mixed-Member Electoral Systems: A Definition and Typology." In *Mixed-Member Electoral Systems: The Best of Both Worlds,* ed. Matthew Soberg Shugart and Martin Wattenberg. Oxford: Oxford University Press.

Skyrms, Brian. 1996. *Evolution and the Social Contract.* Cambridge: Cambridge University Press.

Steiner, J. 1973. *Amicable Agreement versus Majority Rule.* Chapel Hill: University of North Carolina Press.

Still, Jonathon W. 1981. "Political Equality and Election Systems." *Ethics* 91, no. 3: 375–94.

Stokes, Susan. 1998. "Pathologies of Deliberation." In *Deliberative Democracy,* ed. Jon Elster. Cambridge: Cambridge University Press.

Straffin, Philip, Jr. 1977. "Majority Rule and General Decision Rules." *Theory and Decision* 8:351–60.

Strawson, Peter. 1974. *Freedom and Resentment, and Other Essays.* London: Methuen.

Strom, Kaare. 1990. *Minority Government and Majority Rule.* Cambridge: Cambridge University Press.

———. 2000. "Delegation and Accountability in Parliamentary Democracies." *European Journal of Political Research* 37:261–89.

Sugden, Robert. 1985. "Liberty, Preference, and Choice." *Economics and Philosophy* 1, no. 2: 213–29.

Taagepera, Rein, and Matthew Shugart. 1989. *Seats and Votes: The Effects and Determinants of Electoral Systems.* New Haven: Yale University Press.

Taylor, Michael. 1969. "Critique and Comment: Proof of a Theorem on Majority Rule." *Behavioral Science* 14:228–31.

Transparency International. 2005. *Global Corruption Report 2005.* London: Pluto Press.

Tsebelis, George. 1995. "Decision Making in Political Systems: Veto Players in Presidentialism, Parliamentarianism, Multicameralism, and Multipartyism." *British Journal of Political Science* 25:289–326.

———. 2002. *Veto Players: How Political Institutions Work.* New York: Russell Sage Foundation / Princeton University Press.

Tsebelis, George, and Eric Chang. 2001. "Veto Players and the Structure of Budgets in Advanced Industrialized Countries." Mimeo, University of California, Los Angeles.

Ward, Hugh. 1995. "A Contractarian Defense of Ideal Proportional Representation." *Journal of Political Philosophy* 3:86–109.

Warren, Mark. 1988. "Max Weber's Liberalism for a Nietzschean World." *American Political Science Review* 82, no. 1: 31–50.

———. 1992. "Democratic Theory and Self-Transformation." *American Political Science Review* 86, no. 1: 8–23.

———. 1996. "Deliberative Democracy and Authority." *American Political Science Review* 90, no. 1: 46–60.

Weber, Max. 1978. *Economy and Society.* Trans. and ed. Walter Runciman. Cambridge: Cambridge University Press.

Weingast, Barry. 1998. "Political Stability and Civil War: Institutions, Commitment, and American Democracy." In *Analytic Narratives,* ed. Robert Bates, Avner Greif, Margaret Levi, Jean-Laurent Rosenthal, and Barry Weingast. Princeton: Princeton University Press.

Weingast, Barry, Kenneth Shepsle, and Christopher Johnsen. 1981. "The Political Economy of Benefits and Costs." *Journal of Political Economy* 89:642–66.

Williams, Bernard. 1962/1971. "The Idea of Equality." In *Justice and Equality,* ed. Hugo Bedau. Englewood Cliffs, NJ: Prentice-Hall. First printed in *Philosophy, Politics, and Society,* Ser. II, ed. Peter Laslett and W. G. Runciman. Oxford: Basil Blackwell.

Williamson, Oliver. 1975. *Markets and Hierarchies: Analysis and Anti-trust Implications.* New York: Free Press.

Wolff, Robert. 1970. *In Defense of Anarchism.* New York: Harper and Row.

Young, H. Peyton. 1974. "An Axiomatization of Borda's Rule." *Journal of Economic Theory* 9:43–52.

———. 1975. "Social Choice Scoring Functions." *SIAM Journal on Applied Mathematics* 28:824–38.

———. 1995. "Optimal Voting Rules." *Journal of Economic Perspectives* 9, no. 1: 51–64.

Index